MIX AND MATCH
KNIT SWEATER
DESIGNS

RITA MAASSEN

STACKPOLE
BOOKS

Guilford, Connecticut

Published by Stackpole Books

An imprint of The Rowman & Littlefield Publishing Group, Inc.

4501 Forbes Blvd., Ste. 200

Lanham, MD 20706

www.stackpolebooks.com

Distributed by NATIONAL BOOK NETWORK

800-462-6420

The original German edition was published as *Dein Pullover Design*.

Copyright © 2018 frechverlag GmbH, Stuttgart, Germany (www.top-kreativ.de)

This edition is published by arrangement with Claudia Böhme Rights & Literary Agency, Hannover, Germany (www.agency-boehme.com).

Photography: frechverlag GmbH, 70499 Stuttgart, lichtpunkt, Michael Ruder, Stuttgart

Hair and makeup stylist: Charlene Ksiazek, Esslingen

Product management: Mareike Upheber

Editing: Beate Schmitz, Stegen

Typesetting: Petra Theilfarth

Translation: Katharina Sokiran

British Library Cataloguing in Publication Information available

Library of Congress Cataloging-in-Publication Data

Names: Maassen, Rita, author. | Maassen, Rita. Dein Pullover Design.
Title: Mix and match knit sweater designs / Rita Maassen.
Other titles: Dein Pullover Design. English
Description: First edition. | Lanham, MD : Rowman & Littlefield Publishing
   Group, 2020. | The original German edition was published as Dein
   Pullover Design, copyright 2018, Frechverlag GmbH, Stuttgart, Germany. |
   Summary: "This book begins with six basic pullover designs; then the
   author explains her system for mixing the elements. She puts her system
   into practice in 23 unique sweater designs, giving the instructions for
   each so that you may then either follow these patterns as written or do
   your own mixing and matching to create your own unique sweater pattern.
   Over 70,000 different sweaters are possible!"— Provided by publisher.
Identifiers: LCCN 2019052759 (print) | LCCN 2019052760 (ebook) | ISBN
   9780811738743 (paperback) | ISBN 9780811769587 (epub)
Subjects: LCSH: Knitting—Patterns. | Sweaters.
Classification: LCC TT825 .M1312513 2020 (print) | LCC TT825 (ebook) |
   DDC 746.43/2—dc23
LC record available at https://lccn.loc.gov/2019052759
LC ebook record available at https://lccn.loc.gov/2019052760

♾™ The paper used in this publication meets the minimum requirements of American National Standard for Information Sciences—Permanence of Paper for Printed Library Materials, ANSI/NISO Z39.48-1992.

First Edition

*I would like to thank company MEZ GmbH
(www.schachenmayr.de)
for providing yarn support for this book.*

CONTENTS

MIX AND MATCH – STEP BY STEP TO YOUR SWEATER BLISS

KNITTING BASICS – HOW TO WORK

Dear Reader,

Did you ever dream of knitting a sweater entirely to your own spec-ifications? You know this: There are plenty of knitting patterns out there, but in most cases, adapting them to your own needs and ideas is tricky. Sure, you can adjust the length a little bit, or switch out a cuff design. But when it comes to a differently shaped armhole, or to changing a pattern altogether, things can become complicated!

With this book, I want to enable you to design your own sweater in a creative way, using the Mix and Match method. You can pick elements that suit you from an array of different basic designs, and arrange them in your imagination into your perfect sweater. Combine different stitch patterns, adjust the sleeve length, or choose a differ-ent neckline shape—and all elements will fit together perfectly.

A few suggestions for possible combinations are presented in "Mix and Match—Step by Step to Your Sweater Bliss." Perhaps one of these ready-to-use designs is already what you are looking for? If not, you'll find plenty of inspiration for coming up with your own creative solutions.

I wish you much fun on your journey through the world of sweater design!

Yours,

Rita Maaßen

HOW TO USE THIS BOOK

With the help of this guide, it is very easy to design your own sweater. All you need are a notepad and pen. Just work through each section, and write down the steps needed to bring your design idea to life.

1. THE BASIC SWEATER

In the first chapter, I introduce six basic sweaters. The only difference between these basic sweaters is in the stitch patterns used—the garment pattern is the same for all of them. First, pick the design or pattern that comes closest to what you have in mind. Even this can still be changed in a later step.

2. THE BODY SHAPE

Instead of the straight shape of the basic sweaters, all designs can also be knit in an oversized fit, fitted to the body, or as an A-line shape. On pages 68–91, you will find instructions for these modifications to choose from.

3. THE CUFFS

All basic sweaters have ribbed cuffs and hems. If you are not fond of this feature, you can pick out a different cuff or hem design from eight additional suggestions on pages 34–41. Later, when it comes to actually knitting the cuffs or hems, you will just have to make sure that you increase or decrease as many stitches in the last cuff or hem row needed to match the stitch count for your basic sweater, as listed for continuing *after* the cuff or hem.

4. THE NECKLINE

All basic sweaters feature a crewneck with ribbed neckband. On pages 42–46, I introduce additional possibilities for your neckline design. Just pick the one you like best, and write down the appropriate instructions.

5. THE ARMHOLE

You don't like the straight sleeve tops of the basic sweaters and prefer sleeve caps or raglan sleeves? Instructions for these, which can be used with all basic sweaters, can be found on pages 47–58.

6. THE SLEEVE LENGTH

The obligatory long sleeves shown on all basic sweaters may be worked in a ¾ length or as short sleeves for all armhole shapes. How this is done is explained on pages 59–67.

7. THE STITCH PATTERNS

You want to knit a lace sweater for yourself, but can't warm up to the stitch pattern of the basic sweater? No problem: On pages 104–11, four alternate stitch patterns for every basic sweater are shown, which you can use as substitutes without further adjustments.

Now you have gathered all the puzzle pieces needed for your dream sweater. Mark the relevant pages in the book, write down the appropriate instructions on a piece of paper, or use the note-taking form on page 191.

You are all set now to start your project. Before you begin, please take the time to read through the general notes on pages 32–33.

SIZES

Small/Medium/Large (US 6/8, 10/12, 14/16)

Numbers for size Small are listed before the first slash, for size Medium between slashes, and for size Large after the second slash. If only one number is given, it applies to all sizes.

MATERIALS

Schachenmayr Merino Extrafine 120; #3 light weight yarn; 100% wool; 131 yd (120 m), 1.75 oz. (50 g) per skein

- 11/12/13 skeins in #133 burgundy

Circular knitting needles, sizes US 4 (3.5 mm) and US 6 (4.0 mm), each 32 in. (80 cm) long

GAUGE

In stockinette stitch on US 6 (4.0 mm) needles, 22 sts and 30 rows = 4 x 4 in. (10 x 10 cm)

STRAIGHT SLEEVE TOP

STRAIGHT BODY

BASIC SWEATER 2

PRETTY WITH COLORFUL STRIPES

STRAIGHT SLEEVE TOP

STRAIGHT BODY

BASIC SWEATER 3

**NICELY STYLED
WITH BORDER**

STRAIGHT
SLEEVE TOP

STRAIGHT
BODY

BASIC SWEATER 2

PRETTY WITH COLORFUL STRIPES

SIZES

Small/Medium/Large (US 6/8, 10/12, 14/16)
Numbers for size Small are listed before the first slash, for size Medium between slashes, and for size Large after the second slash. If only one number is given, it applies to all sizes.

MATERIALS

Schachenmayr Merino Extrafine 120; #3 light weight yarn; 100% wool; 131 yd (120 m), 1.75 oz. (50 g) per skein

- Main color (MC): 4/5/7 skeins #101 white
- Contrasting color 1 (CC1): 2/3/4 skeins #133 burgundy
- Contrasting color 2 (CC2): 3/4/4 skeins #192 medium gray heathered
- Contrasting color 3 (CC3): 1/2/2 skeins #190 light gray heathered
- Contrasting color 4 (CC4): 1/1/2 skeins #143 pink
- Contrasting color 5 (CC5): 1/1/2 skeins #152 light blue

Circular knitting needles, sizes US 4 (3.5 mm) and US 6 (4.0 mm), each 32 in. (80 cm) long

GAUGE

In stockinette stitch on US 6 (4.0 mm) needles, 22 sts and 30 rows = 4 x 4 in. (10 x 10 cm)

STOCKINETTE STITCH

RS: Knit all sts.
WS: Purl all sts.

RIBBING IN ROWS

RS: Alternate k1, p1.
WS: Work all sts as they appear—knit the knits and purl the purls.

RIBBING IN ROUNDS

All rounds (RS): Alternate k1, p1.

STRIPE SEQUENCE A

Alternate 2 rows in MC (white), 2 rows in CC2 (medium gray heathered).

STRIPE SEQUENCE B

This stripe sequence is worked only once.
18 rows in CC3 (light gray heathered), 6 rows in CC1 (burgundy), 14 rows in CC4 (pink), 6 rows in CC1 (burgundy), 14 rows in MC (white), 12 rows in CC5 (light blue), 22 rows in Stripe Sequence A, 14 rows in CC1 (burgundy), 10 rows in CC2 (medium gray heathered), 10 rows in CC4 (pink), 6 rows in CC1 (burgundy).

STRIPE SEQUENCE C

This stripe sequence is worked only once.
18 rows in Stripe Sequence A, 6 rows in MC (white), 12 rows in CC5 (light blue), 22 rows in Stripe Sequence A, 14 rows in CC1 (burgundy), 10 rows in CC2 (medium gray heathered), 10 rows in CC4 (pink), 6 rows in CC1 (burgundy).

INSTRUCTIONS

BACK

Using US 4 (3.5 mm) needles and MC (white), CO 115/127/131 sts, and for hem ribbing, work 14 rows in ribbing patt; *at the same time*, in the last row, evenly distributed, dec 10/10/8 sts (= 105/117/123 sts). Change to US 6 (4.0 mm) needles, and cont in St st in Stripe Sequence B. After having completed Stripe Sequence B, cont in St st in Stripe Sequence A. At 21/21.3/21.7 in. (53/54/55 cm) (= 158/162/166 rows) from hem ribbing, BO all sts.

FRONT

Work as the Back, but with neckline shaping. For this, after having worked only 19/19.3/19.7 in. (48/49/50 cm) (= 144/148/150 rows) from end of hem ribbing, BO the middle 19/23/25 sts, and continue both sides separately. For the rounded neckline, BO sts at the neck edge in every other row as follows: BO 4 sts once, 3 sts 3/3/2 times, 2 sts 1/1/2 time(s), and 1 st 1/1/2 time(s). At 21/21.3/21.7 in. (53/54/55 cm) (= 158/162/166 rows) from end of hem ribbing, BO the remaining 27/31/33 sts for each shoulder.

SLEEVES (MAKE 2)

Using US 4 (3.5 mm) needles and MC (white), CO 51/55/59 sts, and for cuff ribbing, work 14 rows in ribbing patt; *at the same time*, in the last row, evenly distributed, dec 6/4/4 sts (= 45/51/55 sts). Change to US 6 (4.0 mm) needles, and cont in St st in Stripe Sequence C. After having completed Stripe Sequence C, cont in St st in Stripe Sequence A.

At the same time, for sleeve tapering, after having worked 6/8/8 rows from end of cuff, inc 1 st at each end of the row. Rep these incs in every 6th row 13/10/10 times more and in every 8th row 4/6/6 times more (= 81/85/89 sts). At 16.1/16.5/16.5 in. (41/42/42 cm) (= 124/126/126 rows) from hem ribbing, BO all sts.

FINISHING

Block all pieces to measurements on a soft surface, moisten, and let dry. Close shoulder and side seams from the wrong side, leaving the upper 7.1/7.5/7.9 in. (18/19/20 cm) open for the armholes. Seam the sleeves right sides facing each other and wrong sides facing out, and then sew the sleeves into the armholes from the wrong side.

Using US 4 (3.5 mm) needles and MC (white), pick up and knit 126/130/134 sts from the neckline edge, join into the round, and work 1.2 in. (3 cm) (= 8 rnds) in ribbing pattern. BO all sts in pattern, and weave in ends.

SCHEMATIC

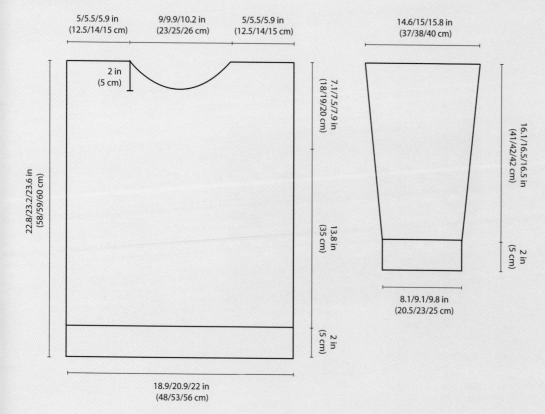

5/5.5/5.9 in (12.5/14/15 cm)

9/9.9/10.2 in (23/25/26 cm)

5/5.5/5.9 in (12.5/14/15 cm)

14.6/15/15.8 in (37/38/40 cm)

2 in (5 cm)

7.1/7.5/7.9 in (18/19/20 cm)

16.1/16.5/16.5 in (41/42/42 cm)

13.8 in (35 cm)

2 in (5 cm)

22.8/23.2/23.6 in (58/59/60 cm)

2 in (5 cm)

8.1/9.1/9.8 in (20.5/23/25 cm)

18.9/20.9/22 in (48/53/56 cm)

BASIC SWEATER 3

NICELY STYLED WITH BORDER

SIZES

Small/Medium/Large (US 6/8, 10/12, 14/16)

Numbers for size Small are listed before the first slash, for size Medium between slashes, and for size Large after the second slash. If only one number is given, it applies to all sizes.

MATERIALS

Schachenmayr Merino Extrafine 120; #3 light weight yarn; 100% wool; 131 yd (120 m), 1.75 oz. (50 g) per skein

- Main color (MC): 8/9/11 skeins #103 linen
- Contrasting color 1 (CC1): 3/3/4 skeins #171 olive
- Contrasting color 2 (CC2): 1/2/2 skeins #143 pink

Circular knitting needles, sizes US 4 (3.5 mm) and US 6 (4.0 mm), each 32 in. (80 cm) long

GAUGE

In stockinette stitch on US 6 (4.0 mm) needles, 22 sts and 30 rows = 4 x 4 in. (10 x 10 cm)

STOCKINETTE STITCH

RS: Knit all sts.
WS: Purl all sts.

RIBBING IN ROWS

RS: Alternate k1, p1.
WS: Work all sts as they appear—knit the knits and purl the purls.

RIBBING IN ROUNDS

All rounds (RS): Alternate k1, p1.

BORDER PATTERN

Work in stockinette stitch from Colorwork Chart A in stranded colorwork pattern. The chart contains both RS and WS rows. Sts are shown as they appear from the RS of the fabric. Begin with the stitch stated in the instructions, work to the end of the patt rep, and then repeat the patt rep widthwise across, ending with the stitch stated in the instructions. Work Rows 1–21 once heightwise.

INSTRUCTIONS

BACK

Using US 4 (3.5 mm) needles, CO 115/127/131 sts, and for hem ribbing, work 14 rows in ribbing patt; *at the same time*, in the last row, evenly distributed, dec 10/10/8 sts (= 105/117/123 sts). Change to US 6 (4.0 mm) needles, and cont in the following pattern: 2 rows in St st in MC (linen); 21 rows in St st in border patt, beginning with the 2nd/18th/15th st of the patt rep; repeat the patt rep widthwise, ending with the 18th/2nd/5th st of the patt rep. After this, work 79 rows in St st in MC (linen); then 21 rows in St st in border patt, beginning with the 2nd/18th/15th st of the patt rep; repeat the patt rep widthwise, ending with the 18th/2nd/5th st of the patt rep. After this, cont in St st in MC (linen). At 21/21.3/21.7 in. (53/54/55 cm) (= 158/162/166 rows) from hem ribbing, BO all sts.

COLORWORK CHART A

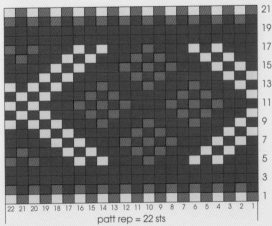

patt rep = 22 sts

KNITTING SYMBOLS

- = St st in MC: linen
- = St st in CC1: olive
- = St st in CC2: pink

FRONT

Work as the Back, but with neckline shaping. For this, after having worked only 19/19.3/19.7 in. (48/49/50 cm) (= 144/148/150 rows) from end of hem ribbing, BO the middle 19/23/25 sts, and continue both sides separately. For the rounded neckline, BO sts at the neck edge in every other row as follows: BO 4 sts once, 3 sts 3/3/2 times, 2 sts 1/1/2 time(s), and 1 st 1/1/2 time(s). At 21/21.3/21.7 in. (53/54/55 cm) (= 158/162/166 rows) from end of hem ribbing, BO the remaining 27/31/33 sts for each shoulder.

SLEEVES (MAKE 2)

Using US 4 (3.5 mm) needles, CO 51/55/59 sts, and for cuff ribbing, work 14 rows in ribbing patt; *at the same time*, in the last row, evenly distributed, dec 6/4/4 sts (= 45/51/55 sts). Change to US 6 (4.0 mm) needles, and cont in the following pattern: 2 rows in St st in MC (linen), 21 rows in St st in Border Patt, beginning with the 10th/7th/5th st of the patt rep, work the patt rep once widthwise, ending with the 10th/13th/15th st of the patt rep. After this, cont in St st in MC (linen).

At the same time, for sleeve tapering, after having worked 6/8/8 rows from end of cuff, inc 1 st at each end of the row. Rep these incs in every 6th row 13/10/10 times more and 4/6/6 times in every 8th row (= 81/85/89 sts). At 16.1/16.5/16.5 in. (41/42/42 cm) (= 124/126/126 rows) from hem ribbing, BO all sts.

FINISHING

Block all pieces to measurements on a soft surface, moisten, and let dry. Close shoulder and side seams from the wrong side, leaving the upper 7.1/7.5/7.9 in. (18/19/20 cm) open for the armholes. Seam the sleeves right sides facing each other and wrong sides facing out, and then sew the sleeves into the armholes from the wrong side.

Using US 4 (3.5 mm) needles and MC (linen), pick up and knit 126/130/134 sts from the neckline, join into the round, and work 1.2 in. (3 cm) (= 8 rnds) in ribbing pattern. BO all sts in pattern, and weave in ends.

SCHEMATIC

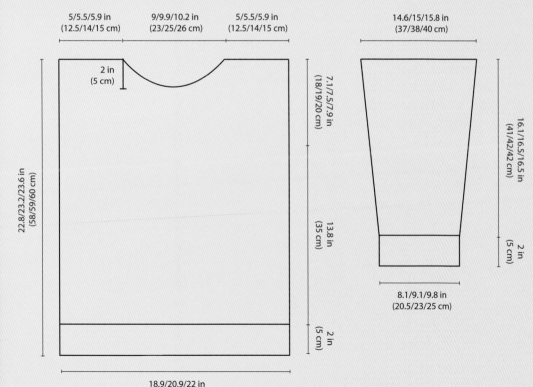

5/5.5/5.9 in (12.5/14/15 cm)

9/9.9/10.2 in (23/25/26 cm)

5/5.5/5.9 in (12.5/14/15 cm)

14.6/15/15.8 in (37/38/40 cm)

2 in (5 cm)

7.1/7.5/7.9 in (18/19/20 cm)

22.8/23.2/23.6 in (58/59/60 cm)

13.8 in (35 cm)

16.1/16.5/16.5 in (41/42/42 cm)

2 in (5 cm)

8.1/9.1/9.8 in (20.5/23/25 cm)

2 in (5 cm)

18.9/20.9/22 in (48/53/56 cm)

BASIC SWEATER 4

PERFECTLY PATTERNED IN STRANDED COLORWORK

STRAIGHT SLEEVE TOP

STRAIGHT BODY

STRAIGHT
SLEEVE TOP

BASIC
SWEATER 5
AIRY AND DELICATE
IN LACE PATTERN

STRAIGHT
BODY

BASIC SWEATER 4

PERFECTLY PATTERNED IN STRANDED COLORWORK

SIZES

Small/Medium/Large (US 6/8, 10/12, 14/16)
Numbers for size Small are listed before the first slash, for size Medium between slashes, and for size Large after the second slash. If only one number is given, it applies to all sizes.

MATERIALS

Schachenmayr Merino Extrafine 120; #3 light weight yarn; 100% wool; 131 yd (120 m), 1.75 oz. (50 g) per skein

- Main color (MC): 8/10/11 skeins #190 light gray heathered
- Contrasting color (CC): 6/8/10 skeins #146 plum

Circular knitting needles, sizes US 4 (3.5 mm) and US 6 (4.0 mm), each 32 in. (80 cm) long

GAUGE

In stranded colorwork pattern on US 6 (4.0 mm) needles, 22 sts and 30 rows = 4 x 4 in. (10 x 10 cm)

STOCKINETTE STITCH

RS: Knit all sts.
WS: Purl all sts.

RIBBING IN ROWS

RS: Alternate k1, p1.
WS: Work all sts as they appear— knit the knits and purl the purls.

RIBBING IN ROUNDS

All rounds (RS): Alternate k1, p1.

STRANDED PATTERN

Work in stockinette stitch in stranded colorwork pattern from Colorwork Chart B. The chart contains both RS and WS rows. Stitches are shown as they appear from the RS of the fabric. Begin with the stitch stated in the instructions, work to the end of the patt rep, and then repeat the patt rep widthwise across, ending with the stitch stated in the instructions. Repeat Rows 1–14 heightwise throughout.

INSTRUCTIONS

BACK

Using US 4 (3.5 mm) needles, CO 115/127/131 sts, and for hem ribbing, work 14 rows in ribbing patt; *at the same time*, in the last row, evenly distributed, dec 10/10/8 sts (= 105/117/123 sts). Change to US 6 (4.0 mm) needles, and cont in St st in stranded pattern, beginning with the 4th/12th/9th st of the chart, and ending with the 10th/2nd/5th st of the chart. After having worked 21/21.3/21.7 in. (53/54/55 cm) (= 158/162/166 rows) from hem ribbing, BO all sts.

FRONT

Work as the Back, but with neckline shaping. For this, after having worked only 19/19.3/19.7 in. (48/49/50 cm) (= 144/148/150 rows) from end of hem ribbing, BO the middle 19/23/25 sts, and continue both sides separately. For the

COLORWORK CHART B

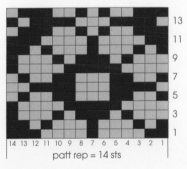

patt rep = 14 sts

KNITTING SYMBOLS

▨ = St st in MC: light gray heathered
■ = St st in CC: plum

rounded neckline, BO sts at the neck edge in every other row as follows: BO 4 sts once, 3 sts 3/3/2 times, 2 sts 1/1/2 time(s), and 1 st 1/1/2 time(s). At 21/21.3/21.7 in. (53/54/55 cm) (= 158/162/166 rows) from end of hem ribbing, BO the remaining 27/31/33 sts for each shoulder.

SLEEVES (MAKE 2)

Using US 4 (3.5 mm) needles, CO 51/55/59 sts in MC (light gray heathered), and for the cuff, work 14 rows in ribbing patt; *at the same time*, in the last row, evenly distributed, dec 6/4/4 sts (= 45/51/55 sts). Change to US 6 (4.0 mm) needles, and cont in St st in stranded pattern, beginning with the 6th/3rd/1st st of the chart, and ending with the 8th/11th/13th st of the chart.

After having worked 6/8/8 rows from end of cuff, for sleeve tapering, inc 1 st at each end of the row. Rep these incs in every 6th row 13/10/10 times more and in every 8th row 4/6/6 times more (= 81/85/89 sts). Incorporate the increased sts into the stranded color-work pattern. At 16.1/16.5/16.5 in. (41/42/42 cm) (= 124/126/126 rows) from hem ribbing, BO all sts.

FINISHING

Block all pieces to measurements on a soft surface, moisten, and let dry. Close shoulder and side seams, leaving the upper 7.1/7.5/7.9 in. (18/19/20 cm) open for the armholes. Close sleeve seams, and then sew the sleeves into the armholes from the wrong side.

Using US 4 (3.5 mm) needles and MC (light gray heathered), pick up and knit 126/130/134 sts from the neckline edge, join into the round, and work 1.2 in. (3 cm) (= 8 rnds) in ribbing pattern. BO all sts in pattern, and weave in ends.

SCHEMATIC

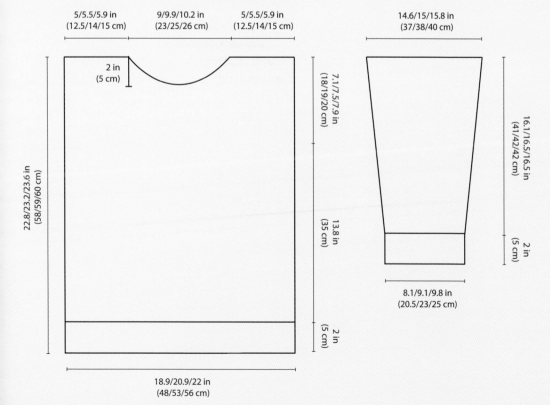

5/5.5/5.9 in (12.5/14/15 cm)
9/9.9/10.2 in (23/25/26 cm)
5/5.5/5.9 in (12.5/14/15 cm)

2 in (5 cm)

22.8/23.2/23.6 in (58/59/60 cm)

7.1/7.5/7.9 in (18/19/20 cm)

13.8 in (35 cm)

2 in (5 cm)

18.9/20.9/22 in (48/53/56 cm)

14.6/15/15.8 in (37/38/40 cm)

16.1/16.5/16.5 in (41/42/42 cm)

2 in (5 cm)

8.1/9.1/9.8 in (20.5/23/25 cm)

BASIC SWEATER 5

AIRY AND DELICATE IN LACE PATTERN

SIZES

Small/Medium/Large (US 6/8, 10/12, 14/16)
Numbers for size Small are listed before the first slash, for size Medium between slashes, and for size Large after the second slash. If only one number is given, it applies to all sizes.

MATERIALS

Schachenmayr Merino Extrafine 120; #3 light weight yarn; 100% wool; 131 yd (120 m), 1.75 oz. (50 g) per skein
• 10/11/13 skeins #101 white
Circular knitting needles, sizes US 4 (3.5 mm) and US 6 (4.0 mm), each 32 in. (80 cm) long

GAUGE

In lace pattern on US 6 (4.0 mm) needles, 20 sts and 28 rows = 4 x 4 in. (10 x 10 cm)

STOCKINETTE STITCH

RS: Knit all sts.
WS: Purl all sts.

RIBBING IN ROWS

RS: Alternate k1, p1.
WS: Work all sts as they appear—knit the knits and purl the purls.

RIBBING IN ROUNDS

All rounds (RS): Alternate k1, p1.

LACE PATTERN

Work from Stitch Pattern Chart A. Only RS rows are shown in the chart; in WS rows, work all sts as they appear, and purl the yarn overs. Begin with the sts before the patt rep, repeat the patt rep widthwise across, and end with the sts after the patt rep. Repeat Rows 1–12 of the chart heightwise throughout.

INSTRUCTIONS

BACK

Using US 4 (3.5 mm) needles, CO 115/127/131 sts, and for hem ribbing, work 14 rows in ribbing patt; *at the same time*, in the last row, evenly distributed, dec 20/22/16 sts (= 95/105/115 sts). Change to US 6 (4.0 mm) needles, and cont in lace pattern. At 21/21.3/21.7 in. (53/54/55 cm) (= 148/152/154 rows) from hem ribbing, BO all sts.

FRONT

Work as the Back, but with neckline shaping. For this, after having worked only 19/19.3/19.7 in. (48/49/50 cm) (= 134/138/140 rows) from end of ribbing, BO the middle 21/21/29 sts, and continue both sides separately. For neckline shaping, BO sts at the neck edge in every other row as follows: BO 3 sts 2/3/2 times, 2 sts 3/2/3 times, and 1 st

STITCH PATTERN CHART A
Stitch count is a multiple of 10 + 15

patt rep = 10 sts

KNITTING SYMBOLS

■ = knit 1 stitch
– = purl 1 stitch
○ = make 1 yarn over
◢ = knit 2 sts together
◣ = slip 1, knit 1, pass the slipped stitch over
▲ = slip 1, knit 2 sts together, pass the slipped stitch over
☐ = no stitch, for better overview only

once. At 21/21.3/21.7 in. (53/54/55 cm) (= 148/152/154 rows) from end of ribbing, BO the remaining 24/28/30 sts for each shoulder.

SLEEVES (MAKE 2)

Using US 4 (3.5 mm) needles, CO 51/55/59 sts, and for the cuff, work 14 rows in ribbing patt; *at the same time,* in the last row, evenly distributed, dec 6/8/10 sts (= 45/47/49 sts). Change to US 6 (4.0 mm) needles, and cont in lace pattern as follows: 0/1/2 st(s) in St st, 45 sts in lace pattern, 0/1/2 st(s) in St st. For sleeve tapering, after having worked 6 rows from end of cuff, inc 1 st at each end of the row. Rep these incs in every 6th row 0/3/4 times more and in every 8th row 12/11/10 times more (= 71/77/79 sts). At 16.1/16.5/16.5 in. (41/42/42 cm) (= 114/118/118 rows) from hem ribbing, BO all sts.

Please note: As soon as you have 49 sts on the needles, the first 2 and the last 2 sts will always be worked in St st. Increases at both ends of the row will then always be worked after or before these 2 sts, and the sts gained from increasing are incorporated into the lace pattern.

FINISHING

Block all pieces to measurements on a soft surface, moisten, and let dry. Close shoulder and side seams from the wrong side, leaving the upper 7.1/7.5/7.9 in. (18/19/20 cm) open for the armholes. Seam the sleeves right sides facing each other and wrong sides facing out, and then sew the sleeves into the armholes from the wrong side.

Using US 4 (3.5 mm) needles, pick up and knit 126/130/134 sts from the neckline edge, join into the round, and work 1.2 in. (3 cm) (= 8 rnds) in ribbing pattern. BO all sts in pattern, and weave in ends.

SCHEMATIC

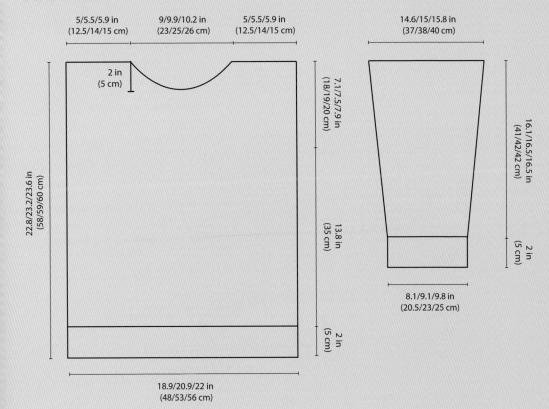

BASIC SWEATER 6

INTRICATELY ENTWINED CABLES

SIZES

Small/Medium/Large (US 6/8, 10/12, 14/16)
Numbers for size Small are listed before the first slash, for size Medium between slashes, and for size Large after the second slash. If only one number is given, it applies to all sizes.

MATERIALS

Schachenmayr Merino Extrafine 120; #3 light weight yarn; 100% wool; 131 yd (120 m), 1.75 oz. (50 g) per skein

• 12/14/16 skeins #133 burgundy

Circular knitting needles, sizes US 4 (3.5 mm) and US 6 (4.0 mm), each 32 in. (80 cm) long

Cable needle (cn)

GAUGE

In Double Seed St on US 6 (4.0 mm) needles, 22 sts and 34 rows = 4 x 4 in. (10 x 10 cm)

In Cable Patt 1 on US 6 (4.0 mm) needles, 58 sts = 8.3 in. (21 cm)

In Cable Patt 2 on US 6 (4.0 mm) needles, 18 sts = 3.2 in. (8 cm)

STOCKINETTE STITCH

RS: Knit all sts.
WS: Purl all sts.

RIBBING IN ROWS

RS: Alternate k1, p1.
WS: Work all sts as they appear—knit the knits and purl the purls.

RIBBING IN ROUNDS

All rounds (RS): Alternate k1, p1.

DOUBLE SEED STITCH

Row 1: Alternate k1, p1.
Row 2: Knit the knits and purl the purls.
Row 3: Alternate p1, k1.
Row 4: Knit the knits and purl the purls.
Rep Rows 1–4 throughout.

CABLE PATTERN 1

Work from Stitch Pattern Chart B. Only RS rows are shown in the chart; in WS rows, work all sts as they appear (knit the knits and purl the purls), and purl the slipped sts. Work the patt rep (58 sts wide) widthwise across once, and then rep Rows 1–12 heightwise throughout.

CABLE PATTERN 2

Work from Stitch Pattern Chart C. Only RS rows are shown in the chart; in WS rows, work all sts as they appear (knit the knits and purl the purls), and purl the slipped sts. Work the patt rep (18 sts wide) widthwise across once, and then rep Rows 1–12 heightwise throughout.

STITCH PATTERN CHART B

cable pattern 1 = 58 sts

STITCH PATTERN CHART C

cable pattern 2 = 18 sts

KNITTING SYMBOLS

■ = knit 1 stitch

▬ = purl 1 stitch

⚏ = slip 1 stitch purlwise with yarn in back of work

= hold 1 stitch on cn in back of work, knit the next 2 stitches, and then knit the stitch from the cn

= hold 2 sts on cn in front of work, purl the next stitch, and then knit the 2 sts from the cn

= hold 2 sts on cn in back of work, knit the next 2 stitches, and then knit the 2 sts from the cn

= hold 4 sts on cn in back of work, knit the next 4 sts, and then knit the 4 sts from the cn

= hold 4 sts on cn in front of work, knit the next 4 sts, and then knit the 4 sts from the cn

**STRAIGHT
SLEEVE TOP**

**STRAIGHT
BODY**

INSTRUCTIONS

BACK

Using US 4 (3.5 mm) needles, CO 115/127/131 sts, and for hem ribbing, work 14 rows in ribbing patt; *at the same time*, in the last row, evenly distributed, inc 1 st (= 116/128/132 sts). Change to US 6 (4.0 mm) needles, and continue in the following pattern: 1 st in St st, 28/34/36 sts in double seed stitch, 58 sts in cable pattern 1, 28/34/36 sts in double seed stitch, 1 st in St st. At 21/21.3/21.7 in. (53/54/55 cm) (= 180/184/188 rows) from hem ribbing, BO all sts.

FRONT

Work as the Back, but with neckline shaping. For this, after having worked only 19/19.3/19.7 in. (48/49/50 cm) (= 164/166/168 rows) from end of ribbing, BO the middle 28/30/30 sts, and continue both sides separately. For neckline shaping, BO sts at the neck edge in every other row as follows: BO 4 sts once, 3 sts twice, 2 sts 3/3/2 times, and 1 st 1/2/4 time(s). At 21/21.3/21.7 in. (53/54/55 cm) (= 180/184/188 rows) from end of ribbing, BO the remaining 27/31/33 sts for each shoulder.

SLEEVES (MAKE 2)

Using US 4 (3.5 mm) needles, CO 51/55/59 sts, and for the cuff, work 14 rows in ribbing patt; *at the same time*, in the last row, evenly distributed, dec 5/3/3 sts (= 46/52/56 sts). Change to US 6 (4.0 mm) needles, and continue in the following pattern: 1 st in St st, 13/16/18 sts in double seed stitch, 18 sts in cable pattern 2, 13/16/18 sts in double seed stitch, and 1 st in St st.

For sleeve tapering, after having worked 6/10/10 rows from end of cuff, inc 1 st at each end of the row. Rep these incs in every 6th row 5/0/0 times more, and then in every 8th row 12/15/15 times (= 82/84/88 sts). After 16.1/16.5/16.5 in. (41/42/42 cm) (= 140/142/142 rows) from end of cuff, BO all sts.

FINISHING

Block all pieces to measurements on a soft surface, moisten, and let dry. Close shoulder and side seams from the wrong side, leaving the upper 7.1/7.5/7.9 in. (18/19/20 cm) open for the armholes. Seam the sleeves right sides facing each other and wrong sides facing out, and then sew the sleeves into the armholes from the wrong side.

Using US 4 (3.5 mm) needles, pick up and knit 126/130/134 sts from the neckline edge, join into the round, and work 1.2 in. (3 cm) (= 8 rnds) in ribbing pattern. BO all sts in pattern, and weave in ends.

SCHEMATIC

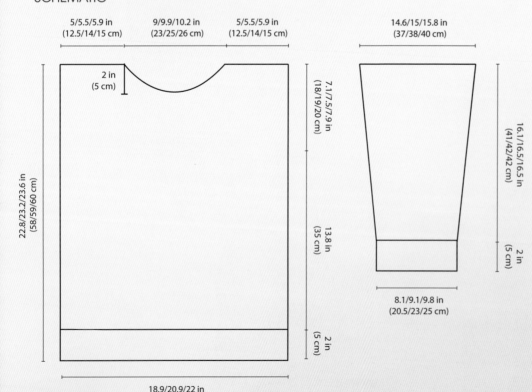

5/5.5/5.9 in (12.5/14/15 cm)
9/9.9/10.2 in (23/25/26 cm)
5/5.5/5.9 in (12.5/14/15 cm)
14.6/15/15.8 in (37/38/40 cm)

2 in (5 cm)

7.1/7.5/7.9 in (18/19/20 cm)

16.1/16.5/16.5 in (41/42/42 cm)

22.8/23.2/23.6 in (58/59/60 cm)

13.8 in (35 cm)

2 in (5 cm)

8.1/9.1/9.8 in (20.5/23/25 cm)

2 in (5 cm)

18.9/20.9/22 in (48/53/56 cm)

STRAIGHT SLEEVE TOP

STRAIGHT BODY

EASY MIX
AND MATCH
SYSTEM –

THE RIGHT INGREDIENTS

BEFORE YOU BEGIN: TIPS AND TRICKS FOR YOUR APPROACH

Before you begin your sweater project, you should consider a few things. I recommend reading these tips thoroughly. If you follow this advice, you will be able to enjoy your sweater for a long time and prevent future disappointments.

THE SIZES

Every basic design and every "add-on"—from the hem ribbing to the sleeve—is always described for three sizes: Small (US 6/8), Medium (US 10/12), and Large (US 14/16). Numbers for size Small are always listed before the first slash; for size Medium, between slashes; and for size Large, after the second slash. If only one number is given, it applies to all sizes.

THE SCHEMATICS

Every design comes with a schematic containing all relevant measurements. Before you reach for the needles, please look at this drawing first. If you are unsure which one of the sizes is best for you, choose a well-fitting sweater from your wardrobe to compare the measurements before deciding which size to make. The schematics apply to garments worked in stockinette stitch. For sweaters with lace or cable patterns, measurements may vary, owing to the different properties of the stitch patterns.

THE GAUGE SWATCH

Gauge swatching is rather unpopular with many knitters, since it takes additional time and prevents us from embarking on the real knitting project right away. Still, do take the time to make a swatch!

For every pattern in this book, a gauge is listed. It tells us how many stitches and rows have to be worked to get a square of 4 x 4 in. (10 x 10 cm). However, personal gauge varies: one knitter might knit rather densely, another more loosely. This impacts the outcome in width and height for each individual stitch. For this reason, even when working the same number of rows and stitches, actual finished measurements may turn out different. The needle size listed in the instructions should be considered a recommendation or suggestion only. If you get a smaller square than 4 x 4 in. (10 x 10 cm) with the listed needle size, you should switch to larger needles; if your square turns out larger, change to a smaller needle size.

For different patterns, a different number of stitches and rows is needed—every stitch pattern has its own gauge. When combining individual parts from different sweaters, it may happen that, for instance, the Front and Back have a different stitch and row count—this should always be retained. If the gauge matches, both pieces will end up having the same measurements later.

Last but not least, much also depends on the yarn used. The sweaters in this book have all been knit in merino wool. This yarn has a smooth structure and is not scratchy, making it suitable even for sensitive skin. Owing to its lower inherent elasticity, merino wool yarn will always grow a little bit after washing (sometimes even more than a little bit). For this reason, it is especially crucial to make a gauge swatch when working with merino wool yarn. Before the swatch can be measured, it is essential to wash it. Only with a properly prepared swatch can you be sure that the sweater will fit correctly after washing and blocking.

Small changes are not restricted to merino wool; other fibers can also grow or shrink to some extent. Therefore, always use your gauge swatch to predict what to expect from the finished garment.

Even when the garment may seem too small (or large) while you knit it up, if your gauge was spot on, your sweater, too, will have the same measurements as listed in the schematic after washing and blocking. Therefore, while knitting, it is more important to orient yourself to the correct number of rows to be worked, rather than watching the centimeters or inches. This way, your sweater will stand up to many washes without losing its perfect fit.

BLOCKING THE PIECES

Knitted garments are elastic and, owing to their own weight, can lose shape, especially after moistening or washing. For this reason, individual parts need to be brought into proper shape through blocking before they can be left to dry. Blocking can be achieved by several techniques. I recommend the following: First, swish the pieces around in lukewarm water and then press out excess water (without wringing!). Now spread out the pieces on a soft surface (for instance, a Styrofoam board, blanket, or foam rubber tiles). Use a measuring tape to check length and width against the measurements given in the schematic for the finished garment. Mark the corner points on the blocking surface with tailor pins, and place individual pieces between the markings. Now, in evenly spaced intervals, also using tailor pins, pin down the pieces along the edges. My tip: To achieve consistent sizes for Front and Back as well as for both sleeves, place these pieces atop each other, and pin them down double layered. In between, check measurements frequently using your measuring tape. Finally, let the pieces dry before seaming them.

Now you are all set to start: Begin with your gauge swatch, and then knit up a dream sweater of your own design.

HEM AND CUFF VARIATIONS

For sleeve cuffs and hem ribbing, first find the body shape and sleeve length you are planning, and follow the instructions.

For all cuff and hem types, in the last WS row, evenly distributed, increase or decrease as many stitches as needed to reach the required stitch count for the sweater after the end of the cuff or hem.

For good stitch definition, it is recommended to always work cuffs and hems with a slightly smaller needle size than the rest of the sweater, for instance US 4 (3.5 mm) instead of US 6 (4.0 mm).

RIBBED HEMS AND CUFFS

(Stitch count is a multiple of 2 + 1.)

RIBBING

RS: Alternate k1, p1.
WS: Work all sts as they appear—knit the knits and purl the purls.

GAUGE

In ribbing patt on US 4 (3.5 mm) needles, 24 sts and 30 rows = 4 x 4 in. (10 x 10 cm)

INSTRUCTIONS FOR FRONT AND BACK

A-LINE SHAPED

CO 177/189/197 sts, and work 14 rows in ribbing patt, in the last row, increasing or decreasing as many sts as needed to reach the required stitch count for the sweater after the hem ribbing.

OVERSIZED BODY SHAPE

CO 167/191/215 sts, and work 14 rows in ribbing patt, in the last row, increasing or decreasing as many sts as needed to reach the required stitch count for the sweater after the hem ribbing.

ALL OTHER BODY SHAPES

CO 115/127/131 sts, and work 14 rows in ribbing patt, in the last row, increasing or decreasing as many sts as needed to reach the required stitch count for the sweater after the hem ribbing.

SLEEVE INSTRUCTIONS

LONG SLEEVE

CO 51/55/59 sts, and work 14 rows in ribbing patt, in the last row, increasing or decreasing as many sts as needed to reach the required stitch count for the sleeve after the cuff.

¾ SLEEVE

CO 65/69/73 sts, and work as described for the long sleeve.

SHORT SLEEVE

CO 79/81/83 sts, and work as described for the long sleeve.

HEMS AND CUFFS IN SEED STITCH

(Stitch count is a multiple of 2 + 1.)

SEED STITCH
In RS and WS rows: Alternate k1, p1.

GAUGE
In seed stitch on US 4 (3.5 mm) needles, 22 sts and 32 rows = 4 x 4 in. (10 x 10 cm)

INSTRUCTIONS FOR FRONT AND BACK

A-LINE SHAPED
CO 163/173/181 sts, and work 16 rows in seed stitch, in the last row, increasing or decreasing as many sts as needed to reach the required stitch count for the sweater after the hem ribbing.

OVERSIZED BODY SHAPE
CO 155/175/197 sts, and work 16 rows in seed stitch, in the last row, increasing or decreasing as many sts as needed to reach the required stitch count for the sweater after the hem ribbing.

ALL OTHER BODY SHAPES
CO 105/117/123 sts, and work 16 rows in seed stitch, in the last row, increasing or decreasing as many sts as needed to reach the required stitch count for the sweater after the hem ribbing.

SLEEVE INSTRUCTIONS

LONG SLEEVE
CO 45/51/55 sts, and work 16 rows in seed stitch, in the last row, increasing or decreasing as many sts as needed to reach the required stitch count for the sleeve after the cuff.

¾ SLEEVE
CO 57/61/65 sts, and work as described for the long sleeve.

SHORT SLEEVE
CO 73/77/81 sts, and work as described for the long sleeve.

HEMS AND CUFFS IN CABLE PATTERN

(Stitch count is a multiple of 10 + 6.)

CABLE PATTERN

Row 1 (RS): *P2, k2, p2, k4, rep from * to last 6 sts of the row, ending with p2, k2, p2.

Row 2 (WS): Knit the knits and purl the purls.

Row 3 (RS): *P2, k2, p2, hold 2 sts on cn in back of work, k2, then k2 from cn, rep from * to last 6 sts of the row, ending with p2, k2, p2.

Row 4 (WS): Knit the knits and purl the purls.

Rep Rows 1–4 throughout.

GAUGE

In cable pattern on US 4 (3.5 mm) needles, 24 sts and 32 rows = 4 x 4 in. (10 x 10 cm)

INSTRUCTIONS FOR FRONT AND BACK

A-LINE SHAPED

CO 176/186/196 sts, and work 16 rows in cable pattern, in the last row, increasing or decreasing as many sts as needed to reach the required stitch count for the sweater after the hem ribbing.

OVERSIZED BODY SHAPE

CO 166/196/216 sts, and work 16 rows in cable pattern, in the last row, increasing or decreasing as many sts as needed to reach the required stitch count for the sweater after the hem ribbing.

ALL OTHER BODY SHAPES

CO 116/126/136 sts, and work 16 rows in cable pattern, in the last row, increasing or decreasing as many sts as needed to reach the required stitch count for the sweater after the hem ribbing.

SLEEVE INSTRUCTIONS

LONG SLEEVE

CO 46/56/66 sts, and work 16 rows in cable pattern, in the last row, increasing or decreasing as many sts as needed to reach the required stitch count for the sleeve after the cuff.

¾ SLEEVE

CO 66/66/76 sts, and work as described for the long sleeve.

SHORT SLEEVE

CO 76/86/86 sts, and work as described for the long sleeve.

HEMS AND CUFFS IN STRANDED PATTERN

(Stitch count is a multiple of 6 + 3.)

STRANDED PATTERN

Work in stockinette in stranded colorwork pattern from Colorwork Chart C. The chart contains both RS and WS rows. Sts are shown as they appear from the RS of the fabric. Repeat the patt rep (6 sts wide) widthwise across the row, ending with the 3 sts after the patt rep. Work Rows 1–6 of the chart twice heightwise.

GARTER STITCH

All rows: Knit all sts on RS and on WS.

GAUGE

In stranded colorwork pattern on US 4 (3.5 mm) needles, 22 sts and 30 rows = 4 x 4 in. (10 x 10 cm)

INSTRUCTIONS FOR FRONT AND BACK

A-LINE SHAPED

Using contrasting color (CC), CO 165/177/183, and work as follows: 4 rows garter st in CC, 12 rows in stranded pattern, 4 rows garter st in CC, in the last row, increasing or decreasing as many sts as needed to reach the required stitch count for the sweater after the hem ribbing.

OVERSIZED BODY SHAPE

Using contrasting color (CC), CO 153/177/201 sts, and work as follows: 4 rows garter st in CC, 12 rows in stranded pattern, 4 rows garter st in CC, in the last row, increasing or decreasing as many sts as needed to reach the required stitch count for the sweater after the hem ribbing.

ALL OTHER BODY SHAPES

Using contrasting color (CC), CO 105/117/123 sts, and work as follows: 4 rows garter st in CC, 12 rows in stranded pattern, 4 rows garter st in CC, in the last row, increasing or decreasing as many sts as needed to reach the required stitch count for the sweater after the hem ribbing.

SLEEVE INSTRUCTIONS

LONG SLEEVE

Using contrasting color (CC), CO 45/51/57 sts, and work as follows: 4 rows garter st in CC, 12 rows in stranded pattern, 4 rows garter st in CC, in the last row, increasing or decreasing as many sts as needed to reach the required stitch count for the sleeve after the cuff.

¾ SLEEVE

CO 57/63/69 sts, and work as described for the long sleeve.

SHORT SLEEVE

CO 69/75/81 sts, and work as described for the long sleeve.

COLORWORK CHART C

1 patt rep = 6 sts

KNITTING SYMBOLS

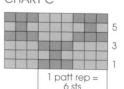

= 1 st in St st in MC
= 1 st in St st in CC

HEMS AND CUFFS IN MOSAIC PATTERN

(Stitch count is a multiple of 2 + 1.)

MOSAIC PATTERN

RS: *K1 in contrasting color (CC), k1 in main color (MC), rep from * across the row, ending with k1 in CC.

WS: *P1 in MC, p1 in CC, rep from * across, ending with p1 in MC.

GARTER STITCH

All rows: Knit all sts on RS and on WS.

GAUGE

In mosaic pattern on US 4 (3.5 mm) needles, 22 sts and 30 rows = 4 x 4 in. (10 x 10 cm)

INSTRUCTIONS FOR FRONT AND BACK

A-LINE SHAPED

Using contrasting color (CC), CO 163/175/181 sts, and work as follows: 4 rows garter st in CC, 10 rows in mosaic pattern, 4 rows garter st in CC, in the last row, increasing or decreasing as many sts as needed to reach the required stitch count for the sweater after the hem ribbing.

OVERSIZED BODY SHAPE

Using contrasting color (CC), CO 153/177/197 sts, and work as follows: 4 rows garter st in CC, 10 rows in mosaic pattern, 4 rows garter st in CC, in the last row, increasing or decreasing as many sts as needed to reach the required stitch count for the sweater after the hem ribbing.

ALL OTHER BODY SHAPES

Using contrasting color (CC), CO 105/117/123 sts, and work as follows: 4 rows garter st in CC, 10 rows in mosaic pattern, 4 rows garter st in CC, in the last row, increasing or decreasing as many sts as needed to reach the required stitch count for the sweater after the hem ribbing.

SLEEVE INSTRUCTIONS

LONG SLEEVE

Using contrasting color (CC), CO 45/51/55 sts, and work as follows: 4 rows garter st in CC, 10 rows in mosaic pattern, 4 rows garter st in CC, in the last row, increasing or decreasing as many sts as needed to reach the required stitch count for the sleeve after the cuff.

¾ SLEEVE

Using contrasting color (CC), CO 57/61/65 sts, and work as described for the long sleeve.

SHORT SLEEVE

Using contrasting color (CC), CO 73/77/81 sts, and work as described for the long sleeve.

HEMS AND CUFFS IN NUPP PATTERN

(Stitch count is a multiple of 11 + 2.)

NUPP PATTERN

Work from Stitch Pattern Chart D. Only RS rows are shown in the chart; in WS rows, purl all sts and yarn overs. Repeat the patt rep widthwise across, ending with the 2 sts after the patt rep.

GARTER STITCH

All rows: Knit all sts on RS and on WS.

GAUGE

In nupp pattern on US 4 (3.5 mm) needles, 21 sts and 29 rows = 4 x 4 in. (10 x 10 cm)

INSTRUCTIONS FOR FRONT AND BACK

A-LINE SHAPED

CO 156/167/178 sts, and work as follows: 4 rows garter st, 16 rows in nupp pattern, 4 rows garter st, in the last row, increasing or decreasing as many sts as needed to reach the required stitch count for the sweater after the hem ribbing.

OVERSIZED BODY SHAPE

CO 145/167/195 sts, and work as follows: 4 rows garter st, 16 rows in nupp pattern, 4 rows garter st, in the last row, increasing or decreasing as many sts as needed to reach the required stitch count for the sweater after the hem ribbing.

ALL OTHER BODY SHAPES

CO 101/112/123 sts, and work as follows: 4 rows garter st, 16 rows in nupp pattern, 4 rows garter st, in the last row, increasing or decreasing as many sts as needed to reach the required stitch count for the sweater after the hem ribbing.

SLEEVE INSTRUCTIONS

LONG SLEEVE

CO 46/46/57 sts, and work as follows: 4 rows garter st, 16 rows in nupp pattern, 4 rows garter st, in the last row, increasing or decreasing as many sts as needed to reach the required stitch count for the sleeve after the cuff.

¾ SLEEVE

CO 57/57/68 sts, and work as described for the long sleeve.

SHORT SLEEVE

CO 68/79/79 sts, and work as described for the long sleeve.

STITCH PATTERN CHART D

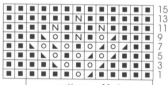

patt rep = 11 sts

KNITTING SYMBOLS

■ = knit 1 stitch

◢ = knit 2 sts together

◣ = slip 1, knit 1, pass the slipped stitch over

○ = make 1 yarn over

N = 1 nupp (= work k1, p1, k1, p1, k1 all into the next st, turn work, purl the 5 nupp sts, turn work again and one after another, pass the 2nd, 3rd, 4th and 5th st over the first one)

HEMS AND CUFFS IN LACE PATTERN

(Stitch count is a multiple of 10 + 13.)

LACE PATTERN

Work from Stitch Pattern Chart E. Only RS rows are shown in the chart; in WS rows, purl all sts and yarn overs. Begin with the 7 sts before the patt rep, repeat the patt rep widthwise, and end with the 6 sts after the patt rep. Work Rows 1–16 once heightwise.

GAUGE

In lace pattern on US 4 (3.5 mm) needles, 21 sts and 32 rows = 4 x 4 in. (10 x 10 cm)

INSTRUCTIONS FOR FRONT AND BACK

A-LINE SHAPED

CO 153/163/173 sts, and work 16 rows from chart, in the last row, increasing or decreasing as many sts as needed to reach the required stitch count for the sweater after the hem.

OVERSIZED BODY SHAPE

CO 143/163/193 sts, and work 16 rows from chart, in the last row, increasing or decreasing as many sts as needed to reach the required stitch count for the sweater after the hem.

ALL OTHER BODY SHAPES

CO 103/113/123 sts, and work 16 rows from chart, in the last row, increasing or decreasing as many sts as needed to reach the required stitch count for the sweater after the hem.

SLEEVE INSTRUCTIONS

LONG SLEEVE

CO 43/53/53 sts, and work 16 rows from chart, in the last row, increasing or decreasing as many sts as needed to reach the required stitch count for the sleeve after the cuff.

¾ SLEEVE

CO 63/63/73 sts, and work as described for the long sleeve.

SHORT SLEEVE

CO 73/83/93 sts, and work as described for the long sleeve.

Please note: These hem and cuff patterns are only conditionally suitable for Basic Sweaters with lace patterns. Due to the different stitch counts in the pattern repeats, the transition from hem or cuff pattern to the stitch pattern in the body of the sweater may turn out slightly shifted. Therefore, for this combination, I recommend working an additional 2–4 rows of garter stitch after the hem and cuffs to achieve a more harmonious transition. More advanced knitters will be able to adjust the hems and cuffs by adding the appropriate number of stitches.

STITCH PATTERN CHART E

	15
	13
	11
	9
	7
	5
	3
	1

patt rep = 10 sts

KNITTING SYMBOLS

▪ = knit 1 stitch

◢ = knit 2 sts together

◣ = slip 1, knit 1, pass the slipped stitch over

○ = make 1 yarn over

▲ = slip 1, knit 2 sts together, pass the slipped stitch over

HEMS AND CUFFS WITH ROLLED EDGE

(Works with any stitch count.)

STOCKINETTE STITCH
RS: Knit all sts.
WS: Purl all sts.

GAUGE
Stockinette stitch on US 4 (3.5 mm) needles, 22 sts and 30 rows = 4 x 4 in. (10 x 10 cm)

INSTRUCTIONS FOR FRONT AND BACK

A-LINE SHAPED
CO 163/175/181 sts, and work 13 rows in St st. Then knit 1 WS row, increasing or decreasing as many sts as needed to reach the required stitch count for the sweater after the hem ribbing.

OVERSIZED BODY SHAPE
CO 153/177/197 sts, and work 13 rows in St st. Then knit 1 WS row, increasing or decreasing as many sts as needed to reach the required stitch count for the sweater after the hem ribbing.

ALL OTHER BODY SHAPES
CO 105/117/123 sts, and work 13 rows in St st. Then knit 1 WS row, increasing or decreasing as many sts as needed to reach the required stitch count for the sweater after the hem ribbing.

SLEEVE INSTRUCTIONS

LONG SLEEVE
CO 45/51/55 sts, and work 13 rows in St st. Then knit 1 WS row, increasing or decreasing as many sts as needed to reach the required stitch count for the sleeve after the cuff.

¾ SLEEVE
CO 57/61/65 sts, and work as described for the long sleeve.

SHORT SLEEVE
CO 73/77/81 sts, and work as described for the long sleeve.

NECKLINE VARIATIONS

On these two pages, you will first learn how to generally incorporate shaping for a round neckline or V-neck when working the Front of your sweater. To create a boatneck, as shown in some patterns, you will not need to add any shaping. The pages after these present a variety of neckband options to choose from.

ROUND NECKLINE/CREWNECK

CREWNECK FOR ALL STOCKINETTE SWEATERS

FRONT WITH STRAIGHT SLEEVE TOP AND ARMHOLE SHAPING

At 19/19.3/19.7 in. (48/49/50 cm) (= 144/148/150 rows) from end of hem ribbing, BO the middle 19/23/25 sts, and continue both sides separately. For the rounded neckline, BO sts at the neck edge in every other row as follows: BO 4 sts once, 3 sts 3/3/2 times, 2 sts 1/1/2 time(s), and 1 st 1/1/2 time(s). At 21/21.3/21.7 in. (53/54/55 cm) (= 158/162/166 rows) from end of ribbing, BO the remaining shoulder sts.

FRONT WITH RAGLAN SLEEVE ARMHOLE SHAPING

At 19/19.3/19.7 in. (48/49/50 cm) (= 144/148/150 rows) from end of hem ribbing, BO the middle 19/23/25 sts, and continue both sides separately. For the rounded neckline, BO sts at the neck edge in every other row as follows: BO 4 sts once, 3 sts 1/2/1 time(s), 2 sts 2/1/2 time(s), and 1 st 1/0/1 time(s). At 20/20.5/21 in. (51/52/53 cm) (= 154/156/158 rows) from end of ribbing, break the working yarn, leaving a not-too-short end, and pull the tail through the last stitch.

CREWNECK FOR SWEATERS WITH LACE PATTERNS

FRONT WITH STRAIGHT SLEEVE TOP AND ARMHOLE SHAPING

At 19/19.3/19.7 in. (48/49/50 cm) (= 134/138/140 rows) from end of ribbing, BO the middle 21/21/29 sts, and continue both sides separately. For the rounded neckline, BO sts at the neck edge in every other row as follows: BO 3 sts 2/3/2 times, 2 sts 3/2/3 times, and 1 st once. At 21/21.3/21.7 in. (53/54/55 cm) (= 148/152/154 rows) from end of ribbing, BO the remaining shoulder sts.

FRONT WITH RAGLAN SLEEVE ARMHOLE SHAPING

At 19/19.3/19.7 in. (48/49/50 cm) (= 134/138/140 rows) from end of ribbing, BO the middle 21/21/29 sts, and continue both sides separately. For the rounded neckline, BO sts at the neck edge in every other row as follows: BO 3 sts 2/3/2 times, and then 2 sts 1/0/2 time(s). At 20/20.5/21 in. (51/52/53 cm) (= 142/146/150 rows) from end of ribbing, break the working yarn, leaving a not-too-short end, and pull the tail through the last stitch.

CREWNECK FOR SWEATERS WITH CABLE PATTERN

FRONT WITH STRAIGHT SLEEVE TOP AND ARMHOLE SHAPING

At 19/19.3/19.7 in. (48/49/50 cm) (= 164/166/168 rows) from end of ribbing, BO the middle 28/30/30 sts, and continue both sides separately. For the rounded neckline, BO sts at the neck edge in every other row as follows: BO 4 sts once, 3 sts twice, 2 sts 3/3/2 times, and 1 st 1/2/4 time(s). At 21/21.3/21.7 in. (53/54/55 cm) (= 180/184/188 rows) from end of ribbing, BO the remaining shoulder sts.

FRONT WITH RAGLAN SLEEVE ARMHOLE SHAPING

At 19/19.3/19.7 in. (48/49/50 cm) (= 164/166/168 rows) from end of ribbing, BO the middle 28/30/32 sts, and continue both sides separately. For the rounded neckline, BO sts at the neck edge in every other row as follows: BO 4 sts once, 3 sts twice, and 2 sts twice. At 20/20.5/21 in. (51/52/53 cm) (= 174/176/180 rows) from end of ribbing, break the working yarn, leaving a not-too-short end, and pull the tail through the last stitch.

V-NECK

V-NECK FOR ALL STOCKINETTE SWEATERS

FRONT WITH STRAIGHT SLEEVE TOP AND ARMHOLE SHAPING

At 13.8/13.8/14.2 in. (35/35/36 cm) (= 106/106/108 rows) from end of ribbing, BO 1 st in the middle, and continue both sides separately. For the sloped neckline, at the neck edge, in every RS row, work accented decrease of 1 st each 25/27/28 times. At 21/21.3/21.7 in. (53/54/55 cm) (= 158/162/166 rows) from end of ribbing, BO the remaining shoulder sts.

FRONT WITH RAGLAN SLEEVE ARMHOLE SHAPING

At 14.4/14.2/14.2 in. (36.5/36/36 cm) (= 110/108/108 rows) from end of ribbing, BO 1 st in the middle, and continue both sides separately. For the sloped neckline, on both sides of the neck edge, in every RS row, work accented decrease of 1 st each 21/23/24 times. At 20/20.5/21 in. (51/52/53 cm) (= 154/156/158 rows) from end of ribbing, break the working yarn, leaving a not-too-short end, and pull the tail through the last stitch.

V-NECK FOR SWEATERS WITH LACE PATTERNS

FRONT WITH STRAIGHT SLEEVE TOP AND ARMHOLE SHAPING

At 14.2/14.6/13.8 in. (36/37/35 cm) (= 100/102/98 rows) from end of ribbing, BO 1 st in the middle, and continue both sides separately. For the sloped neckline, at the neck edge, in every RS row, work accented decrease of 1 st each 23/24/27 times. At 21/21.3/21.7 in. (53/54/55 cm) (= 148/152/154 rows) from end of ribbing, BO the remaining shoulder sts.

FRONT WITH RAGLAN SLEEVE ARMHOLE SHAPING

At 15/15.4/13.8 in. (38/39/35 cm) (= 106/108/100 rows) from end of ribbing, BO 1 st in the middle, and continue both sides separately. For the sloped neckline, on both sides of the neck edge, in every RS row, work accented decrease of 1 st each 18/19/24 times. At 20/20.5/21 in. (51/52/53 cm) (= 144/148/150 rows) from end of ribbing, break the working yarn, leaving a not-too-short end, and pull the tail through the last stitch.

V-NECK IN SWEATERS WITH CABLE PATTERN

FRONT WITH STRAIGHT SLEEVE TOP AND ARMHOLE SHAPING

At 13.8/13.8/14.2 in. (35/35/36 cm) (= 118/118/120 rows) from end of ribbing, BO 2 sts in the middle and continue both sides separately. For the sloped neckline, at the neck edge, in every RS row, work accented decrease of 1 st each 30/32/33 times. At 21/21.3/21.7 in. (53/54/55 cm) (= 180/184/188 rows) from end of ribbing, BO the remaining shoulder sts.

FRONT WITH RAGLAN SLEEVE ARMHOLE SHAPING

At 13.8/13.8/14.2 in. (35/35/36 cm) (= 118/118/120 rows) from end of ribbing, BO 2 sts in the middle and continue both sides separately. For the sloped neckline, on both sides of the neck edge, in every RS row, work accented decrease of 1 st each 27/28/29 times. At 20/20.5/21 in. (51/52/53 cm) (= 174/176/180 rows) from end of ribbing, break the working yarn, leaving a not-too-short end, and pull the tail through the last stitch.

ACCENTED DECREASES

Accented decreases are always worked in RS rows, at both ends of the row, as follows: K1, skp, work in pattern to last 3 sts of the row, then k2tog, k1. In WS rows, always purl the first 2 sts and the last 2 sts of the row. In RS rows without decreases, always knit the first 2 sts and the last 2 sts of the row.

NECKBAND VARIATIONS

For good stitch definition, it is recommended to always work neckbands with a slightly smaller needle size than the rest of the sweater—for instance, US 4 (3.5 mm) instead of US 6 (4.0 mm).

ROUND NECKLINE/CREWNECK WITH RIBBED NECKBAND

(Stitch count is a multiple of 2.)

RIBBING
All rounds (RS): Alternate k1, p1.

GAUGE
In ribbing patt on US 4 (3.5 mm) needles, 24 sts and 30 rows = 4 x 4 in. (10 x 10 cm)

INSTRUCTIONS
Pick up and knit 126/130/134 sts around the neckline edge, join into the round, and work 1.2 in. (3 cm) (= 8 rnds) in ribbing pattern. BO all sts in pattern, and weave in ends.

ROUND NECKLINE/CREWNECK WITH ROLLED EDGE

(Works for any stitch count.)

STOCKINETTE STITCH
All rounds (RS): Knit all stitches.

GAUGE
Stockinette stitch on US 4 (3.5 mm) needles, 22 sts and 30 rows = 4 x 4 in. (10 x 10 cm)

INSTRUCTIONS
Pick up and knit 126/130/134 sts around the neckline edge, join into the round, and purl 1 rnd. Then work 16 rnds in St st. BO all sts, and weave in ends.

ROUND NECKLINE/CREWNECK WITH TURTLENECK

(Stitch count is a multiple of 2.)

RIBBING

All rounds (RS): Alternate k1, p1.

GAUGE

In ribbing patt on US 4 (3.5 mm) needles, 24 sts and 30 rows = 4 x 4 in. (10 x 10 cm)

INSTRUCTIONS

Pick up and knit 126/130/134 sts around the neckline edge, join into the round, and, for the turtleneck, work in ribbing patt for 9.5 in. (24 cm) (= 72 rnds). BO all sts in pattern, and weave in ends.

ROUND NECKLINE/CREWNECK WITH MOCK TURTLENECK

(Stitch count is a multiple of 6.)

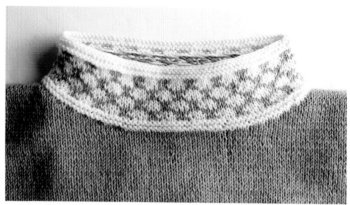

GARTER STITCH

Knit all odd-numbered rnds; purl all even-numbered rnds.

STRANDED PATTERN

Work from Colorwork Chart C. The chart shows all rounds as the stitches appear on the RS of the fabric. Repeat the patt rep (6 sts wide) around. Rep Rnds 1–6 heightwise 2 times.

GAUGE

In stranded colorwork pattern on US 4 (3.5 mm) needles, 22 sts and 30 rows = 4 x 4 in. (10 x 10 cm)

INSTRUCTIONS

Using contrasting color (CC), pick up and knit 120/126/132 sts around the neckline edge, join into the round, and work as follows: 4 rnds garter st in CC, 12 rnds in stranded colorwork pattern, 4 rnds garter st in CC. BO all sts, and weave in ends.

COLORWORK
CHART C
(IN ROUNDS)

KNITTING SYMBOLS

▨ = 1 st in St st in MC
☐ = 1 st in St st in CC

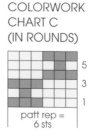

patt rep = 6 sts

V-NECK WITH RIBBED NECKBAND FOR ALL SWEATER SHAPES

(Stitch count is a multiple of 2.)

RIBBING
All rounds (RS):
Alternate k1, p1.

GAUGE
In ribbing on US 4 (3.5 mm) needles, 24 sts and 30 rows = 4 x 4 in. (10 x 10 cm)

FINISHING FOR STRAIGHT ARMHOLE AND ARMHOLE SHAPING

Beginning at the left shoulder, pick up and knit 156/162/168 sts around the V-neck neckline edge as follows: 52/54/56 sts to 1 st before the deepest point of the V-neck, 1 st from the tip of the V-neck, 52/54/56 sts up to the right shoulder, and 51/53/55 sts along the Back neckline. Join into the round, and work ribbing as follows:

Rnd 1: Work in ribbing.

Rnd 2: Work in ribbing to 1 st before the tip of the V-neck, work cdd over 3 sts (= slip 2 sts together knitwise, knit the next st, and pass the slipped sts over the knitted one), ribbing to end of rnd.

Rnd 3: Knit the knits and purl the purls.

Rep Rnds 2 and 3 twice more, and then BO all sts in pattern.

Weave in ends.

FINISHING FOR RAGLAN-SHAPED ARMHOLE

Beginning at the right edge of the Back neckline, pick up and knit 156/162/168 sts around the V-neck neckline edge as follows: 51/53/55 sts along the Back neckline, 52/54/56 sts from the sts of the left sleeve and the left Front to 1 st before the deepest point of the V-neck, 1 st from the tip of the V-neck, 52/54/56 sts from the sts of the right Front and the sts of the right sleeve. Join into the round, and work ribbing as follows:

Rnd 1: Work in ribbing.

Rnd 2: Work in ribbing to 1 st before the tip of the V-neck, work cdd over 3 sts (= slip 2 sts together knitwise, knit the next st, and pass the slipped sts over the knitted one), ribbing to end of rnd.

Rnd 3: Knit the knits and purl the purls.

Rep Rnds 2 and 3 twice more, and then BO all sts in pattern.

Weave in ends.

ARMHOLES

All Basic Sweaters in this book have armholes with drop shoulders. As an alternative, every design can be worked with sleeve caps or raglan sleeves instead. This chapter covers the method for sweaters with long sleeves. Other sleeve options are explained in detail in the "Sleeve Lengths" section on page 59. Because sweaters with oversized fit are always worked with drop shoulders, these will not be addressed in this chapter at all.

First, instructions for the Front and Back of the appropriate Basic Sweater are followed to the armholes, and then armholes are worked as described below:

SLEEVE SHAPE 1: SLEEVE CAP SHAPES

ARMHOLE SHAPING FOR STOCKINETTE SWEATERS (EXCEPT OVERSIZED FIT)

FRONT AND BACK

For armhole shaping, after having worked 13.8 in. (35 cm) (= 104 rows) from end of ribbing, BO 3/4/5 sts at each end of the row. After this, in every other row, BO another 2 sts twice and 1 st 2/2/0 times. For the Front, *at the same time*, work neckline shaping for the desired neckline shape. At 21/21.3/21.7 in. (53/54/55 cm) (= 158/162/166 rows) from end of ribbing, BO remaining sts.

SLEEVES

The matching sleeve for this armhole shape can be found in the "Sleeve Lengths" section, beginning on page 59. All sleeve shapes with a sleeve cap from these pages will fit into this armhole.

ARMHOLE SHAPING FOR SWEATERS WITH LACE PATTERNS (EXCEPT OVERSIZED FIT)

FRONT AND BACK

For armhole shaping, after having worked 13.8 in. (35 cm) (= 98 rows) from end of ribbing, BO 3/4/5 sts at each end of the row. After this, in every other row, BO another 2 sts twice and 1 st 1/2/1 time(s). For the Front, *at the same time*, work neckline shaping for the desired neckline shape. At 21/21.3/21.7 in. (53/54/55 cm) (= 148/152/154 rows) from end of ribbing, BO remaining sts.

SLEEVES

The matching sleeve for this armhole shape can be found in the "Sleeve Lengths" section, beginning on page 59. All sleeve shapes with a sleeve cap from these pages will fit into this armhole.

ARMHOLE SHAPING FOR SWEATERS WITH CABLE PATTERN (EXCEPT OVERSIZED FIT)

FRONT AND BACK

For armhole shaping, after having worked 13.6/13.8/13.8 in. (34.5/35/35 cm) (= 118/120/120 rows) from end of ribbing, BO 3/4/5 sts at each end of the row. After this, in every other row, BO another 2 sts twice and 1 st 2/2/1 time(s). For the Front, *at the same time*, work neckline shaping for the desired neckline shape. At 21/21.3/21.7 in. (53/54/55 cm) (= 180/184/188 rows) from end of ribbing, BO remaining sts.

SLEEVES

The matching sleeve for this armhole shape can be found in the "Sleeve Lengths" section, beginning on page 59. All sleeve shapes with a sleeve cap from these pages will fit into this armhole.

Please note: Armholes for sweaters with stripes, borders, and stranded color-work patterns are worked the same as for sleeves worked in stockinette stitch. How to incorporate the different stitch patterns into the sleeves is explained in detail in the "Sleeve Lengths" section.

SLEEVE SHAPE 1: BASIC SWEATERS 1–4 WITH SLEEVE CAP

Please note: For Basic Sweaters 2–4, armhole decreases are worked the same as described here for a stockinette sweater. The patterns for Front and Back are adjusted for the decreases. How to adjust the stitch pattern for the sleeves is explained in detail in the "Sleeve Lengths" section, beginning on page 59.

STOCKINETTE STITCH
RS: Knit all sts.
WS: Purl all sts.

RIBBING IN ROWS
RS: Alternate k1, p1.
WS: Work all sts as they appear—knit the knits and purl the purls.

RIBBING IN ROUNDS
All rounds (RS): Alternate k1, p1.

INSTRUCTIONS

BACK
Using US 4 (3.5 mm) needles, CO 115/127/131 sts, and for hem ribbing, work 14 rows in ribbing patt; *at the same time*, in the last row, evenly distributed, dec 10/10/8 sts (= 105/117/123 sts). Change to US 6 (4.0 mm) needles, and continue in St st.

For armhole shaping, after having worked 13.8 in. (35 cm) (= 104 rows) from end of ribbing, BO 3/4/5 sts at each end of the row. After this, in every other row, BO another 2 sts twice and 1 st 2/2/0 times. At 21/21.3/21.7 in. (53/54/55 cm) (= 158/162/166 rows) from hem ribbing, BO all sts.

FRONT
Work as the Back, but with neckline shaping. For this, after having worked 19/19.3/19.7 in. (48/49/50 cm) (= 144/148/150 rows) from end of hem ribbing, BO the middle 19/23/25 sts, and continue both sides separately. For the rounded neckline, BO sts at the neck edge in every other row as follows: BO 4 sts once, 3 sts 3/3/2 times, 2 sts 1/1/2 time(s), and 1 st 1/1/2 time(s). At 21/21.3/21.7 in. (53/54/55 cm) (= 158/162/166 rows) from end of ribbing, BO the remaining 18/21/24 sts for each shoulder.

SLEEVES (MAKE 2)
Using US 4 (3.5 mm) needles, CO 51/55/59 sts, and for the cuff, work 14 rows in ribbing patt; in the last WS row, evenly distributed, dec 6/4/4 sts (= 45/51/55 sts). Change to US 6 (4.0 mm) needles, and continue in St st. For sleeve tapering, after having worked 6/8/8 rows from end of cuff, inc 1 st at each end of the row. Rep these incs in every 6th row 7/2/0 times more and in every 8th row 7/1/12 time(s) (= 75/79/81 sts).

For the sleeve cap, at a height of 15/15.4/15.4 in. (38/39/39 cm) (= 116/118/118 rows) from end of cuff, BO 3/4/5 sts at each end of the row. After this, BO sts at each end of the row in every other row as follows: BO 2 sts twice, 1 st 10/12/14 times, 2 sts 5/4/3 times, and 3 sts once. At sleeve cap height of 4.7/5.1/5.5 in. (12/13/14 cm) (= 38/40/42 rows), BO the remaining 15/17/17 sts.

FINISHING
Block all pieces to measurements on a soft surface, moisten, and let dry. Close shoulder and side seams from the wrong side. Seam the sleeves right sides facing each other and wrong sides facing out, and then sew the sleeves into the armholes from the wrong side.

Using US 4 (3.5 mm) needles, pick up and knit 126/130/134 sts from the neckline edge, join into the round, and work 1.2 in. (3 cm) (= 8 rnds) in ribbing pattern. BO all sts in pattern, and weave in ends.

SCHEMATIC

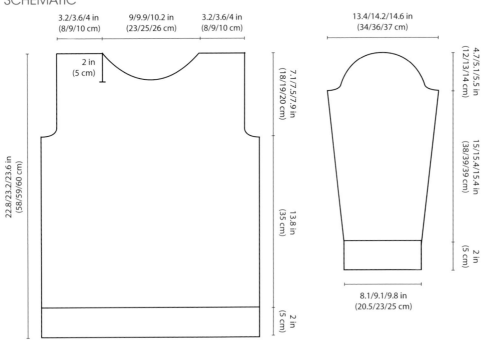

3.2/3.6/4 in (8/9/10 cm)
9/9.9/10.2 in (23/25/26 cm)
3.2/3.6/4 in (8/9/10 cm)

2 in (5 cm)

7.1/7.5/7.9 in (18/19/20 cm)

22.8/23.2/23.6 in (58/59/60 cm)

13.8 in (35 cm)

2 in (5 cm)

18.9/20.9/22 in (48/53/56 cm)

13.4/14.2/14.6 in (34/36/37 cm)

4.7/5.1/5.5 in (12/13/14 cm)

15/15.4/15.4 in (38/39/39 cm)

2 in (5 cm)

8.1/9.1/9.8 in (20.5/23/25 cm)

SIZES

Small/Medium/Large (US 6/8, 10/12, 14/16) Numbers for size Small are listed before the first slash, for size Medium between slashes, and for size Large after the second slash. If only one number is given, it applies to all sizes.

MATERIALS

Schachenmayr Merino Extrafine 120; #3 light weight yarn; 100% wool; 131 yd (120 m), 1.75 oz. (50 g) per skein

• 11/12/13 skeins #156 cloud heathered

Circular knitting needles, sizes US 4 (3.5 mm) and US 6 (4.0 mm), each 32 in. (80 cm) long

GAUGE

In stockinette stitch on US 6 (4.0 mm) needles, 22 sts and 30 rows = 4 x 4 in. (10 x 10 cm)

STRAIGHT BODY

SLEEVE WITH SLEEVE CAP

SLEEVE SHAPE 1: BASIC SWEATER 5 WITH SLEEVE CAP

SIZES

Small/Medium/Large (US 6/8, 10/12, 14/16)

Numbers for size Small are listed before the first slash, for size Medium between slashes, and for size Large after the second slash. If only one number is given, it applies to all sizes.

MATERIALS

Schachenmayr Merino Extrafine 120; #3 light weight yarn; 100% wool; 131 yd (120 m), 1.75 oz. (50 g) per skein

- 10/11/13 skeins in color of choice

Circular knitting needles, sizes US 4 (3.5 mm) and US 6 (4.0 mm), each 32 in. (80 cm) long

GAUGE

In lace pattern on US 6 (4.0 mm) needles, 20 sts and 28 rows = 4 x 4 in. (10 x 10 cm)

STITCH PATTERN CHART A

Page 52

STOCKINETTE STITCH

RS: Knit all sts.
WS: Purl all sts.

RIBBING IN ROWS

RS: Alternate k1, p1.
WS: Work all sts as they appear—knit the knits and purl the purls.

RIBBING IN ROUNDS

All rounds (RS): Alternate k1, p1.

LACE PATTERN

Work from Stitch Pattern Chart A. Only RS rows are shown in the chart; in WS rows, work all sts as they appear, and purl the yarn overs. Begin with the sts before the patt rep, repeat the patt rep widthwise across, and end with the sts after the patt rep. Repeat Rows 1–12 of the chart heightwise throughout.

INSTRUCTIONS

BACK

Using US 4 (3.5 mm) needles, CO 115/127/131 sts, and for hem ribbing, work 14 rows in ribbing patt; *at the same time*, in the last row, evenly distributed, dec 20/22/16 sts (= 95/105/115 sts). Change to US 6 (4.0 mm) needles, and cont in lace pattern.

For armhole shaping, after having worked 13.8 in. (35 cm) (= 98 rows) from end of ribbing, BO 3/4/5 sts at each end of the row. After this, in every other row, BO another 2 sts twice and 1 st 1/2/1 time(s). At 21/21.3/21.7 in. (53/54/55 cm) (= 148/152/154 rows) from end of ribbing, BO remaining sts.

FRONT

Work as the Back, but with neckline shaping. For this, after having worked only 19/19.3/19.7 in. (48/49/50 cm) (= 134/138/140 rows) from end of ribbing, BO the middle 21/21/29 sts, and continue both sides separately. For the rounded neckline, BO sts at the neck edge in every other row as follows: BO 3 sts 2/3/2 times, 2 sts 3/2/3 times, and 1 st once. At 21/21.3/21.7 in. (53/54/55 cm) (= 148/152/154 rows) from end of ribbing, BO the remaining shoulder sts.

SLEEVES (MAKE 2)

Using US 4 (3.5 mm) needles, CO 51/55/59 sts, and for the cuff, work 14 rows in ribbing patt; in the last WS row, evenly distributed, dec 6/8/10 sts (= 45/47/49 sts). Cont in lace pattern as follows: 0/1/2 st(s) in St st, 45 sts in lace pattern from Stitch Pattern Chart A, 0/1/2 st(s) in St st. For sleeve tapering,

after having worked 6 rows from end of cuff, inc 1 st at each end of the row. Rep these incs in every 6th row 0/4/9 times more and in every 8th row 11/9/5 times more (= 69/75/79 sts).

For the sleeve cap, at a height of 15/15.4/15.4 in. (38/39/39 cm) (= 106/110/110 rows) from end of cuff, BO sts at both ends of the row as follows: BO 3/4/5 sts each once; then, in every other row, 2 sts twice, 1 st 9/10/12 times, 2 sts 4/4/3 times, and 3 sts once. At sleeve cap height of 4.7/5.1/5.5 in. (12/13/14 cm) (= 34/36/38 rows), BO the remaining 15/17/19 sts.

FINISHING

Block all pieces to measurements on a soft surface, moisten, and let dry. Close shoulder and side seams from the wrong side. Seam the sleeves right sides facing each other and wrong sides facing out, and then sew the sleeves into the armholes from the wrong side.

Using US 4 (3.5 mm) needles, pick up and knit 126/130/134 sts from the neckline edge, join into the round, and work 1.2 in. (3 cm) (= 8 rnds) in ribbing pattern. BO all sts in pattern, and weave in ends.

SLEEVE SHAPE 1:
BASIC SWEATER 6 WITH SLEEVE CAP

SIZES

Small/Medium/Large (US 6/8, 10/12, 14/16)

Numbers for size Small are listed before the first slash, for size Medium between slashes, and for size Large after the second slash. If only one number is given, it applies to all sizes.

MATERIALS

Schachenmayr Merino Extrafine 120; #3 light weight yarn; 100% wool; 131 yd (120 m), 1.75 oz. (50 g) per skein
- 12/14/16 skeins in color of choice

Circular knitting needles, US 4 (3.5 mm) and US 6 (4.0 mm), each 32 in. (80 cm) long

Cable needle (cn)

GAUGE

In double seed stitch on US 6 (4.0 mm) needles, 22 sts and 34 rows = 4 x 4 in. (10 x 10 cm)

In cable pattern 1 on US 6 (4.0 mm) needles, 58 sts = 8.3 in. (21 cm)

In cable pattern 2 on US 6 (4.0 mm) needles, 18 sts = 3.2 in. (8 cm)

STITCH PATTERN CHARTS B AND C
Page 52

STOCKINETTE STITCH

RS: Knit all sts.
WS: Purl all sts.

RIBBING IN ROWS

RS: Alternate k1, p1.
WS: Work all sts as they appear— knit the knits and purl the purls.

RIBBING IN ROUNDS

All rounds (RS): Alternate k1, p1.

DOUBLE SEED STITCH

Row 1: Alternate k1, p1.
Row 2: Knit the knits and purl the purls.
Row 3: Alternate p1, k1.
Row 4: Knit the knits and purl the purls.
Rep Rows 1–4 throughout.

CABLE PATTERN 1

Work from Stitch Pattern Chart B. Only RS rows are shown in the chart; in WS rows, work all sts as they appear (knit the knits and purl the purls), and purl the slipped sts. Work the patt rep (58 sts wide) widthwise across once, and then rep Rows 1–12 heightwise throughout.

CABLE PATTERN 2

Work from Stitch Pattern Chart C. Only RS rows are shown in the chart; in WS rows, work all sts as they appear (knit the knits and purl the purls), and purl the slipped sts. Work the patt rep (18 sts wide) widthwise across once, and then rep Rows 1–12 heightwise throughout.

INSTRUCTIONS

BACK

Using US 4 (3.5 mm) needles, CO 115/127/131 sts, and for hem ribbing, work 14 rows in ribbing patt; *at the same time*, in the last row, evenly distributed, inc 1 st (= 116/128/132 sts). Change to US 6 (4.0 mm) needles, and continue in the following pattern: 1 st in St st, 28/34/36 sts in double seed stitch, 58 sts in cable pattern 1, 28/34/36 sts in double seed stitch, 1 st in St st.

For armhole shaping, after having worked 13.8 in. (35 cm) (= 118/120/120 rows) from end of ribbing, BO 3/4/5 sts at each end of the row. After this, in every other row, BO another 2 sts twice and 1 st 2/2/1 time(s). At 21/21.3/21.7 in. (53/54/55 cm) (= 180/184/188 rows) from end of ribbing, BO remaining sts.

FRONT

Work as the Back, but with neckline shaping. For this, after having worked only 19/19.3/19.7 in. (48/49/50 cm) (= 164/166/168 rows) from end of ribbing, BO the middle 28/30/30 sts, and continue both sides separately. For the rounded neckline, BO sts at the neck edge in every other row as follows: BO 4 sts once, 3 sts twice, 2 sts 3/3/2 times, and 1 st 1/2/4 time(s). At 21/21.3/21.7 in. (53/54/55 cm) (= 180/184/188 rows) from end of ribbing, BO the remaining shoulder sts.

SLEEVES (MAKE 2)

Using US 4 (3.5 mm) needles, CO 51/55/59 sts, and for the cuff, work 14 rows in ribbing patt; in the last WS row, evenly distributed, dec 5/3/3 sts (= 46/52/56 sts). After this, change to US 6 (4.0 mm) needles, and continue in the following pattern: 1 st in St st, 13/16/18 sts in double seed stitch, 18 sts in cable pattern 2 from Stitch Pattern Chart C, 13/16/18 sts in double seed stitch, 1 st in St st. For sleeve tapering, after having worked 6/10/10 rows from end of cuff, inc 1 st at each end of the row. Rep these incs in every 6th row 8/0/0 times more and in every 8th row 8/14/14 times more (= 80/82/86 sts).

For the sleeve cap, at 15/15.4/15.4 in. (38/39/39 cm) (= 130/132/132 rows) from end of ribbing, BO sts at both ends of the row as follows: 3/4/5 sts each once, and then, in every other row, 2 sts twice, 1 st 12/16/19 times, 2 sts 3/2/2 times, and 3 sts 2/1/0 time(s). At sleeve cap height of 4.7/5.1/5.5 in. (12/13/14 cm) (= 40/44/48 rows), BO the remaining 18/20/22 sts.

FINISHING

Block all pieces to measurements on a soft surface, moisten, and let dry. Close shoulder and side seams from the wrong side. Seam the sleeves right sides facing each other and wrong sides facing out, and then sew the sleeves into the armholes from the wrong side.

Using US 4 (3.5 mm) needles, pick up and knit 126/130/134 sts from the neckline edge, join into the round, and work 1.2 in. (3 cm) (= 8 rnds) in ribbing pattern. BO all sts in pattern, and weave in ends.

STITCH PATTERN CHART A
Stitch count is a multiple of 10 + 15.

patt rep = 10 sts

KNITTING SYMBOLS

■ = knit 1 stitch

− = purl 1 stitch

○ = make 1 yarn over

◢ = knit 2 sts together

◣ = slip 1, knit 1, pass the slipped stitch over

▲ = slip 1, knit 2 sts together, pass the slipped stitch over

☐ = no stitch, for better overview only

STITCH PATTERN CHART B

cable pattern 1 = 58 sts

STITCH PATTERN CHART C

cable pattern 2 = 18 sts

KNITTING SYMBOLS

■ = knit 1 stitch

− = purl 1 stitch

ɑɪ = slip 1 stitch purlwise with yarn in back of work

= hold 1 stitch on cn in back of work, knit the next 2 stitches, and then knit the stitch from the cn

= hold 2 sts on cn in front of work, purl the next stitch, and then knit the 2 sts from the cn

= hold 2 sts on cn in back of work, knit the next 2 stitches, and then knit the 2 sts from the cn

= hold 4 sts on cn in back of work, knit the next 4 sts, and then knit the 4 sts from the cn

= hold 4 sts on cn in front of work, knit the next 4 sts, and then knit the 4 sts from the cn

SLEEVE SHAPE 2: RAGLAN SHAPES

RAGLAN SLEEVE FOR STOCKINETTE SWEATERS (EXCEPT OVERSIZED FIT)

FRONT AND BACK

For the raglan sleeve, after having worked 13.8 in. (35 cm) (= 104 rows) from end of ribbing, BO 6/7/8 sts at each end of the row. After this, BO sts at both ends of the row in every other row as follows: BO 3 sts once and 2 sts once. Then, at both ends of the row, in every other row, work accented decrease of 1 st each 16/21/22 times, and then in every 4th row 3/1/1 time(s) more. On the Front, work neckline shaping *at the same time*, so that only 1 st remains on each side in the end. At 20/20.5/21 in. (51/52/53 cm) (= 154/156/158 rows) from end of ribbing, BO the remaining sts on the Back; for the Front, break the working yarn with a not-too-short end, and pull the tail through the last stitch.

SLEEVES

The matching sleeve for this armhole shape can be found in the "Sleeve Lengths" section, beginning on page 59. All raglan sleeves from that page will fit into this armhole.

RAGLAN SLEEVE FOR SWEATERS WITH LACE PATTERNS (EXCEPT OVERSIZED FIT)

FRONT AND BACK

For the raglan sleeve, after having worked 13.8 in. (35 cm) (= 98 rows) from end of ribbing, BO 6/7/8 sts at each end of the row. After this, BO sts at both ends of the row in every other row as follows: BO 3 sts once and 2 sts once. Then, at both ends of the row, in every other row, work accented decrease of 1 st each 15/19/16 times, and then in every 4th row 2/1/3 time(s) more. At 20/20.5/21 in. (51/52/53 cm) (= 142/146/148 rows) from end of ribbing, BO the remaining sts on the Back; for the Front, break the working yarn with a not-too-short end, and pull the tail through the last stitch.

SLEEVES

The matching sleeve for this armhole shape can be found in the "Sleeve Lengths" section, beginning on page 59. All raglan sleeves from that page will fit into this armhole.

RAGLAN SLEEVE FOR SWEATERS WITH CABLE PATTERNS (EXCEPT OVERSIZED FIT)

FRONT AND BACK

For the raglan sleeve, after having worked 13.8 in. (35 cm) (= 118 rows) from end of ribbing, BO 6/7/8 sts at each end of the row. After this, BO sts at both ends of the row in every other row as follows: BO 3 sts once and 2 sts once. Then, at both ends of the row, in every other row, work accented decrease of 1 st each 11/18/16 times, and then in every 4th row 7/4/6 time(s) more. On the Front, work neckline shaping *at the same time*, so that only 1 st remains on each side in the end. At 20/20.5/21 in. (51/52/53 cm) (= 174/176/180 rows) from end of ribbing, BO the remaining sts on the Back; for the Front, break the working yarn with a not-too-short end, and pull the tail through the last stitch.

SLEEVES

The matching sleeve for this armhole shape can be found in the "Sleeve Lengths" section, beginning on page 59. All raglan sleeves from that page will fit into this armhole.

Please note: The armholes for the sweater with stripes, border, and stranded colorwork pattern are worked the same as for stockinette sweaters. How to incorporate the different stitch patterns into the sleeves is explained in the "Sleeve Lengths" section, beginning on page 61.

ACCENTED DECREASES

Accented decreases are always worked in RS rows, at both ends of the row as follows: K1, skp, work in pattern to last 3 sts of the row, then k2tog, k1. In WS rows, always purl the first 2 sts and the last 2 sts of the row. In RS rows without decreases, always knit the first 2 sts and the last 2 sts of the row.

SLEEVE SHAPE 2:
BASIC SWEATERS 1-4 WITH RAGLAN SLEEVE

Please note: For Basic Sweaters 2–4, raglan decreases are worked the same way as described here for a stockinette sweater. The patterns for Front and Back are adjusted for the decreases. How to adjust the stitch pattern for the sleeves is explained in detail in the "Sleeve Lengths" section, beginning on page 59.

STOCKINETTE STITCH
RS: Knit all sts.
WS: Purl all sts.

RIBBING IN ROWS
RS: Alternate k1, p1.
WS: Work all sts as they appear—knit the knits and purl the purls.

RIBBING IN ROUNDS
All rounds (RS): Alternate k1, p1.

ACCENTED DECREASES
Accented decreases are always worked in RS rows, at both ends of the row as follows: K1, skp, cont in St st to last 3 sts of the row, then k2tog, k1. In WS rows, always purl the first 2 sts and the last 2 sts of the row. In RS rows without decreases, always knit the first 2 sts and the last 2 sts of the row.

SCHEMATIC

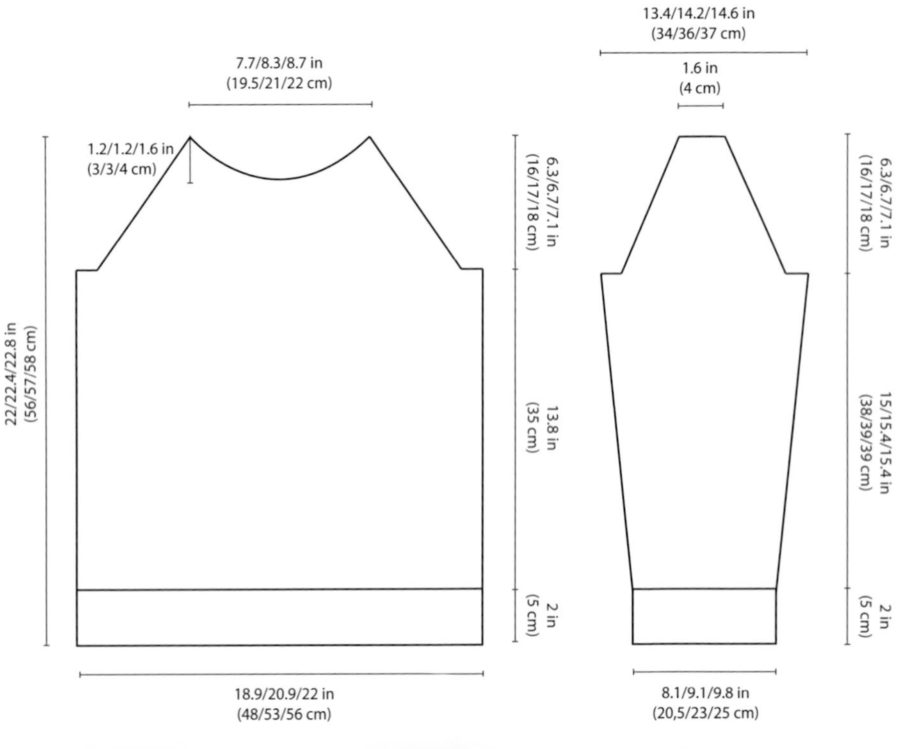

INSTRUCTIONS

BACK
Using US 4 (3.5 mm) needles, CO 115/127/131 sts, and for hem ribbing, work 14 rows in ribbing patt; *at the same time*, in the last row, evenly distributed, dec 10/10/8 sts (= 105/117/123 sts). Change to US 6 (4.0 mm) needles, and continue in St st.

For the raglan sleeve, after having worked 13.8 in. (35 cm) (= 104 rows) from end of ribbing, BO 6/7/8 sts at each end of the row. After this, BO sts at both ends of the row in every other row as follows: BO 3 sts once and 2 sts once. Then, at both ends of the row, in every other row, work accented decrease of 1 st each 16/21/22 times, and then in every 4th row 3/1/1 time(s) more. At 20/20.5/21 in. (51/52/53 cm) (= 154/156/158 rows) from end of ribbing, BO the remaining 45/49/51 sts.

FRONT
Work as the Back, but with neckline shaping. For this, after having worked only 19/19.3/19.7 in. (48/49/50 cm) (= 144/148/150 rows) from end of hem ribbing, BO the middle 19/23/25 sts, and

continue both sides separately. For the rounded neckline, BO sts at the neck edge in every other row as follows: 4 sts once, 3 sts 1/2/1 time(s), 2 sts 2/1/2 time(s), and 1 st 1/0/1 time(s). At 20/20.5/21 in. (51/52/53 cm) (= 154/156/158 rows) from end of ribbing, break the working yarn, leaving a not-too-short end, and pull the tail through the last stitch.

SLEEVES (MAKE 2)
Using US 4 (3.5 mm) needles, CO 51/55/59 sts, and for the cuff, work 14 rows in ribbing patt; *at the same time*, in the last row, evenly distributed, dec 6/4/4 sts (= 45/51/55 sts). Change to US 6 (4.0 mm) needles, and continue in St st. For sleeve tapering, after having worked 6/8/8 rows from end of cuff, inc 1 st at each end of the row. Rep these incs in every 6th row 7/2/0 times more and in every 8th row 7/11/12 times more (= 75/79/81 sts).

For raglan shaping, after 15/15.4/15.4 in. (38/39/39 cm) (= 116/118/118 rows) from end of ribbing, BO 6/7/8 sts at each end of the row. After this, BO sts at each end of the row in every other row as follows: 3 sts once and 2 sts once. Then, at each end of the row, in every other row, work accented decrease of 1 st each 22/23/23 times, and then in every 4th row 0/0/1 time(s) more. At raglan height 6.3/6.7/7.1 in. (16/17/18 cm) (= 50/52/54 rows), BO the remaining 9 sts.

FINISHING
Block all pieces to measurements on a soft surface, moisten, and let dry. Right sides facing each other and wrong sides facing out, sew the sleeves to the Front and Back along the raglan lines. Close side and sleeve seams from the wrong side.

Using US 4 (3.5 mm) needles, pick up and knit 126/130/134 sts from the neckline edge, join into the round, and work 1.2 in. (3 cm) (= 8 rnds) in ribbing pattern. BO all sts in pattern, and weave in ends.

7.7/8.3/8.7 in (19.5/21/22 cm)

1.2/1.2/1.6 in (3/3/4 cm)

22/22.4/22.8 in (56/57/58 cm)

18.9/20.9/22 in (48/53/56 cm)

13.4/14.2/14.6 in (34/36/37 cm)

1.6 in (4 cm)

6.3/6.7/7.1 in (16/17/18 cm)

13.8 in (35 cm)

2 in (5 cm)

6.3/6.7/7.1 in (16/17/18 cm)

15/15.4/15.4 in (38/39/39 cm)

2 in (5 cm)

8.1/9.1/9.8 in (20.5/23/25 cm)

SIZES

Small/Medium/Large (US 6/8, 10/12, 14/16) Numbers for size Small are listed before the first slash, for size Medium between slashes, and for size Large after the second slash. If only one number is given, it applies to all sizes.

MATERIALS

Schachenmayr Merino Extrafine 120; #3 light weight yarn; 100% wool; 131 yd (120 m), 1.75 oz. (50 g) per skein

- 11/12/13 skeins #157 harmony heathered

Circular knitting needles, sizes US 4 (3.5 mm) and US 6 (4.0 mm), each 32 in. (80 cm) long

GAUGE

In stockinette stitch on US 6 (4.0 mm) needles, 22 sts and 30 rows = 4 x 4 in. (10 x 10 cm)

RAGLAN SLEEVE

STRAIGHT BODY

SLEEVE SHAPE 2:
BASIC SWEATER 5 WITH RAGLAN SLEEVE

SIZES

Small/Medium/Large (US 6/8, 10/12, 14/16)

Numbers for size Small are listed before the first slash, for size Medium between slashes, and for size Large after the second slash. If only one number is given, it applies to all sizes.

MATERIALS

Schachenmayr Merino Extrafine 120; #3 light weight yarn; 100% wool; 131 yd (120 m), 1.75 oz. (50 g) per skein

- 10/11/13 skeins in color of choice

Circular knitting needles, US 4 (3.5 mm) and US 6 (4.0 mm), each 32 in. (80 cm) long

GAUGE

In lace pattern on US 6 (4.0 mm) needles, 20 sts and 28 rows = 4 x 4 in. (10 x 10 cm)

STITCH PATTERN CHART

Page 58

STOCKINETTE STITCH

RS: Knit all sts.

WS: Purl all sts.

RIBBING IN ROWS

RS: Alternate k1, p1.

WS: Work all sts as they appear—knit the knits and purl the purls.

RIBBING IN ROUNDS

All rounds (RS): Alternate k1, p1.

LACE PATTERN

Work from Stitch Pattern Chart A. Only RS rows are shown in the chart; in WS rows, work all sts as they appear, and purl the yarn overs. Begin with the sts before the patt rep, repeat the patt rep widthwise across, and end with the sts after the patt rep. Repeat Rows 1–12 of the chart heightwise throughout.

ACCENTED DECREASES

Accented decreases are always worked in RS rows, at both ends of the row as follows: K1, skp, work in pattern to last 3 sts of the row, then k2tog, k1. In WS rows, always purl the first 2 sts and the last 2 sts of the row. In RS rows without decreases, always knit the first 2 sts and the last 2 sts of the row.

INSTRUCTIONS

BACK

With US 4 (3.5 mm) needles, CO 115/127/131 sts, and for hem ribbing, work 14 rows in ribbing patt; *at the same time*, in the last row, evenly distributed, dec 20/22/16 sts (= 95/105/115 sts). Change to US 6 (4.0 mm) needles, and cont in lace pattern.

For the raglan sleeve, after having worked 13.8 in. (35 cm) (= 98 rows) from end of ribbing, BO at both ends of the row as follows: BO 6/7/8 sts each once; then, in every other row, 3 sts once, and then 2 sts once. Then work accented decrease of 1 st at each end of the row in every other row as follows: 15/19/16 times, and then in every 4th row 2/1/3 time(s) more. At 20/20.5/21 in. (51/52/53 cm) (= 142/146/148 rows) from hem ribbing, BO all sts.

FRONT

Work as the Back, but with neckline shaping. For this, after having worked only 19/19.3/19.7 in. (48/49/50 cm) (= 134/138/140 rows) from end of ribbing, BO the middle 21/21/29 sts, and continue both sides separately. For the rounded neckline, BO sts at the neck edge in every other row as follows: 3 sts 2/3/2 times and 2 sts 1/0/2 time(s). At 20/20.5/21 in. (51/52/53 cm) (= 142/

146/150 rows) from end of ribbing, break the working yarn, leaving a not-too-short end, and pull the tail through the last stitch.

SLEEVES (MAKE 2)

With US 4 (3.5 mm) needles, CO 51/55/59 sts, and for the cuff, work 14 rows in ribbing patt; *at the same time*, in the last row, evenly distributed, dec 6/8/10 sts (= 45/47/49 sts). Cont in lace pattern as follows: 0/1/2 st(s) in St st, 45 sts in lace pattern from Stitch Pattern Chart A, 0/1/2 st(s) in St st. For sleeve tapering, after having worked 6 rows from end of cuff, inc 1 st at each end of the row. Rep these incs in every 6th row 0/4/9 times more and in every 8th row 11/9/5 times more (= 69/75/79 sts).

For raglan shaping, at 15/15.4/15.4 in. (38/39/39 cm) (= 106/110/110 rows) from end of ribbing, BO at both ends of the row as follows: BO 6/7/8 sts each once; then, in every other row, 3 sts once, and then 2 sts once. Then, at both ends of the row, in every other row, work accented decrease of 1 st each 19/21/22 times. At 6.3/6.7/7.1 in. (16/17/18 cm) (= 44/48/52 rows) raglan height, BO the remaining 9 sts.

FINISHING

Block all pieces to measurements on a soft surface, moisten, and let dry. Right sides facing each other and wrong sides facing out, sew the sleeves to the Front and Back along the raglan lines. Close side and sleeve seams from the wrong side.

Using US 4 (3.5 mm) needles, pick up and knit 126/130/134 sts from the neckline edge, join into the round, and work 1.2 in. (3 cm) (= 8 rnds) in ribbing pattern. BO all sts in pattern, and weave in ends.

SLEEVE SHAPE 2:
BASIC SWEATER 6 WITH RAGLAN SLEEVE

SIZES

Small/Medium/Large (US 6/8, 10/12, 14/16)

Numbers for size Small are listed before the first slash, for size Medium between slashes, and for size Large after the second slash. If only one number is given, it applies to all sizes.

MATERIALS

Schachenmayr Merino Extrafine 120; #3 light weight yarn; 100% wool; 131 yd (120 m), 1.75 oz. (50 g) per skein

• 12/14/16 skeins in color of choice

Circular knitting needles, US 4 (3.5 mm) and US 6 (4.0 mm), each 32 in. (80 cm) long

Cable needle

GAUGE

In double seed stitch on US 6 (4.0 mm) needles, 22 sts and 34 rows = 4 x 4 in. (10 x 10 cm)

In cable pattern 1 on US 6 (4.0 mm) needles, 58 sts = 8.3 in. (21 cm)

In cable pattern 2 on US 6 (4.0 mm) needles, 18 sts = 3.2 in. (8 cm)

STITCH PATTERN CHARTS

Page 58

STOCKINETTE STITCH

RS: Knit all sts.
WS: Purl all sts.

RIBBING IN ROWS

RS: Alternate k1, p1.
WS: Work all sts as they appear— knit the knits and purl the purls.

RIBBING IN ROUNDS

All rounds (RS): Alternate k1, p1.

DOUBLE SEED STITCH

Row 1: Alternate k1, p1.
Row 2: Knit the knits and purl the purls.
Row 3: Alternate p1, k1.
Row 4: Knit the knits and purl the purls.
Rep Rows 1–4 throughout.

CABLE PATTERN 1

Work from Stitch Pattern Chart B. Only RS rows are shown in the chart; in WS rows, work all sts as they appear (knit the knits and purl the purls), and purl the slipped sts. Work the patt rep (58 sts wide) widthwise across once, and then rep Rows 1–12 heightwise throughout.

CABLE PATTERN 2

Work from Stitch Pattern Chart C. Only RS rows are shown in the chart; in WS rows, work all sts as they appear (knit the knits and purl the purls), and purl the slipped sts. Work the patt rep (18 sts wide) widthwise across once, and then rep Rows 1–12 heightwise throughout.

INSTRUCTIONS

BACK

Using US 4 (3.5 mm) needles, CO 115/127/131 sts, and for hem ribbing, work 14 rows in ribbing patt; *at the same time*, in the last row, inc 1 st (= 116/128/132 sts). Change to US 6 (4.0 mm) needles, and continue in the following pattern: 1 st in St st, 28/34/36 sts in double seed stitch, 58 sts in cable pattern 1, 28/34/36 sts in double seed stitch, 1 st in St st.

For the raglan sleeve, after having worked 13.8 in. (35 cm) (= 118 rows) from end of ribbing, BO sts at both ends of the row as follows: 6/7/8 sts each once; then, in every other row, 3 sts once, and then 2 sts once. Then, at both ends of the row, in every other row, work accented decrease of 1 st each 11/18/16 times, and then in every 4th row 7/4/6 time(s) more. After having worked 20/20.5/21 in. (51/52/53 cm) (= 174/176/180 rows) from hem ribbing, BO all sts.

FRONT

Work as the Back, but with neckline shaping. For this, after having worked 19/19.3/19.7 in. (48/49/50 cm) (= 164/166/168 rows) from end of ribbing, BO the middle 28/30/32 sts and continue both sides separately. For the rounded neckline, BO sts at the neck edge in every other row as follows: 4 sts once, 3 sts twice, and 2 sts twice. After having worked 20/20.5/21 in. (51/52/53 cm) (= 174/176/180 rows) from end of ribbing, break the working yarn, leaving a not-too-short end, and pull the tail through the last stitch.

SLEEVES (MAKE 2)

Using US 4 (3.5 mm) needles, CO 51/55/59 sts, and for the cuff, work 14 rows in ribbing patt; *at the same time*, in the last row, evenly distributed, dec 5/3/3 sts (= 46/52/56 sts). Change to US 6 (4.0 mm) needles, and continue in the following pattern: 1 st in St st, 13/16/18 sts in double seed stitch, 18 sts in cable pattern 2, 13/16/18 sts in double seed stitch, 1 st in St st.

For sleeve tapering, after having worked 6/10/10 rows from end of cuff, inc 1 st at each end of the row. Rep these incs in every 6th row 8/0/0 times more and in every 8th row 8/14/14 times more (= 80/82/86 sts).

For raglan shaping, after having worked 15/15.4/15.4 in. (38/39/39 cm) (= 130/132/132 rows) from end of ribbing, BO at both ends of the row as follows: BO 6/7/8 sts each once; then, in every other row, 3 sts once, and then 2 sts once. Then, at both ends of the row, in every other row, work accented decrease of 1 st each 25/24/24 times, and in every 4th row 0/1/2 times(s). At raglan height 6.3/6.7/7.1 in. (16/17/18 cm) (= 56/58/62 rows), BO the remaining 8 sts.

FINISHING

Block all pieces to measurements on a soft surface, moisten, and let dry. Right sides facing each other and wrong sides facing out, sew the sleeves to the Front and Back along the raglan lines. Close side and sleeve seams from the wrong side.

Using US 4 (3.5 mm) needles, pick up and knit 126/130/134 sts from the neckline edge, join into the round, and work 1.2 in. (3 cm) (= 8 rnds) in ribbing pattern. BO all sts in pattern, and weave in ends.

STITCH PATTERN CHART A
Stitch count is a multiple of 10 + 15

11
9
7
5
3
1

patt rep = 10 sts

KNITTING SYMBOLS

- ■ = knit 1 stitch
- – = purl 1 stitch
- O = make 1 yarn over
- ◢ = knit 2 sts together

- ◣ = slip 1, knit 1, pass the slipped stitch over
- ▲ = slip 1, knit 2 sts together, pass the slipped stitch over
- □ = no stitch, for better overview only

STITCH PATTERN CHART B

11
9
7
5
3
1

cable pattern 1 = 58 sts

STITCH PATTERN CHART C

11
9
7
5
3
1

cable pattern 2 = 18 sts

KNITTING SYMBOLS

- ■ = knit 1 stitch
- – = purl 1 stitch
- ▣ = slip 1 stitch purlwise with yarn in back of work
- = hold 1 stitch on cn in back of work, knit the next 2 stitches, and then knit the stitch from the cn
- = hold 2 sts on cn in front of work, purl the next stitch, and then knit the 2 sts from the cn
- = hold 2 sts on cn in back of work, knit the next 2 stitches, and then knit the 2 sts from the cn
- = hold 4 sts on cn in back of work, knit the next 4 sts, and then knit the 4 sts from the cn
- = hold 4 sts on cn in front of work, knit the next 4 sts, and then knit the 4 sts from the cn

SLEEVE LENGTHS

STRAIGHT SLEEVE TOP

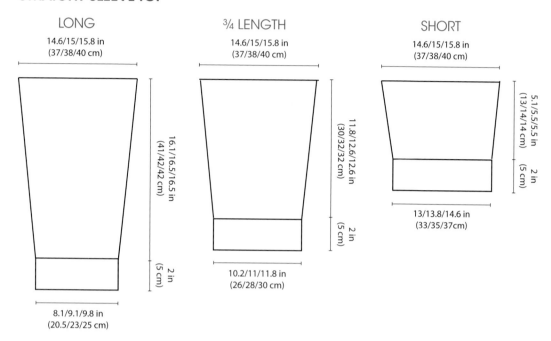

LONG
14.6/15/15.8 in
(37/38/40 cm)

16.1/16.5/16.5 in
(41/42/42 cm)

2 in
(5 cm)

8.1/9.1/9.8 in
(20.5/23/25 cm)

¾ LENGTH
14.6/15/15.8 in
(37/38/40 cm)

11.8/12.6/12.6 in
(30/32/32 cm)

2 in
(5 cm)

10.2/11/11.8 in
(26/28/30 cm)

SHORT
14.6/15/15.8 in
(37/38/40 cm)

5.1/5.5/5.5 in
(13/14/14 cm)

2 in
(5 cm)

13/13.8/14.6 in
(33/35/37cm)

SLEEVE WITH SLEEVE CAP

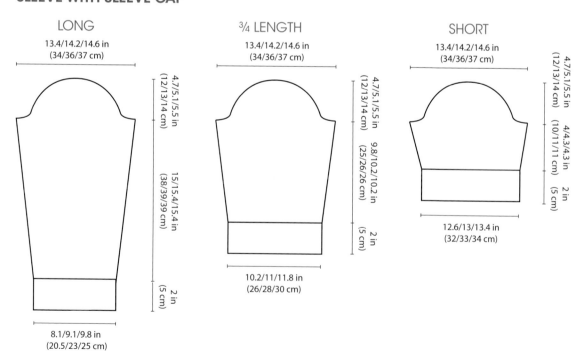

LONG
13.4/14.2/14.6 in
(34/36/37 cm)

4.7/5.1/5.5 in
(12/13/14 cm)

15/15.4/15.4 in
(38/39/39 cm)

2 in
(5 cm)

8.1/9.1/9.8 in
(20.5/23/25 cm)

¾ LENGTH
13.4/14.2/14.6 in
(34/36/37 cm)

4.7/5.1/5.5 in
(12/13/14 cm)

9.8/10.2/10.2 in
(25/26/26 cm)

2 in
(5 cm)

10.2/11/11.8 in
(26/28/30 cm)

SHORT
13.4/14.2/14.6 in
(34/36/37 cm)

4.7/5.1/5.5 in
(12/13/14 cm)

4/4.3/4.3 in
(10/11/11 cm)

2 in
(5 cm)

12.6/13/13.4 in
(32/33/34 cm)

SLEEVE WITH RAGLAN SHAPING

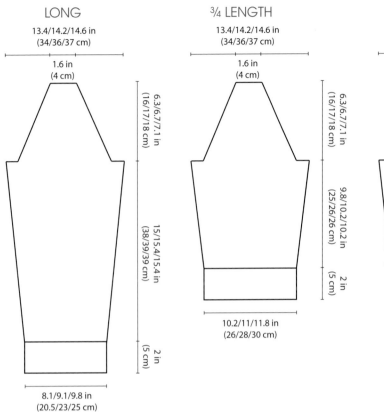

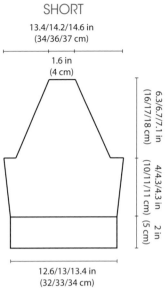

LONG

13.4/14.2/14.6 in
(34/36/37 cm)

1.6 in
(4 cm)

6.3/6.7/7.1 in
(16/17/18 cm)

15/15.4/15.4 in
(38/39/39 cm)

2 in
(5 cm)

8.1/9.1/9.8 in
(20.5/23/25 cm)

¾ LENGTH

13.4/14.2/14.6 in
(34/36/37 cm)

1.6 in
(4 cm)

6.3/6.7/7.1 in
(16/17/18 cm)

9.8/10.2/10.2 in
(25/26/26 cm)

2 in
(5 cm)

10.2/11/11.8 in
(26/28/30 cm)

SHORT

13.4/14.2/14.6 in
(34/36/37 cm)

1.6 in
(4 cm)

6.3/6.7/7.1 in
(16/17/18 cm)

4/4.3/4.3 in
(10/11/11 cm)

2 in
(5 cm)

12.6/13/13.4 in
(32/33/34 cm)

OVERSIZED SLEEVE

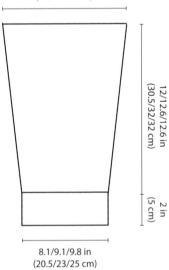

13/14.2/15 in
(33/36/38 cm)

12/12.6/12.6 in
(30.5/32/32 cm)

2 in
(5 cm)

8.1/9.1/9.8 in
(20.5/23/25 cm)

SLEEVE LENGTHS FOR ALL STOCKINETTE SWEATERS

SWEATER WITH DROP SHOULDER

LONG SLEEVE IN STOCKINETTE

First, work the desired sleeve cuff; in the last row, increase or decrease as many sts as needed for a total of 45/51/55 sts on the needles. After this, cont in St st. For sleeve tapering, after having worked 6/8/8 rows from end of cuff, inc 1 st at each end of the row. Rep these incs in every 6th row 13/10/10 times more and in every 8th row 4/6/6 times more (= 81/85/89 sts). At 16.1/16.5/16.5 in. (41/42/42 cm) (= 124/126/126 rows) from end of cuff, BO all sts.

LONG SLEEVE WITH BORDER

Work the same as sleeve for stockinette sweaters, but after end of cuff, cont in the following pattern sequence: 2 rows in St st in MC; 21 rows in St st in border patt from Colorwork Chart A: beginning with the 10th/7th/5th st of the chart, work to the end of the patt rep, and then repeat the patt rep widthwise across, ending with the 10th/13th/15th st of the chart. Incorporate the increased sts into the stitch pattern. After this, work in MC in St st.

LONG SLEEVE IN STRANDED COLORWORK PATTERN

Work the same as sleeve for stockinette sweaters, but after end of cuff, cont in St st in stranded colorwork pattern from Colorwork Chart B: beginning with the 6th/3rd/1st st of the chart, work to the end of the patt rep, and then repeat the patt rep widthwise across, ending with the 8th/11th/13th st of the patt rep. Incorporate the increased sts into the stitch pattern.

LONG SLEEVE WITH STRIPES

Stripe Sequence A = Alternate 2 rows in MC, 2 rows in CC2. Work the same as sleeve for stockinette sweaters, but after end of cuff, cont in St st in the following stripe sequence: 18 rows in stripe sequence A, 6 rows in MC, 12 rows in CC5, 22 rows in stripe sequence A, 14 rows in CC1, 10 rows in CC2, 10 rows in CC4, 6 rows in CC1. This stripe sequence is worked only once. After its completion, finish the sleeve in St st in stripe sequence A.

¾ SLEEVE IN STOCKINETTE

First, work the desired sleeve cuff; in the last row, increase or decrease as many sts as needed for a total of 57/61/65 sts on the needles. After this, cont in St st. For sleeve tapering, after having worked 8 rows from end of cuff, inc 1 st at each

end of the row. Rep these incs in every 6th row 7/5/5 times more and in every 8th row 4/6/6 times more (= 81/85/89 sts). At 11.8/12.6/12.6 in. (30/32/32 cm) (= 90/94/94 rows) from end of cuff, BO all sts.

¾ SLEEVE WITH BORDER

Work the same as sleeve for stockinette sweaters, but after end of cuff, cont in the following pattern sequence: 2 rows in St st in MC; 21 rows in St st in border patt from Colorwork Chart A, beginning with the 4th/2nd/22nd st of the patt rep, work to the end of the patt rep, and then repeat the patt rep widthwise across, ending with the 16th/18th/20th st of the patt rep. Incorporate the increased sts into the stitch pattern. After this, work in MC in St st.

¾ SLEEVE IN STRANDED COLORWORK PATTERN

Work the same as sleeve for stockinette sweaters, but after end of cuff, cont in St st in stranded colorwork pattern from Colorwork Chart B, beginning with the 7th/5th/3rd st of the patt rep, work to the end of the patt rep, and then repeat the patt rep widthwise across, ending with the 7th/9th/11th st of the patt rep. Incorporate the increased sts into the stitch pattern.

¾ SLEEVE WITH STRIPES

Stripe Sequence A = Alternate 2 rows in MC, 2 rows in CC2. Work the same as sleeve for stockinette sweaters, but after end of cuff, cont in St st in the following stripe sequence: 18 rows in stripe sequence A, 6 rows in MC, 12 rows in CC5, 22 rows in stripe sequence A, 14 rows in CC1, 10 rows in CC2, 8/10/10 rows in CC4, 0/2/2 rows in CC1. This stripe sequence is worked only once.

SHORT SLEEVE IN STOCKINETTE

First, work the desired sleeve cuff; in the last row, increasing or decreasing as needed for a total of 73/77/81 sts on the needles. After this, cont in St st. For sleeve tapering, after having worked 8 rows from end of cuff, inc 1 st at each end of the row. Rep these incs in every 8th row 3 times more (= 81/85/89 sts). At 5.1/5.5/5.5 in. (13/14/14 cm) (= 40/44/44 rows) from end of cuff, BO all sts.

SHORT SLEEVE WITH BORDER

Work the same as sleeve for stockinette sweaters, but after end of cuff, cont in the following pattern sequence: 2 rows in St st in MC; 21 rows in St st in border patt from Colorwork Chart A, beginning with the 18th/16th/14th st of the patt rep, work to the end of the patt rep, and then repeat the patt rep widthwise across, ending with the 2nd/4th/6th st of the patt rep. Incorporate the increased sts into the stitch pattern. After this, work in MC in St st.

SHORT SLEEVE IN STRANDED COLORWORK PATTERN

Work the same as sleeve for stockinette sweaters, but after end of cuff, cont in St st in stranded colorwork pattern from Colorwork Chart B, beginning with the 13th/11th/9th st of the patt rep, work to the end of the patt rep, and then repeat the patt rep widthwise across, ending with the 1st/3rd/5th st of the patt rep. Incorporate the increased sts into the stitch pattern.

SHORT SLEEVE WITH STRIPES

Stripe Sequence A = Alternate 2 rows in MC, 2 rows in CC2. Work the same as sleeve for stockinette sweaters, but after end of cuff, cont in St st in the following stripe sequence: 18 rows in stripe sequence A, 6 rows in MC, 12 rows in CC5, 4/8/8 rows in stripe sequence A. This stripe sequence is worked only once.

SWEATER WITH SLEEVE CAP OR RAGLAN SHAPING

LONG SLEEVE IN STOCKINETTE

First, work the desired sleeve cuff; in the last row, increase or decrease as many sts as needed for a total of 45/51/55 sts on the needles. After this, cont in St st. For sleeve tapering, after having worked 6/8/8 rows from end of cuff, inc 1 st at each end of the row. Rep these incs in every 6th row 7/2/0 times more and in every 8th row 7/11/12 times more (= 75/79/81 sts). After this, work either a sleeve cap or raglan shaping as follows:

To work sleeve cap, at a height of 15/15.4/15.4 in. (38/39/39 cm) (= 116/118/118 rows) from end of ribbing, BO 3/4/5 sts at each end of the row. After this, BO sts at both ends of the row in every other row as follows: 2 sts twice, 1 st 10/12/14 times, 2 sts 5/4/3 times, and 3 sts once. At sleeve cap height of 4.7/5.1/5.5 in. (12/13/14 cm) (= 38/40/42 rows), BO the remaining 15/17/17 sts.

To work raglan shaping, at a height of 15/15.4/15.4 in. (38/39/39 cm) (= 116/118/118 rows) from end of ribbing, BO 6/7/8 sts at each end of the row. After this, BO sts at both ends of the row in every other row as follows: 3 sts once and 2 sts once. Then, at both ends of the row, in every other row, work accented decrease of 1 st each 22/23/23 times, and then in every 4th row 0/0/1 time(s) more. At raglan height 6.3/6.7/7.1 in. (16/17/18 cm) (= 50/52/54 rows), BO the remaining 9 sts.

LONG SLEEVE WITH BORDER

Work the same as sleeve for stockinette sweaters, but after end of cuff, cont in the following pattern sequence: 2 rows

in St st in MC; 21 rows in St st in border patt from Colorwork Chart A, beginning with the 10th/7th/5th st of the patt rep, work to the end of the patt rep, and then repeat the patt rep widthwise across, ending with the 10th/13th/15th st of the patt rep. Incorporate the increased sts into the stitch pattern. After this, first work 11.8/12.2/12.2 in. (30/31/31 cm) (= 91/93/93 rows) in MC in St st; then another 21 rows in St st in border patt, beginning with the 17th/15th/14th st of the patt rep; work to the end of the patt rep, and then repeat the patt rep widthwise across, ending with the 3rd/5th/6th st of the patt rep. Finish the sleeve in MC in St st.

LONG SLEEVE IN STRANDED COLORWORK PATTERN

Work the same as sleeve for stockinette sweaters, but after end of cuff, cont in St st in stranded colorwork pattern from Colorwork Chart B, beginning with the 6th/3rd/1st st of the patt rep, work to the end of the patt rep, and then repeat the patt rep widthwise across, ending with the 8th/11th/13th st of the patt rep. Incorporate the increased sts into the stitch pattern.

LONG SLEEVE WITH STRIPES

Stripe Sequence A = Alternate 2 rows in MC, 2 rows in CC2. Work the same as sleeve for stockinette sweaters, but after end of cuff, cont in St st in the following stripe sequence: 18 rows in stripe sequence A, 6 rows in MC, 12 rows in CC5, 22 rows in stripe sequence A, 14 rows in CC1, 10 rows in CC2, 10 rows in CC4, 6 rows in CC1, 16 rows in stripe sequence A, 4/6/6 rows in CC1, 10 rows in CC2, 10 rows in CC4, 6 rows in CC1. This stripe sequence is worked only once. After its completion, finish the sleeve in St st in stripe sequence A.

¾ SLEEVE IN STOCKINETTE

First, work the desired sleeve cuff; in the last row, increase or decrease as many sts as needed for a total of 57/61/65 sts on the needles. After this, cont in St st. For sleeve tapering, after having worked 2/4/8 rows from end of hem ribbing, inc 1 st at each end of the row. Rep these incs in every 6th row 1/0/0 time(s) more and in every 8th row 7/8/7 times more (= 75/79/81 sts). At 9.9/10.2/10.2 in. (25/26/26 cm) (= 76/78/78 rows) from end of ribbing, work either sleeve cap or raglan shaping as for the long sleeve.

¾ SLEEVE WITH BORDER

Work the same as sleeve for stockinette sweaters, but after having worked 9.5 in. (24 cm) (= 74 rows) from end of cuff, work 21 rows in St st in border patt from Colorwork Chart A, beginning with the 17th/15th/14th st of the patt rep, work to the end of the patt rep, and then repeat the patt rep widthwise across, ending with the 3rd/5th/6th st of the patt rep. Finish the sleeve in MC in St st.

¾ SLEEVE IN STRANDED COLORWORK PATTERN

Work the same as sleeve for stockinette sweaters, but after end of cuff, cont in St st in stranded colorwork pattern from

Colorwork Chart B, beginning with the 7th/5th/3rd st of the patt rep, work to the end of the patt rep, and then repeat the patt rep widthwise across, ending with the 7th/9th/11th st of the patt rep. Incorporate the increased sts into the stitch pattern.

¾ SLEEVE WITH STRIPES

Stripe Sequence A = Alternate 2 rows in MC, 2 rows in CC2. Work the same as sleeve for stockinette sweaters, but after end of cuff, cont in St st in the following stripe sequence: 18 rows in stripe sequence A, 14 rows in CC1, 10 rows in CC2, 10 rows in CC4, 6 rows in CC1, 16 rows in stripe sequence A, 4/6/6 rows in CC1, 10 rows in CC2, 10 rows in CC4, 6 rows in CC1. This stripe sequence is worked only once. After its completion, finish the sleeve in St st in stripe sequence A.

SHORT SLEEVE IN STOCKINETTE

First, work the desired sleeve cuff; in the last row, increase or decrease as many sts as needed for a total of 69/73/75 sts on the needles. After this, cont in St st. For sleeve tapering, after having worked 2/6/2 rows from end of cuff, inc 1 st at each end of the row. Rep these incs in every 8th row 2 times more (= 75/79/81 sts).

At 4/4.3/4.3 in. (10/11/11 cm) (= 30/32/32 rows) from end of ribbing, work either sleeve cap or raglan shaping as for the long sleeve.

SHORT SLEEVE WITH BORDER

Work the same as sleeve for stockinette sweaters, but after having worked 3.6 in. (9 cm) (= 28 rows) from end of cuff, work 21 rows in St st in border patt from Colorwork Chart A, beginning with the 17th/15th/14th st of the patt rep, work to the end of the patt rep, and then repeat the patt rep widthwise across, ending with the 3rd/5th/6th st of the patt rep. Finish the sleeve in MC in St st.

SHORT SLEEVE IN STRANDED COLORWORK PATTERN

Work the same as sleeve for stockinette sweaters, but after end of cuff, cont in St st in stranded colorwork pattern from Colorwork Chart B, beginning with the 1st/13th/12th st of the patt rep, work to the end of the patt rep, and then repeat the patt rep widthwise across, ending with the 13th/1st/2nd st of the patt rep. Incorporate the increased sts into the stitch pattern.

SHORT SLEEVE WITH STRIPES

Stripe Sequence A = Alternate 2 rows in MC, 2 rows in CC2. Work the same as sleeve for stockinette sweaters, but after end of cuff, cont in St st in the following stripe sequence: 6 rows in CC4, 6 rows in CC1, 16 rows in stripe sequence A, 4/6/6 rows in CC1, 10 rows in CC2, 10 rows in CC4, 6 rows in CC1. This stripe sequence is worked only once. After its completion, finish the sleeve in St st in stripe sequence A.

SLEEVE FOR SWEATERS WITH OVERSIZED FIT

Please note: All sweaters with oversized fit in this book have drop shoulders and straight long sleeves, which means that options for ¾ sleeve, short sleeve, sleeve cap, and raglan shaping are not possible.

LONG SLEEVE FOR OVERSIZED FIT IN STOCKINETTE

First, work the desired sleeve cuff; in the last row, increase or decrease as many sts as needed for a total of 45/51/55 sts on the needles. After this, cont in St st. For sleeve tapering, after having worked 6/8/8 rows from end of cuff, inc 1 st at each end of the row. Rep these incs in every 6th row 13/10/10 times more and in every 8th row 0/3/3 times more (= 73/79/83 sts). At 12/12.6/12.6 in. (30.5/32/32 cm) (= 92/98/98 rows) from end of cuff, BO all sts.

LONG SLEEVE FOR OVERSIZED FIT WITH BORDER

Work the same as sleeve for oversized stockinette sweaters, but after end of cuff, cont in the following patt: 2 rows in St st in MC, 21 rows in St st in border patt from Colorwork Chart A, beginning with the 10th/7th/5th st of the chart, work to the end of the patt rep, and then repeat the patt rep widthwise across, ending with the 10th/13th/15th st of the chart. Incorporate the increased sts into the stitch pattern. Finish the sleeve in MC in St st.

LONG SLEEVE FOR OVERSIZED FIT IN STRANDED COLORWORK PATTERN

Work the same as sleeve for oversized stockinette sweaters, but after end of cuff, cont in St st in stranded colorwork pattern from Colorwork Chart B, beginning with the 6th/3rd/1st st of the chart, work to the end of the patt rep, and then repeat the patt rep widthwise across, ending with the 8th/11th/13th st of the chart. Incorporate the increased sts into the stitch pattern.

LONG SLEEVE FOR OVERSIZED FIT WITH STRIPES

Stripe Sequence A = Alternate 2 rows in MC, 2 rows in CC2. Work the same as sleeve for oversized stockinette sweaters, but after end of cuff, cont in St st in the following stripe sequence: 18 rows in stripe sequence A, 6 rows in MC, 12 rows in CC5, 22 rows in stripe sequence A, 14 rows in CC1, 10 rows in CC2, 10 rows in CC4, 0/0/4 rows in stripe sequence A. This stripe sequence is worked only once. After its completion, finish the sleeve for sizes Medium and Large in St st in stripe sequence A.

SLEEVE LENGTHS FOR SWEATERS WITH LACE PATTERNS

Please note: The following applies to all sleeves with lace patterns: As soon as there are 49 sts on the needles after completion of the cuff, the first 2 and the last 2 sts will always be worked in St st. Increases at both ends of the row will then always be worked after or before these 2 sts, and the sts gained from increasing are incorporated into the lace pattern.

SWEATER WITH DROP SHOULDER

LONG SLEEVE

First, work the desired sleeve cuff; in the last row, increase or decrease as many sts as needed for a total of 45/47/49 sts on the needles. Cont in lace pattern as follows: 0/1/2 st(s) in St st, 45 sts in lace pattern from Stitch Pattern Chart A, 0/1/2 st(s) in St st. For sleeve tapering, after having worked 6 rows from end of cuff, inc 1 st at each end of the row. Rep these incs at both ends of the row in every 6th row 0/3/4 times more and in every 8th row 12/11/10 times more (= 71/77/79 sts). At 16.1/16.5/16.5 in. (41/42/42 cm) (= 114/118/118 rows) from cuff, BO all sts.

¾ SLEEVE

First, work the desired sleeve cuff; in the last row, increase or decrease as many sts as needed for a total of 55/57/59 sts on the needles. Cont in lace pattern as follows: 0/1/2 st(s) in St st, 55 sts in lace pattern from Stitch Pattern Chart A, 0/1/2 st(s) in St st. For sleeve tapering, after having worked 8/4/6 rows from end of cuff, inc 1 st at each end of the row. Rep these incs in every 6th row 0/0/1 time(s) more, in every 8th row 3/9/8 times more, and in every 10th row 4/0/0 times more (= 71/77/79 sts). At 11.8/12.6/12.6 in. (30/32/32 cm) (= 82/84/84 rows) from cuff, BO all sts.

SHORT SLEEVE

First, work the desired sleeve cuff; in the last row, increase or decrease as many sts as needed for a total of 65/67/69 sts on the needles. Cont in lace pattern as follows: 0/1/2 st(s) in St st, 65 sts in lace pattern from Stitch Pattern Chart A, 0/1/2 st(s) in St st. For sleeve tapering, after having worked 6 rows from end of cuff, inc 1 st at each end of the row. Rep these incs in every 6th row 0/4/4 times more and in every 8th row 2/0/0 times more (= 71/77/79 sts). At 5.1/5.5/5.5 in. (13/14/14 cm) (= 36/38/38 rows) from cuff, BO all sts.

SWEATER WITH EITHER SLEEVE CAP OR RAGLAN SHAPING

LONG SLEEVE

First, work the desired sleeve cuff; in the last row, increase or decrease as many sts as needed for a total of 45/47/49 sts on the needles. Cont in lace pattern as follows: 0/1/2 st(s) in St st, 45 sts in lace pattern from Stitch Pattern Chart A, 0/1/2 st(s) in St st. For sleeve tapering, after having worked 6 rows from end of cuff, inc 1 st at each end of the row. Rep these incs in every 6th row 0/4/9 times more and in every 8th row 11/9/5 times more (= 69/75/79 sts). After this, work either sleeve cap or raglan shaping as follows:

To work sleeve cap, at a height of 15/15.4/15.4 in. (38/39/39 cm) (= 106/110/110 rows) from end of cuff, BO sts at both ends of the row as follows: BO 3/4/5 sts each once; then, in every other row, 2 sts twice, 1 st 9/10/12 times, 2 sts 4/4/3 times, and 3 sts once. At sleeve cap height of 4.7/5.1/5.5 in. (12/13/14 cm) (= 34/36/38 rows), BO the remaining 15/17/19 sts.

To work raglan shaping, at a height of 15/15.4/15.4 in. (38/39/39 cm) (= 106/110/110 rows) from end of cuff, BO at each end of the row as follows: BO 6/7/8 sts each once; then, in every other row, 3 sts once, and then 2 sts once. Then work accented decrease of 1 st at each end of the row in every other row 19/21/22 times. At raglan height of 6.3/6.7/7.1 in. (16/17/18 cm) (= 44/48/52 rows), BO the remaining 9 sts.

¾ SLEEVE

First, work the desired sleeve cuff; in the last row, increase or decrease as many sts as needed for a total of 55/57/59 sts on the needles. Cont in lace pattern as follows: 0/1/2 st(s) in St st, 55 sts in lace pattern from Stitch Pattern Chart A, 0/1/2 st(s) in St st. For sleeve tapering, after having worked 8/8/6 rows from end of cuff, inc 1 st at each end of the row. Rep these incs in every 6th row 0/0/6 times more and in every 8th row 6/8/3 times more (= 69/75/79 sts). At 9.9/10.2/10.2 in. (25/26/26 cm) (= 70/72/72 rows) from end of cuff, work either sleeve cap or raglan shaping as for long sleeve.

SHORT SLEEVE

First, work the desired sleeve cuff; in the last row, increase or decrease as many sts as needed for a total of 65/67/69 sts on the needles. Cont in lace pattern as follows: 0/1/2 st(s) in St st, 65 sts in lace pattern from Stitch Pattern Chart A, 0/1/2 st(s) in St st. For sleeve tapering, after having worked 8/6/4 rows from end of cuff, inc 1 st at each end of the row. Rep these incs in every 4th row 0/0/1 time(s) more, in every 6th row 0/3/3 times more, and in every 8th row 1/0/0 time(s) more (= 69/75/79 sts). At 4/4.3/4.3 in. (10/11/11 cm) (= 28/30/30 rows) from end of cuff, work either sleeve cap or raglan shaping as for long sleeve.

LONG SLEEVE FOR SWEATERS WITH OVERSIZED FIT

Please note: All sweaters with oversized fit in this book have drop shoulders and straight long sleeves, which means that options for ¾ sleeve, short sleeve, sleeve cap, and raglan shaping are not possible.

First, work the desired sleeve cuff; in the last row, increase or decrease as many sts as needed for a total of 45/47/49 sts on the needles. After this, cont in lace pattern from Stitch Pattern Chart A as follows: 0/1/2 st(s) in St st, 45 sts in lace pattern, 0/1/2 st(s) in St st. For sleeve tapering, after having worked 6/8/8 rows from end of cuff, inc 1 st at each end of the row. Rep these incs in every 6th row 3/10/6 times more and in every 8th row 7/2/6 times more (= 67/73/75 sts). At 12/12.6/13.4 in. (30.5/32/34 cm) (= 86/90/96 rows) from end of cuff, BO all sts.

SLEEVE LENGTHS FOR SWEATERS WITH CABLE PATTERNS

SWEATER WITH DROP SHOULDERS

LONG SLEEVE

First, work the desired sleeve cuff; in the last row, increase or decrease as many sts as needed for a total of 46/52/56 sts on the needles. After this, cont in the following pattern sequence: 1 st in St st, 13/16/18 sts in double seed stitch, 18 sts in cable pattern from Stitch Pattern Chart C, 13/16/18 sts in double seed stitch, 1 st in St st. For sleeve tapering, after having worked 6/10/10 rows from end of cuff, inc 1 st at each end of the row. Rep these incs in every 6th row 5/0/0 times more and in every 8th row 12/15/15 times more (= 82/84/88 sts). At 16.1/16.5/16.5 in. (41/42/42 cm) (= 140/142/142 rows) from end of cuff, BO all sts.

¾ SLEEVE

First, work the desired sleeve cuff; in the last row, increase or decrease as many sts as needed for a total of 60/64/68 sts on the needles. After this, cont in the following pattern sequence: 1 st in St st, 20/22/24 sts in double seed stitch, 18 sts in cable pattern from Stitch Pattern Chart C, 20/22/24 sts in double seed stitch, 1 st in St st. For sleeve tapering, after having worked 14/16/10 rows from end of cuff, inc 1 st at each end of the row. Rep these incs in every 8th row 10/9/1 time(s) more and in every 10th row 0/0/8 times more (= 82/84/88 sts). At 11.8/12.6/12.6 in. (30/32/32 cm) (= 102/108/108 rows) from end of cuff, BO all sts.

SHORT SLEEVE

First, work the desired sleeve cuff; in the last row, increase or decrease as many sts as needed for a total of 72/76/80 sts on the needles. After this, cont in the following pattern sequence: 1 st in St st, 26/28/30 sts in double seed stitch, 18 sts in cable pattern from Stitch Pattern Chart C, 26/28/30 sts in double seed stitch, 1 st in St st. For sleeve tapering, after having worked 6/6/16 rows from end of cuff, inc 1 st at each end of the row. Rep these incs in every 8th row 4/0/0 times more and in every 10th row 0/3/3 times more (= 82/84/88 sts). At 5.1/5.5/5.5 in. (13/14/14 cm) (= 44/48/48 rows) from end of cuff, BO all sts.

SWEATER WITH EITHER SLEEVE CAP OR RAGLAN SHAPING

LONG SLEEVE

First, work the desired sleeve cuff; in the last row, increase or decrease as many sts as needed for a total of 46/52/56 sts on the needles. After this, cont in the following pattern sequence: 1 st in St st, 13/16/18 sts in double seed stitch, 18 sts in cable pattern from Stitch Pattern Chart C, 13/16/18 sts in double seed stitch, 1 st in St st. For sleeve tapering, after having worked 6/10/10 rows from end of cuff, inc 1 st at each end of the row. Rep these incs in every 6th row 8/0/0 times more and in every 8th row 8/14/14 times more (= 80/82/86 sts). After this, work either sleeve cap or raglan shaping as follows:

To work sleeve cap, at a height of 15/15.4/15.4 in. (38/39/39 cm) (= 130/132/132 rows) from end of cuff, BO sts at both ends of the row as follows: 3/4/5 sts each once, and then, in every other row, 2 sts twice, 1 st 12/16/19 times, 2 sts 3/2/2 times, and 3 sts 2/1/0 time(s). At sleeve cap height of 4.7/5.1/5.5 in. (12/13/14 cm) (= 40/44/48 rows), BO the remaining 18/20/22 sts.

To work raglan shaping, at a height of 15/15.4/15.4 in. (38/39/39 cm) (= 130/132/132 rows) from end of cuff, BO at both ends of the row as follows: BO 6/7/8 sts each once; then, in every other row, 3 sts once, and then 2 sts once. Then work accented decrease of 1 st at each end of the row in every other row as follows: 25/24/24 times, and then in every 4th row 0/1/2 time(s). At raglan height 6.3/6.7/7.1 in. (16/17/18 cm) (= 56/58/62 rows), BO the remaining 8 sts.

¾ SLEEVE

First, work the desired sleeve cuff; in the last row, increase or decrease as many sts as needed for a total of 60/64/68 sts on the needles. After this, cont in the following pattern sequence: 1 st in St st, 20/22/24 sts in double seed stitch, 18 sts in cable pattern from Stitch Pattern Chart C, 20/22/24 sts in double seed stitch, 1 st in St st. For sleeve tapering, after having worked 6 rows from end of cuff, inc 1 st at each end of the row. Rep these incs in every 8th row 9/4/5 times more and in every 10th row 0/4/3 times more (= 80/82/86 sts). At 9.9/10.2/10.2 in. (25/26/26 cm) (= 86/90/90 rows) from end of ribbing, work either sleeve cap or raglan shaping as for the long sleeve.

SHORT SLEEVE

First, work the desired sleeve cuff; in the last row, increase or decrease as many sts as needed for a total of 72/76/80 sts on the needles. After this, cont in the following pattern sequence: 1 st in St st, 26/28/30 sts in double seed stitch, 18 sts in cable pattern from Stitch Pattern Chart C, 26/28/30 sts in double seed stitch, 1 st in St st. For sleeve tapering, after having worked 4/6/6 rows from end of cuff, inc 1 st at each end of the row. Rep these incs in every 8th row 3/0/0 times more and in every 10th row 0/2/2 times more (= 80/82/86 sts). At 4/4.3/4.3 in. (10/11/11 cm) (= 34/38/38 rows) from end of cuff, work either sleeve cap or raglan shaping as for the long sleeve.

LONG SLEEVE FOR SWEATERS WITH OVERSIZED FIT

Please note: All sweaters with oversized fit in this book have drop shoulders and straight long sleeves, which means that options for ¾ sleeve, short sleeve, sleeve cap, and raglan shaping are not possible.

First, work the desired sleeve cuff; in the last row, increase or decrease as many sts as needed for a total of 46/52/56 sts on the needles. After this, cont in the following pattern sequence: 1 st in St st, 13/16/18 sts in double seed stitch, 18 sts in cable pattern from Stitch Pattern Chart C, 13/16/18 sts in double seed stitch, 1 st in St st. For sleeve tapering, after having worked 6/10/10 rows from end of cuff, inc 1 st at each end of the row (= 48/54/58 sts). Rep these incs in every 6th row 8/0/0 times more and in every 8th row 5/11/12 times more (= 74/76/82 sts). At 12/12.6/12.6 in. (30.5/32/32 cm) (= 104/108/108 rows) from end of cuff, BO the remaining 74/76/82 sts.

BODY SHAPES

OVERSIZED BODY SHAPE

STOCKINETTE STITCH

RS: Knit all sts.
WS: Purl all sts.

RIBBING IN ROWS

RS: Alternate k1, p1.
WS: Work all sts as they appear—knit the knits and purl the purls.

RIBBING IN ROUNDS

All rounds (RS): Alternate k1, p1.

INSTRUCTIONS

BACK

Using US 4 (3.5 mm) needles, CO 167/191/215 sts, and for hem ribbing, work 14 rows in ribbing patt; *at the same time*, in the last row, evenly distributed, dec 14/14/18 sts (= 153/177/197 sts). Change to US 6 (4.0 mm) needles, and continue in St st. At 21/21.3/21.7 in. (53/54/55 cm) (= 158/162/166 rows) from hem ribbing, BO all sts.

FRONT

Work as the Back, but with neckline shaping. For this, after having worked only 19/19.3/19.7 in. (48/49/50 cm) (= 144/148/150 rows) from end of hem ribbing, BO the middle 19/23/25 sts, and continue both sides separately. For the rounded neckline, BO sts at the neck edge in every other row as follows: BO 4 sts once, 3 sts 3/3/2 times, 2 sts 1/1/2 time(s), and 1 st 1/1/2 time(s). At 21/21.3/21.7 in. (53/54/55 cm) (= 158/162/166 rows) from end of ribbing, BO the remaining 51/61/70 sts for each shoulder.

SLEEVES (MAKE 2)

Using US 4 (3.5 mm) needles, CO 51/55/59 sts, and for the cuff, work 14 rows in ribbing; in the last WS row, evenly distributed, dec 6/4/4 sts (= 45/51/55 sts). Change to US 6 (4.0 mm) needles, and continue in St st. *At the same time*, for sleeve tapering, after having worked 6/8/8 rows from end of cuff, inc 1 st at each end of the row. Rep these incs in every 6th row 13/10/10 times more and in every 8th row 0/3/3 times more (= 73/79/83 sts). At 12/12.6/12.6 in. (30.5/32/32 cm) (= 92/98/98 rows) from end of cuff, BO all sts.

FINISHING

Block all pieces to measurements on a soft surface, moisten, and let dry. Close shoulder and side seams from the wrong side, leaving the upper 6.5/7.1/7.5 in. (16.5/18/19 cm) open for the armholes. Seam the sleeves right sides facing each other and wrong sides facing out, and then sew the sleeves into the armholes from the wrong side.

Using US 4 (3.5 mm) needles, pick up and knit 126/130/134 sts from the neckline edge, join into the round, and work 1.2 in. (3 cm) (= 8 rnds) in ribbing pattern. BO all sts, and weave in ends.

SCHEMATIC

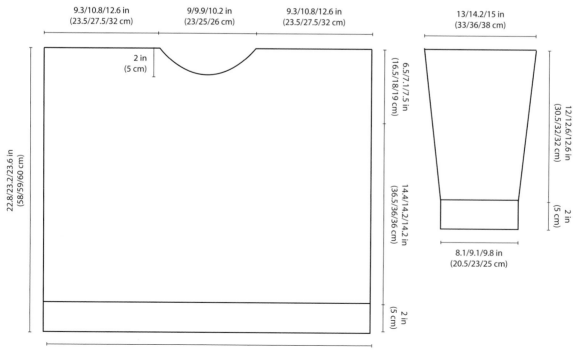

**STRAIGHT
SLEEVE TOP**

SIZES

Small/Medium/Large
(US 6/8, 10/12, 14/16)
Numbers for size Small
are listed before the first
slash, for size Medium
between slashes, and for
size Large after the sec-
ond slash. If only one
number is given, it ap-
plies to all sizes.

MATERIALS

Schachenmayr Merino
Extrafine 120; #3 light
weight yarn; 100% wool;
131 yd (120 m), 1.75 oz.
(50 g) per skein
- 12/13/14 skeins #166
  ocean blue heathered

Circular knitting needles,
sizes US 4 (3.5 mm) and
US 6 (4.0 mm), each 40 in.
(100 cm) long

GAUGE

In stockinette stitch
on US 6 (4.0 mm)
needles, 22 sts and
30 rows = 4 x 4 in.
(10 x 10 cm)

**OVERSIZED
BODY
SHAPE**

OVERSIZED WITH COLORFUL STRIPES

SIZES

Small/Medium/Large (US 6/8, 10/12, 14/16)

Numbers for size Small are listed before the first slash, for size Medium between slashes, and for size Large after the second slash. If only one number is given, it applies to all sizes.

MATERIALS

Schachenmayr Merino Extrafine 120; #3 light weight yarn; 100% wool; 131 yd (120 m), 1.75 oz. (50 g) per skein

- Main color (MC): 5/6/7 skeins in your choice of color
- Contrasting color 1 (CC1): 3/4/5 skeins in your choice of color
- Contrasting color 2 (CC2): 4/5/5 skeins in your choice of color
- Contrasting color 3 (CC3): 2/2/2 skeins in your choice of color
- Contrasting color 4 (CC4): 2/2/3 skeins in your choice of color
- Contrasting color 5 (CC5): 2/2/3 skeins in your choice of color

Circular knitting needles, US 4 (3.5 mm) and US 6 (4.0 mm), each 40 in. (100 cm) long

GAUGE

In stockinette stitch on US 6 (4.0 mm) needles, 22 sts and 30 rows = 4 x 4 in. (10 x 10 cm)

STOCKINETTE STITCH

RS: Knit all sts.
WS: Purl all sts.

RIBBING IN ROWS

RS: Alternate k1, p1.
WS: Work all sts as they appear—knit the knits and purl the purls.

RIBBING IN ROUNDS

All rounds (RS): Alternate k1, p1.

STRIPE SEQUENCE A

Alternate 2 rows in MC, 2 rows in CC2.

STRIPE SEQUENCE B

This stripe sequence is worked only once. 18 rows in CC3, 6 rows in CC1, 14 rows in CC4, 6 rows in CC1, 14 rows in MC, 12 rows in CC5, 22 rows in stripe sequence A, 14 rows in CC1, 10 rows in CC2, 10 rows in CC4, 6 rows in CC1.

STRIPE SEQUENCE C

This stripe sequence is worked only once. 18 rows in stripe sequence A, 6 rows in MC, 12 rows in CC5, 22 rows in stripe sequence A, 14 rows in CC1, 10 rows in CC2, 10 rows in CC4, 0/4/4 rows in CC1.

INSTRUCTIONS

BACK

Using US 4 (3.5 mm) needles, CO 167/191/215 sts, and for hem ribbing, work 14 rows in ribbing patt; *at the same time*, in the last row, evenly distributed, dec 14/14/18 sts (= 153/177/197 sts). Change to US 6 (4.0 mm) needles, and cont in St st in stripe sequence B. After having completed stripe sequence B, cont in St st in stripe sequence A. At 21/21.3/21.7 in. (53/54/55 cm) (= 158/162/166 rows) from hem ribbing, BO all sts.

FRONT

Work as the Back, but with neckline shaping. For this, after having worked only 19/19.3/19.7 in. (48/49/50 cm) (= 144/148/150 rows) from end of hem ribbing, BO the middle 19/23/25 sts, and continue both sides separately. For the rounded neckline, BO sts at the neck edge in every other row as follows: BO 4 sts once, 3 sts 3/3/2 times, 2 sts 1/1/2 time(s), and 1 st 1/1/2 time(s). At 21/21.3/21.7 in. (53/54/55 cm) (= 158/162/166 rows) from end of ribbing, BO the remaining 51/61/70 sts for each shoulder.

SLEEVES (MAKE 2)

Using US 4 (3.5 mm) needles, CO 51/55/59 sts, and for the cuff, work 14 rows in ribbing; in the last WS row, evenly distributed, dec 6/4/4 sts (= 45/51/55 sts). Change to US 6 (4.0 mm) needles, and cont in St st in stripe sequence C. *At the same time*, for sleeve tapering, after having worked 6/8/8 rows from end of cuff, inc 1 st at each end of the row. Rep these incs in every 6th row 13/10/10 times more and in every 8th row 0/3/3 times more (= 73/79/83 sts). At 12/12.6/12.6 in. (30.5/32/32 cm) (= 92/98/98 rows) from end of cuff, BO all sts.

FINISHING

Block all pieces to measurements on a soft surface, moisten, and let dry. Close shoulder and side seams from the wrong side, leaving the upper 6.5/7.1/7.5 in. (16.5/18/19 cm) open for the armholes. Seam the sleeves right sides facing each other and wrong sides facing out, and then sew the sleeves into the armholes from the wrong side.

Using US 4 (3.5 mm) needles, pick up and knit 126/130/134 sts from the neckline edge, join into the round, and work 1.2 in. (3 cm) (= 8 rnds) in ribbing pattern. BO all sts, and weave in ends.

OVERSIZED WITH BORDER

SIZES

Small/Medium/Large (US 6/8, 10/12, 14/16)

Numbers for size Small are listed before the first slash, for size Medium between slashes, and for size Large after the second slash. If only one number is given, it applies to all sizes.

MATERIALS

Schachenmayr Merino Extrafine 120; #3 light weight yarn; 100% wool; 131 yd (120 m), 1.75 oz. (50 g) per skein

- Main color (MC): 11/12/13 skeins in your choice of color
- Contrasting color 1 (CC1): 4/4/5 skeins in your choice of color
- Contrasting color 2 (CC2): 1/2/2 skeins in your choice of color

Circular knitting needles, US 4 (3.5 mm) and US 6 (4.0 mm), each 40 in. (100 cm) long

GAUGE

In stockinette stitch on US 6 (4.0 mm) needles, 22 sts and 30 rows = 4 x 4 in. (10 x 10 cm)

COLORWORK CHART A

Page 75

STOCKINETTE STITCH

RS: Knit all sts.
WS: Purl all sts.

RIBBING IN ROWS

RS: Alternate k1, p1.
WS: Work all sts as they appear—knit the knits and purl the purls.

RIBBING IN ROUNDS

All rounds (RS): Alternate k1, p1.

BORDER PATTERN

Work in stockinette stitch from Colorwork Chart A. The chart contains both RS and WS rows. Sts are shown as they appear from the RS of the fabric. Begin with the stitch stated in the instructions, work to the end of the patt rep, and then repeat the patt rep widthwise across, ending with the stitch stated in the instructions. Work Rows 1–21 once heightwise.

INSTRUCTIONS

BACK

Using US 4 (3.5 mm) needles, CO 167/191/215 sts, and for hem ribbing, work 14 rows in ribbing patt; *at the same time*, in the last row, evenly distributed, dec 14/14/18 sts (= 153/177/197 sts). Change to US 6 (4.0 mm) needles, and cont as follows: 2 rows in St st in MC; 21 rows in St st in border patt, beginning with the 22nd/10th/19th st of the patt rep and ending with the 20th/10th/17th st of the patt rep; then work 79 rows in St st in MC; 21 rows in St st in border patt, beginning with the 22nd/10th/19th st of the patt rep and ending with the 20th/10th/17th st of the patt rep. After this, work in MC in St st. At 21/21.3/21.7 in. (53/54/55 cm) (= 158/162/166 rows) from hem ribbing, BO all sts.

FRONT

Work as the Back, but with neckline shaping. For this, after having worked only 19/19.3/19.7 in. (48/49/50 cm) (= 144/148/150 rows) from end of hem ribbing, BO the middle 19/23/25 sts, and continue both sides separately. For the rounded neckline, BO sts at the neck edge in every other row as follows: BO 4 sts once, 3 sts 3/3/2 times, 2 sts 1/1/2 time(s), and 1 st 1/1/2 time(s). At 21/21.3/21.7 in. (53/54/55 cm) (=

158/162/166 rows) from end of ribbing, BO the remaining 51/61/70 sts for each shoulder.

SLEEVES (MAKE 2)

Using US 4 (3.5 mm) needles, CO 51/55/59 sts, and for the cuff, work 14 rows in ribbing; in the last WS row, evenly distributed, dec 6/4/4 sts (= 45/51/55 sts). Change to US 6 (4.0 mm) needles, and cont as follows: 2 rows in St st in MC; 21 rows in St st in border patt, beginning with the 10th/7th/5th st of the patt rep, ending with the 10th/13th/15th st of the patt rep. After this, work in MC in St st. *At the same time*, for sleeve tapering, after having worked 6/8/8 rows from end of cuff, inc 1 st at each end of the row. Rep these incs in every 6th row 13/10/10 times more and in every 8th row 0/3/3 times more (= 73/79/83 sts). At 12/12.6/12.6 in. (30.5/32/32 cm) (= 92/98/98 rows) from end of cuff, BO all sts.

FINISHING

Block all pieces to measurements on a soft surface, moisten, and let dry. Close shoulder and side seams from the wrong side, leaving the upper 6.5/7.1/7.5 in. (16.5/18/19 cm) open for the armholes. Seam the sleeves right sides facing each other and wrong sides facing out, and then sew the sleeves into the armholes from the wrong side.

Using US 4 (3.5 mm) needles, pick up and knit 126/130/134 sts from the neckline edge, join into the round, and work 1.2 in. (3 cm) (= 8 rnds) in ribbing pattern. BO all sts, and weave in ends.

OVERSIZED WITH STRANDED PATTERN

SIZES

Small/Medium/Large (US 6/8, 10/12, 14/16)

Numbers for size Small are listed before the first slash, for size Medium between slashes, and for size Large after the second slash. If only one number is given, it applies to all sizes.

MATERIALS

Schachenmayr Merino Extrafine 120; #3 light weight yarn; 100% wool; 131 yd (120 m), 1.75 oz. (50 g) per skein

- Main color (MC): 10/12/13 skeins in your choice of color
- Contrasting color (CC): 6/8/10 skeins in your choice of color

Circular knitting needles, US 4 (3.5 mm) and US 6 (4.0 mm), each 40 in. (100 cm) long

GAUGE

In stranded colorwork pattern on US 6 (4.0 mm) needles, 22 sts and 30 rows = 4 x 4 in. (10 x 10 cm)

COLORWORK CHART B

Page 75

STOCKINETTE STITCH

RS: Knit all sts.
WS: Purl all sts.

RIBBING IN ROWS

RS: Alternate k1, p1.
WS: Work all sts as they appear—knit the knits and purl the purls.

RIBBING IN ROUNDS

All rounds (RS): Alternate k1, p1.

STRANDED PATTERN

Work in stockinette stitch in stranded colorwork pattern from Colorwork Chart B. The chart contains both RS and WS rows. Sts are shown as they appear from the RS of the fabric. Begin with the stitch stated in the instructions, work to the end of the patt rep, and then repeat the patt rep widthwise across, ending with the stitch stated in the instructions. Repeat Rows 1–14 heightwise throughout.

INSTRUCTIONS

BACK

Using US 4 (3.5 mm) needles, CO 167/191/215 sts, and for hem ribbing, work 14 rows in ribbing patt; *at the same time*, in the last row, evenly distributed, dec 14/14/18 sts (= 153/177/197 sts). Change to US 6 (4.0 mm) needles, and cont in St st in stranded colorwork pattern from Colorwork Chart B, beginning with the 1st/3rd/7th st of the patt rep and ending with the 13th/11th/7th st of the patt rep. At 21/21.3/21.7 in. (53/54/55 cm) (= 158/162/166 rows) from hem ribbing, BO all sts.

FRONT

Work as the Back, but with neckline shaping. For this, after having worked only 19/19.3/19.7 in. (48/49/50 cm) (= 144/148/150 rows) from end of hem ribbing, BO the middle 19/23/25 sts, and continue both sides separately. For the rounded neckline, BO sts at the neck edge in every other row as follows: BO 4 sts once, 3 sts 3/3/2 times, 2 sts 1/1/2 time(s), and 1 st 1/1/2 time(s).

At 21/21.3/21.7 in. (53/54/55 cm) (= 158/162/166 rows) from end of ribbing, BO the remaining 51/61/70 sts for each shoulder.

SLEEVES (MAKE 2)

Using US 4 (3.5 mm) needles, CO 51/55/59 sts, and for the cuff, work 14 rows in ribbing; in the last WS row, evenly distributed, dec 6/4/4 sts (= 45/51/55 sts). Change to US 6 (4.0 mm) needles, and cont in St st in stranded colorwork pattern from Colorwork Chart B, beginning with the 6th/3rd/1st st of the patt rep and ending with the 8th/11th/13th st of the patt rep. *At the same time*, for sleeve tapering, after having worked 6/8/8 rows from end of cuff, inc 1 st at each end of the row. Rep these incs in every 6th row 13/10/10 times more and in every 8th row 0/3/3 times more (= 73/79/83 sts). At 12/12.6/12.6 in. (30.5/32/32 cm) (= 92/98/98 rows) from end of cuff, BO all sts.

FINISHING

Block all pieces to measurements on a soft surface, moisten, and let dry. Close shoulder and side seams from the wrong side, leaving the upper 6.5/7.1/7.5 in. (16.5/18/19 cm) open for the armholes. Seam the sleeves right sides facing each other and wrong sides facing out, and then sew the sleeves into the armholes from the wrong side.

Using US 4 (3.5 mm) needles, pick up and knit 126/130/134 sts from the neckline edge, join into the round, and work 1.2 in. (3 cm) (= 8 rnds) in ribbing pattern. BO all sts, and weave in ends.

OVERSIZED WITH LACE PATTERN

SIZES

Small/Medium/Large (US 6/8, 10/12, 14/16)

Numbers for size Small are listed before the first slash, for size Medium between slashes, and for size Large after the second slash. If only one number is given, it applies to all sizes.

MATERIALS

Schachenmayr Merino Extrafine 120; #3 light weight yarn; 100% wool; 131 yd (120 m), 1.75 oz. (50 g) per skein

- 13/14/15 skeins in your choice of color

Circular knitting needles, US 4 (3.5 mm) and US 6 (4.0 mm), each 40 in. (100 cm) long

GAUGE

In lace pattern on US 6 (4.0 mm) needles, 20 sts and 28 rows = 4 x 4 in. (10 x 10 cm)

STITCH PATTERN CHART A

Page 75

STOCKINETTE STITCH

RS: Knit all sts.
WS: Purl all sts.

RIBBING IN ROWS

RS: Alternate k1, p1.
WS: Work all sts as they appear— knit the knits and purl the purls.

RIBBING IN ROUNDS

All rounds (RS): Alternate k1, p1.

LACE PATTERN

Work from Stitch Pattern Chart A. Only RS rows are shown in the chart; in WS rows, work all sts as they appear, and purl the yarn overs. Begin with the sts before the patt rep, repeat the patt rep widthwise across, and end with the sts after the patt rep. Repeat Rows 1–12 of the chart heightwise throughout.

INSTRUCTIONS

BACK

Using US 4 (3.5 mm) needles, CO 167/191/215 sts, and for hem ribbing, work 14 rows in ribbing patt; *at the same time*, in the last row, evenly distributed, dec 22/26/30 sts (= 145/165/185 sts). Cont in lace pattern. At 21/21.3/21.7 in. (53/54/55 cm) (= 148/152/154 rows) from hem ribbing, BO all sts.

FRONT

Work as the Back, but with neckline shaping. For this, after having worked only 19/19.3/19.7 in. (48/49/50 cm) (= 134/138/140 rows) from end of ribbing, BO the middle 21/21/29 sts, and continue both sides separately. For the rounded neckline, BO sts at the neck edge in every other row as follows: BO 3 sts 2/3/2 times, 2 sts 3/2/3 times, and 1 st once. At 21/21.3/21.7 in. (53/54/55 cm) (= 148/152/154 rows) from end of ribbing BO the remaining 49/58/65 sts for each shoulder.

SLEEVES (MAKE 2)

CO 51/55/59 sts, and for the cuff, work 14 rows in ribbing patt; *at the same time*, in the last row, evenly distributed, dec 6/8/10 sts (= 45/47/49 sts). Cont in the following patt: 0/1/2 st(s) in St st, 45 sts in lace pattern, 0/1/2 st(s) in St st. *At the same time*, for sleeve tapering, after having worked 6 rows from end of cuff, inc 1 st at each end of the row. Rep these incs in every 6th row 0/3/4 times more and in every 8th row 9/8/7 times more (= 65/71/73 sts). At 12/12.6/12.6 in. (30.5/32/32 cm) (= 86/90/90 rows) from end of cuff, BO all sts.

Please note: As soon as you have 49 sts on the needles, always work the first 2 sts and the last 2 sts of the row in St st. Increases at both ends of the row will then always be worked after or before these 2 sts, and the sts gained from increasing are incorporated into the lace pattern.

FINISHING

Block all pieces to measurements on a soft surface, moisten, and let dry. Close shoulder and side seams from the wrong side, leaving the upper 6.5/7.1/7.5 in. (16.5/18/19 cm) open for the armholes. Seam the sleeves right sides facing each other and wrong sides facing out, and then sew the sleeves into the armholes from the wrong side.

Using US 4 (3.5 mm) needles, pick up and knit 126/130/134 sts from the neckline edge, join into the round, and work 1.2 in. (3 cm) (= 8 rnds) in ribbing pattern. BO all sts, and weave in ends.

OVERSIZED WITH CABLE PATTERN

SIZES

Small/Medium/Large (US 6/8, 10/12, 14/16)

Numbers for size Small are listed before the first slash, for size Medium between slashes, and for size Large after the second slash. If only one number is given, it applies to all sizes.

MATERIALS

Schachenmayr Merino Extrafine 120; #3 light weight yarn; 100% wool; 131 yd (120 m), 1.75 oz. (50 g) per skein

- 14/16/17 skeins in your choice of color

Circular knitting needles, US 4 (3.5 mm) and US 6 (4.0 mm), each 40 in. (100 cm) long

Cable needle (cn)

GAUGE

In double seed stitch on US 6 (4.0 mm) needles, 22 sts and 34 rows = 4 x 4 in. (10 x 10 cm)

In cable pattern 1 on US 6 (4.0 mm) needles, 58 sts = 8.3 in. (21 cm)

In cable pattern 2 on US 6 (4.0 mm) needles, 18 sts = 3.1 in. (8 cm)

STITCH PATTERN CHARTS B AND C
Page 75

STOCKINETTE STITCH

RS: Knit all sts.
WS: Purl all sts.

RIBBING IN ROWS

RS: Alternate k1, p1.
WS: Work all sts as they appear—knit the knits and purl the purls.

RIBBING IN ROUNDS

All rounds (RS): Alternate k1, p1.

DOUBLE SEED STITCH

Row 1: Alternate k1, p1.
Row 2: Knit the knits and purl the purls.
Row 3: Alternate p1, k1.
Row 4: Knit the knits and purl the purls.
Rep Rows 1–4 throughout.

CABLE PATTERN 1

Work from Stitch Pattern Chart B. Only RS rows are shown in the chart; in WS rows, work all sts as they appear (knit the knits and purl the purls), and purl the slipped sts. Work the patt rep (58 sts wide) widthwise across once, and then rep Rows 1–12 heightwise throughout.

CABLE PATTERN 2

Work from Stitch Pattern Chart C. Only RS rows are shown in the chart; in WS rows, work all sts as they appear (knit the knits and purl the purls), and purl the slipped sts. Work the patt rep (18 sts wide) widthwise across once, and then rep Rows 1–12 heightwise throughout.

INSTRUCTIONS

BACK

Using US 4 (3.5 mm) needles, CO 167/191/215 sts, and for hem ribbing, work 14 rows in ribbing patt; *at the same time*, in the last row, evenly distributed, dec 3/3/7 sts (= 164/188/208 sts). Change to US 6 (4.0 mm) needles, and continue in the following pattern: 1 st in St st, 52/64/74 sts in double seed stitch, 58 sts in cable pattern from Stitch Pattern Chart B, 52/64/74 sts in double seed stitch, 1 st in St st. At 21/21.3/21.7 in. (53/54/55 cm) (= 180/184/188 rows) from hem ribbing, BO all sts.

FRONT

Work as the Back, but with neckline shaping. For this, after having worked only 19/19.3/19.7 in. (48/49/50 cm) (= 164/166/168 rows) from end of ribbing, BO the middle 28/30/30 sts, and continue both sides separately. For the rounded neckline, BO sts at the neck edge in every other row as follows: BO 4 sts once, 3 sts twice, 2 sts 3/3/2 times, and 1 st 1/2/4 time(s). At 21/21.3/21.7 in. (53/54/55 cm) (= 180/184/188 rows) from end of ribbing, BO the remaining 51/61/71 sts for each shoulder.

SLEEVES (MAKE 2)

Using US 4 (3.5 mm) needles, CO 51/55/59 sts, and for the cuff, work 14 rows in ribbing; in the last WS row, evenly distributed, dec 5/3/3 sts (= 46/52/56 sts). Change to US 6 (4.0 mm) needles, and continue in the following pattern: 1 st in St st, 13/16/18 sts in double seed stitch, 18 sts in cable pattern from Stitch Pattern Chart C, 13/16/18 sts in double seed stitch, 1 st in St st. *At the same time,* for sleeve tapering, after having worked 6/10/10 rows from end of cuff, inc 1 st at each end of the row. Rep these incs in every 6th row 5/0/0 times more and in every 8th row 8/11/12 times more (= 74/76/82 sts). At 12/12.6/12.6 in. (30.5/32/32 cm) (= 104/108/108 rows) from end of cuff, BO all sts.

FINISHING

Block all pieces to measurements on a soft surface, moisten, and let dry. Close shoulder and side seams from the wrong side, leaving the upper 6.5/7.1/7.5 in. (16.5/18/19 cm) open for the armholes. Seam the sleeves right sides facing each other and wrong sides facing out, and then sew the sleeves into the armholes from the wrong side.

Using US 4 (3.5 mm) needles, pick up and knit 126/130/134 sts from the neckline edge, join into the round, and work 1.2 in. (3 cm) (= 8 rnds) in ribbing pattern. BO all sts, and weave in ends.

STITCH PATTERN AND COLORWORK CHARTS

COLORWORK CHART A

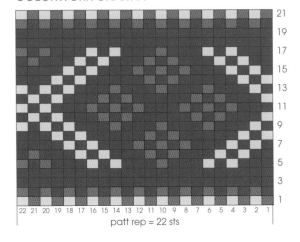

patt rep = 22 sts

KNITTING SYMBOLS

= St st in MC
= St st in CC1
= St st in CC2

COLORWORK CHART B

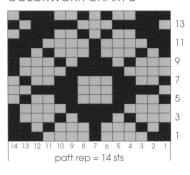

patt rep = 14 sts

KNITTING SYMBOLS

= St st in MC
= St st in CC

STITCH PATTERN CHART A

Stitch count is a multiple of 10 + 15

patt rep = 10 sts

KNITTING SYMBOLS

= knit 1 st
= purl 1 st
= make 1 yarn over
= knit 2 sts together
= slip 1, knit 1, pass the slipped st over
= slip 1, knit 2 sts together, pass the slipped st over
= no st, for better overview only

STITCH PATTERN CHART B

cable pattern 1 = 58 sts

STITCH PATTERN CHART C

cable pattern 2 = 18 sts

KNITTING SYMBOLS

= knit 1 st
= purl 1 st
= slip 1 st purlwise with yarn in back of work
= hold 1 st on cn in back of work, knit the next 2 sts, and then knit the st from the cn
= hold 2 sts on cn in front of work, purl the next st, and then knit the 2 sts from the cn

= hold 2 sts on cn in back of work, knit the next 2 sts, and then knit the 2 sts from the cn
= hold 4 sts on cn in back of work, knit the next 4 sts, and then knit the 4 sts from the cn
= hold 4 sts on cn in front of work, knit the next 4 sts, and then knit the 4 sts from the cn

A-LINE SHAPED

STOCKINETTE STITCH

RS: Knit all sts.
WS: Purl all sts.

RIBBING IN ROWS

RS: Alternate k1, p1.
WS: Work all sts as they appear—knit the knits and purl the purls.

RIBBING IN ROUNDS

All rounds (RS): Alternate k1, p1.

ACCENTED DECREASES

Accented decreases are always worked in RS rows, at both ends of the row as follows: K1, skp, cont in St st to last 3 sts of the row, then k2tog, k1. In WS rows, always purl the first 2 sts and the last 2 sts of the row. In RS rows without decreases, always knit the first 2 sts and the last 2 sts of the row.

INSTRUCTIONS

BACK

Using US 4 (3.5 mm) needles, CO 177/189/197 sts, and for hem ribbing, work 14 rows in ribbing patt; *at the same time*, in the last row, evenly distributed, dec 14/14/16 sts (= 163/175/181 sts). Change to US 6 (4.0 mm) needles, and continue in St st. *At the same time*, for the sloped sides, after having worked 4/2/4 rows from end of hem ribbing, work 1 accented decrease at each end of the row. Rep accented decreases at both ends of the row alternatingly in every 2nd and every 4th row a total of 28 times more (= 105/117/123 sts). After this, cont even in St st without further decreases. At 21/21.3/21.7 in. (53/54/55 cm) (= 158/162/166 rows) from hem ribbing, BO all sts.

FRONT

Work as the Back, but with neckline shaping. For this, after having worked only 19/19.3/19.7 in. (48/49/50 cm) (= 144/148/150 rows) from end of hem ribbing, BO the middle 19/23/25 sts, and continue both sides separately. For the rounded neckline, BO sts at the neck edge in every other row as follows: BO 4 sts once, 3 sts 3/3/2 times, 2 sts 1/1/2 time(s), and 1 st 1/1/2 time(s). At 21/21.3/21.7 in. (53/54/55 cm) (= 158/162/166 rows) from end of ribbing, BO the remaining 27/31/33 sts for each shoulder.

SLEEVES (MAKE 2)

Using US 4 (3.5 mm) needles, CO 51/55/59 sts, and for the cuff, work 14 rows in ribbing patt; *at the same time*, in the last row, evenly distributed, dec 6/4/4 sts (= 45/51/55 sts). Change to US 6 (4.0 mm) needles, and continue in St st. For sleeve tapering, after having worked 6/8/8 rows from end of cuff, inc 1 st at each end of the row. Rep these incs in every 6th row 13/10/10 times more and in every 8th row 4/6/6 times more (= 81/85/89 sts). At 16.1/16.5/16.5 in. (41/42/42 cm) (= 124/126/126 rows) from end of cuff, BO all sts.

FINISHING

Block all pieces to measurements on a soft surface, moisten, and let dry. Close shoulder and side seams from the wrong side, leaving the upper 7.1/7.5/7.9 in. (18/19/20 cm) open for the armholes. Seam the sleeves right sides facing each other and wrong sides facing out, and then sew the sleeves into the armholes from the wrong side.

Using US 4 (3.5 mm) needles, pick up and knit 126/130/134 sts from the neckline edge, join into the round, and work 1.2 in. (3 cm) (= 8 rnds) in ribbing pattern. BO all sts, and weave in ends.

SCHEMATIC

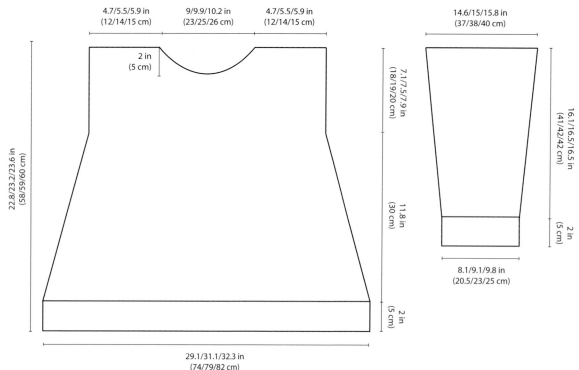

4.7/5.5/5.9 in (12/14/15 cm)
9/9.9/10.2 in (23/25/26 cm)
4.7/5.5/5.9 in (12/14/15 cm)
2 in (5 cm)
22.8/23.2/23.6 in (58/59/60 cm)
2 in (5 cm)
29.1/31.1/32.3 in (74/79/82 cm)

14.6/15/15.8 in (37/38/40 cm)
7.1/7.5/7.9 in (18/19/20 cm)
16.1/16.5/16.5 in (41/42/42 cm)
11.8 in (30 cm)
2 in (5 cm)
8.1/9.1/9.8 in (20.5/23/25 cm)

SIZES

Small/Medium/Large (US 6/8, 10/12, 14/16)

Numbers for size Small are listed before the first slash, for size Medium between slashes, and for size Large after the second slash. If only one number is given, it applies to all sizes.

MATERIALS

Schachenmayr Merino Extrafine 120; #3 light weight yarn; 100% wool; 131 yd (120 m), 1.75 oz. (50 g) per skein

- 11/12/13 skeins #171 olive

Circular knitting needles, US 4 (3.5 mm) and US 6 (4.0 mm), each 32 in. (80 cm) long

GAUGE

In stockinette stitch on US 6 (4.0 mm) needles, 22 sts and 30 rows = 4 x 4 in. (10 x 10 cm)

STRAIGHT SLEEVE TOP

A-LINE SHAPE

A-LINE SHAPED WITH COLORFUL STRIPES

SIZES

Small/Medium/Large (US 6/8, 10/12, 14/16)

Numbers for size Small are listed before the first slash, for size Medium between slashes, and for size Large after the second slash. If only one number is given, it applies to all sizes.

MATERIALS

Schachenmayr Merino Extrafine 120; #3 light weight yarn; 100% wool; 131 yd (120 m), 1.75 oz. (50 g) per skein

- Main color (MC): 4/5/7 skeins in color of your choice
- Contrasting color 1 (CC1): 2/3/4 skeins in color of your choice
- Contrasting color 2 (CC2): 3/4/4 skeins in color of your choice
- Contrasting color 3 (CC3): 1/2/2 skeins in color of your choice
- Contrasting color 4 (CC4): 1/1/2 skeins in color of your choice
- Contrasting color 5 (CC5): 1/1/2 skeins in color of your choice

Circular knitting needles, US 4 (3.5 mm) and US 6 (4.0 mm), each 32 in. (80 cm) long

GAUGE

In stockinette stitch on US 6 (4.0 mm) needles, 22 sts and 30 rows = 4 x 4 in. (10 x 10 cm)

STOCKINETTE STITCH

RS: Knit all sts.
WS: Purl all sts.

RIBBING IN ROWS

RS: Alternate k1, p1.
WS: Work all sts as they appear— knit the knits and purl the purls.

RIBBING IN ROUNDS

All rounds (RS): Alternate k1, p1.

ACCENTED DECREASES

Accented decreases are always worked in RS rows, at both ends of the row as follows: K1, skp, cont in St st to last 3 sts of the row, then k2tog, k1. In WS rows, always purl the first 2 sts and the last 2 sts of the row. In RS rows without decreases, always knit the first 2 sts and the last 2 sts of the row.

STRIPE SEQUENCE A

Alternate 2 rows in MC, 2 rows in CC2.

STRIPE SEQUENCE B

This stripe sequence is worked only once. 18 rows in CC3, 6 rows in CC1, 14 rows in CC4, 6 rows in CC1, 14 rows in MC, 12 rows in CC5, 22 rows in stripe sequence A, 14 rows in CC1, 10 rows in CC2, 10 rows in CC4, 6 rows in CC1.

STRIPE SEQUENCE C

This stripe sequence is worked only once. 18 rows in stripe sequence A, 6 rows in MC, 12 rows in CC5, 22 rows in stripe sequence A, 14 rows in CC1, 10 rows in CC2, 10 rows in CC4, 6 rows in CC1, 14 rows in stripe sequence A, 10 rows in CC4, 6 rows in CC1.

INSTRUCTIONS

BACK

Using US 4 (3.5 mm) needles, CO 177/189/197 sts, and for hem ribbing, work 14 rows in ribbing patt; *at the same time*, in the last row, evenly distributed, dec 14/14/16 sts (= 163/175/181 sts). Change to US 6 (4.0 mm) needles, and cont in St st in stripe sequence B. After having completed stripe sequence B, cont in St st in stripe sequence A. *At the same time*, for the sloped sides, after having worked 4/2/4 rows from end of hem ribbing, work 1 accented decrease at each end of the row. Rep accented decreases at both ends of the row alternatingly in every 2nd and every 4th row a total of 28 times more (= 105/117/123 sts). After this, cont even in St st without further decreases. At 21/21.3/21.7 in. (53/54/55 cm) (= 158/162/166 rows) from hem ribbing, BO all sts.

FRONT

Work as the Back, but with neckline shaping. For this, after having worked only 19/19.3/19.7 in. (48/49/50 cm) (= 144/148/150 rows) from end of hem ribbing, BO the middle 19/23/25 sts, and continue both sides separately. For the rounded neckline, BO sts at the neck edge in every other row as follows: BO 4 sts once, 3 sts 3/3/2 times, 2 sts 1/1/2 time(s), and 1 st 1/1/2 time(s). At 21/21.3/21.7 in. (53/54/55 cm) (= 158/162/166 rows) from end of ribbing, BO the remaining 27/31/33 sts for each shoulder.

SLEEVES (MAKE 2)

Using US 4 (3.5 mm) needles, CO 51/55/59 sts, and for the cuff, work 14 rows in ribbing patt; *at the same time*, in the last row, evenly distributed, dec 6/4/4 sts (= 45/51/55 sts). Change to US 6 (4.0 mm) needles, and cont in St st in stripe sequence C. After having completed stripe sequence C, cont in St st in stripe sequence A. For sleeve tapering, after having worked 6/8/8 rows from end of cuff, inc 1 st at each end of the row. Rep these incs in every 6th row 13/10/10 times more and in every 8th row 4/6/6 times more (= 81/85/89 sts). At 16.1/16.5/16.5 in. (41/42/42 cm) (= 124/126/126 rows) from end of cuff, BO all sts.

FINISHING

Block all pieces to measurements on a soft surface, moisten, and let dry. Close shoulder and side seams from the wrong side, leaving the upper 7.1/7.5/7.9 in. (18/19/20 cm) open for the armholes. Seam the sleeves right sides facing each other and wrong sides facing out, and then sew the sleeves into the armholes from the wrong side.

Using US 4 (3.5 mm) needles, pick up and knit 126/130/134 sts from the neckline edge, join into the round, and work 1.2 in. (3 cm) (= 8 rnds) in ribbing pattern. BO all sts, and weave in ends.

A-LINE SHAPED WITH BORDER

SIZES

Small/Medium/Large (US 6/8, 10/12, 14/16)

Numbers for size Small are listed before the first slash, for size Medium between slashes, and for size Large after the second slash. If only one number is given, it applies to all sizes.

MATERIALS

Schachenmayr Merino Extrafine 120; #3 light weight yarn; 100% wool; 131 yd (120 m), 1.75 oz. (50 g) per skein

- Main color (MC): 11/12/13 skeins in color of your choice
- Contrasting color 1 (CC1): 4/4/5 skeins in color of your choice
- Contrasting color 2 (CC2): 1/2/2 skeins in color of your choice

Circular knitting needles, US 4 (3.5 mm) and US 6 (4.0 mm), each 32 in. (80 cm) long

GAUGE

In stockinette stitch on US 6 (4.0 mm) needles, 22 sts and 30 rows = 4 x 4 in. (10 x 10 cm)

COLORWORK CHART A

Page 83

STOCKINETTE STITCH

RS: Knit all sts.
WS: Purl all sts.

RIBBING IN ROWS

RS: Alternate k1, p1.
WS: Work all sts as they appear—knit the knits and purl the purls.

RIBBING IN ROUNDS

All rounds (RS): Alternate k1, p1.

ACCENTED DECREASES

Accented decreases are always worked in RS rows, at both ends of the row as follows: K1, skp, cont in St st to last 3 sts of the row, then k2tog, k1. In WS rows, always purl the first 2 sts and the last 2 sts of the row. In RS rows without decreases, always knit the first 2 sts and the last 2 sts of the row.

BORDER PATTERN

Work in stockinette stitch from Colorwork Chart A. The chart contains both RS and WS rows. Sts are shown as they appear from the RS of the fabric. Begin with the stitch stated in the instructions, work to the end of the patt rep, and then repeat the patt rep widthwise across, ending with the stitch stated in the instructions. Work Rows 1–21 once heightwise.

INSTRUCTIONS

BACK

Using US 4 (3.5 mm) needles, CO 177/189/197 sts, and for hem ribbing, work 14 rows in ribbing patt; *at the same time*, in the last row, evenly distributed, dec 14/14/16 sts (= 163/175/181 sts). Change to US 6 (4.0 mm) needles, and cont as follows: 2 rows in St st in MC; 21 rows in St st in border patt, beginning with the 17th/11th/8th st of the patt rep and ending with the 3rd/9th/12th st of the patt rep; 79 rows in St st in MC; 21 rows in St st in border patt, beginning with the 2nd/18th/15th st of the patt rep; repeat the patt rep widthwise, ending with the 18th/2nd/5th st of the patt rep. After this, work in MC in St st. *At the same time*, for the sloped sides, after having worked 4/2/4 rows from end of hem ribbing, work 1 accented decrease at each end of the row. Rep accented decreases at both ends of the row alternatingly in every 2nd and every 4th row a total of 28 times more (= 105/117/123 sts). After this, cont even in St st without further decreases. At 21/21.3/21.7 in. (53/54/55 cm) (= 158/162/166 rows) from hem ribbing, BO all sts.

FRONT

Work as the Back, but with neckline shaping. For this, after having worked only 19/19.3/19.7 in. (48/49/50 cm) (= 144/148/150 rows) from end of hem

ribbing, BO the middle 19/23/25 sts, and continue both sides separately. For the rounded neckline, BO sts at the neck edge in every other row as follows: BO 4 sts once, 3 sts 3/3/2 times, 2 sts 1/1/2 time(s), and 1 st 1/1/2 time(s). At 21/21.3/21.7 in. (53/54/55 cm) (= 158/162/166 rows) from end of ribbing, BO the remaining 27/31/33 sts for each shoulder.

SLEEVES (MAKE 2)

Using US 4 (3.5 mm) needles, CO 51/55/59 sts, and for the cuff, work 14 rows in ribbing patt; *at the same time*, in the last row, evenly distributed, dec 6/4/4 sts (= 45/51/55 sts). Change to US 6 (4.0 mm) needles, and cont in St st as follows: 2 rows in St st in MC; 21 rows in St st in border patt, beginning with the 10th/7th/5th st of the patt rep; work the patt rep once, ending with the 10th/13th/15th st of the patt rep. After this, work in MC in St st. For sleeve tapering, after having worked 6/8/8 rows from end of cuff, inc 1 st at each end of the row. Rep these incs in every 6th row 13/10/10 times more and in every 8th row 4/6/6 times more (= 81/85/89 sts). At 16.1/16.5/16.5 in. (41/42/42 cm) (= 124/126/126 rows) from end of cuff, BO all sts.

FINISHING

Block all pieces to measurements on a soft surface, moisten, and let dry. Close shoulder and side seams from the wrong side, leaving the upper 7.1/7.5/7.9 in. (18/19/20 cm) open for the armholes. Seam the sleeves right sides facing each other and wrong sides facing out, and then sew the sleeves into the armholes from the wrong side.

Using US 4 (3.5 mm) needles, pick up and knit 126/130/134 sts from the neckline edge, join into the round, and work 1.2 in. (3 cm) (= 8 rnds) in ribbing pattern. BO all sts, and weave in ends.

A-LINE SHAPED WITH STRANDED PATTERN

SIZES

Small/Medium/Large (US 6/8, 10/12, 14/16)

Numbers for size Small are listed before the first slash, for size Medium between slashes, and for size Large after the second slash. If only one number is given, it applies to all sizes.

MATERIALS

Schachenmayr Merino Extrafine 120; #3 light weight yarn; 100% wool; 131 yd (120 m), 1.75 oz. (50 g) per skein

- Main color (MC): 10/12/13 skeins in color of your choice
- Contrasting color (CC): 6/8/10 skeins in color of your choice

Circular knitting needles, sizes US 4 (3.5 mm) and US 6 (4.0 mm), each in 32 in. (80 cm) and 40 in. (100 cm) long

GAUGE

In stranded colorwork pattern on US 6 (4.0 mm) needles, 22 sts and 30 rows = 4 x 4 in. (10 x 10 cm)

COLORWORK CHART B

Page 83

STOCKINETTE STITCH

RS: Knit all sts.

WS: Purl all sts.

RIBBING IN ROWS

RS: Alternate k1, p1.

WS: Work all sts as they appear— knit the knits and purl the purls.

RIBBING IN ROUNDS

All rounds (RS): Alternate k1, p1.

ACCENTED DECREASES

Accented decreases are always worked in RS rows, at both ends of the row as follows: K1, skp, work in pattern to last 3 sts of the row, then k2tog, k1. In WS rows, always purl the first 2 sts and the last 2 sts of the row. In RS rows without decreases, always knit the first 2 sts and the last 2 sts of the row.

STRANDED PATTERN

Work in stockinette stitch from Colorwork Chart B. The chart contains both RS and WS rows. Sts are shown as they appear from the RS of the fabric. Begin with the stitch stated in the instructions, work to the end of the patt rep, and then repeat the patt rep widthwise across, ending with the stitch stated in the instructions. Repeat Rows 1–14 heightwise throughout.

INSTRUCTIONS

BACK

Using US 4 (3.5 mm) needles, CO 177/189/197 sts, and for hem ribbing, work 14 rows in ribbing patt; *at the same time*, in the last row, evenly distributed, dec 14/14/16 sts (= 163/175/181 sts). Change to US 6 (4.0 mm) needles, and cont in St st in stranded colorwork pattern from Colorwork Chart B, beginning with the 10th/4th/1st st of the patt rep and ending with the 4th/10th/13th st of the patt rep. *At the same time*, for the sloped sides, after having worked 4/2/4 rows from end of hem ribbing, work 1 accented decrease at each end of the row. Rep accented decreases at both ends of the row a total of 28 times more, alternatingly in every 2nd and every 4th row (= 105/117/123 sts). After this, cont even in St st without further decreases. At 21/21.3/21.7 in. (53/54/55 cm) (= 158/162/166 rows) from hem ribbing, BO all sts.

FRONT

Work as the Back, but with neckline shaping. For this, after having worked only 19/19.3/19.7 in. (48/49/50 cm) (= 144/148/150 rows) from end of hem ribbing, BO the middle 19/23/25 sts, and continue both sides separately. For the rounded neckline, BO sts at the neck edge in every other row as follows: BO 4 sts once, 3 sts 3/3/2 times, 2 sts 1/1/2 time(s), and 1 st 1/1/2 time(s). At 21/21.3/21.7 in. (53/54/55 cm) (= 158/162/166 rows) from end of ribbing, BO the remaining 27/31/33 sts for each shoulder.

SLEEVES (MAKE 2)

Using US 4 (3.5 mm) needles, CO 51/55/59 sts, and for the cuff, work 14 rows in ribbing patt; *at the same time*, in the last row, evenly distributed, dec 6/4/4 sts (= 45/51/55 sts). Change to US 6 (4.0 mm) needles, and cont in St st in stranded colorwork pattern from Colorwork Chart B, beginning with the 10th/4th/1st st of the patt rep and ending with the 4th/10th/13th st of the patt rep. *At the same time*, for sleeve tapering, after having worked 6/8/8 rows from end of cuff, inc 1 st at each end of the row. Rep these incs in every 6th row 13/10/10 times more and in every 8th row 4/6/6 times more (= 81/85/89 sts). At 16.1/16.5/16.5 in. (41/42/42 cm) (= 124/126/126 rows) from end of cuff, BO all sts.

FINISHING

Block all pieces to measurements on a soft surface, moisten, and let dry. Close shoulder and side seams from the wrong side, leaving the upper 7.1/7.5/7.9 in. (18/19/20 cm) open for the armholes. Seam the sleeves right sides facing each other and wrong sides facing out, and then sew the sleeves into the armholes from the wrong side.

Using US 4 (3.5 mm) needles, pick up and knit 126/130/134 sts from the neckline edge, join into the round, and work 1.2 in. (3 cm) (= 8 rnds) in ribbing pattern. BO all sts, and weave in ends.

A-LINE SHAPED WITH LACE PATTERN

SIZES

Small/Medium/Large (US 6/8, 10/12, 14/16)

Numbers for size Small are listed before the first slash, for size Medium between slashes, and for size Large after the second slash. If only one number is given, it applies to all sizes.

MATERIALS

Schachenmayr Merino Extrafine 120; #3 light weight yarn; 100% wool; 131 yd (120 m), 1.75 oz. (50 g) per skein

- 13/14/15 skeins in color of your choice

Circular knitting needles, US 4 (3.5 mm) and US 6 (4.0 mm), each 32 in. (80 cm) long

GAUGE

In lace pattern on US 6 (4.0 mm) needles, 20 sts and 28 rows = 4 x 4 in. (10 x 10 cm)

STITCH PATTERN CHART A

Page 83

STOCKINETTE STITCH

RS: Knit all sts.
WS: Purl all sts.

RIBBING IN ROWS

RS: Alternate k1, p1.
WS: Work all sts as they appear— knit the knits and purl the purls.

RIBBING IN ROUNDS

All rounds (RS): Alternate k1, p1.

ACCENTED DECREASES

Accented decreases are always worked in RS rows, at both ends of the row, as follows: K1, skp, work in pattern to last 3 sts of the row, then k2tog, k1. In WS rows, always purl the first 2 sts and the last 2 sts of the row. In RS rows without decreases, always knit the first 2 sts and the last 2 sts of the row.

LACE PATTERN

Work from Stitch Pattern Chart A. Only RS rows are shown in the chart; in WS rows, work all sts as they appear, and purl the yarn overs. Begin with the sts before the patt rep, repeat the patt rep widthwise across, and end with the sts after the patt rep. Repeat Rows 1–12 of the chart heightwise throughout.

INSTRUCTIONS

BACK

Using US 4 (3.5 mm) needles, CO 177/189/197 sts, and work 14 rows in ribbing patt; *at the same time*, in the last row, evenly distributed, dec 32/34/32 sts (= 145/155/165 sts). Change to US 6 (4.0 mm) needles, and cont in lace pattern. *At the same time*, for the sloped sides, after having worked 4 rows from end of hem ribbing, work 1 accented decrease at each end of the row. Rep accented decreases at both ends of the row in every 4th row 8 times more, and then alternatingly in every 2nd and every 4th row a total of 16 times more (= 95/105/115 sts). After this, cont even in lace pattern without further decreases. At 21/21.3/21.7 in. (53/54/55 cm) (= 148/152/154 rows) from hem ribbing, BO all sts.

FRONT

Work as the Back, but with neckline shaping. For this, after having worked only 19/19.3/19.7 in. (48/49/50 cm) (= 134/138/140 rows) from end of ribbing, BO the middle 21/21/29 sts, and continue both sides separately. For the rounded neckline, BO sts at the neck edge in every other row as follows: BO 3 sts 2/3/2 times, 2 sts 3/2/3 times, and 1 st once. At 21/21.3/21.7 in. (53/54/55 cm) (= 148/152/154 rows) from end of ribbing, BO the remaining 24/28/30 sts for each shoulder.

SLEEVES (MAKE 2)

Using US 4 (3.5 mm) needles, CO 51/55/59 sts, and for the cuff, work 14 rows in ribbing patt; *at the same time*, in the last row, evenly distributed, dec 6/8/10 sts (= 45/47/49 sts). Change to US 6 (4.0 mm) needles, and cont in the following pattern: 0/1/2 st(s) in St st, 45 sts in lace pattern, 0/1/2 st(s) in St st. *At the same time*, for sleeve tapering, after having worked 6 rows from end of cuff, inc 1 st at each end of the row. Rep these incs in every 6th row 0/3/4 times more and in every 8th row 12/11/10 times more (= 71/77/79 sts). At 16.1/16.5/16.5 in. (41/42/42 cm) (= 114/118/118 rows) from end of cuff, BO all sts.

Please note: As soon as you have 49 sts on the needles, always work the first 2 sts and the last 2 sts of the row in St st. Increases at both ends of the row will then always be worked after or before these 2 sts, and the sts gained from increasing are incorporated into the lace pattern.

FINISHING

Block all pieces to measurements on a soft surface, moisten, and let dry. Close shoulder and side seams from the wrong side, leaving the upper 7.1/7.5/7.9 in. (18/19/20 cm) open for the armholes. Seam the sleeves right sides facing each other and wrong sides facing out, and then sew the sleeves into the armholes from the wrong side.

Using US 4 (3.5 mm) needles, pick up and knit 126/130/134 sts from the neckline edge, join into the round, and work 1.2 in. (3 cm) (= 8 rnds) in ribbing pattern. BO all sts, and weave in ends.

A-LINE SHAPED WITH CABLE PATTERN

SIZES

Small/Medium/Large (US 6/8, 10/12, 14/16)

Numbers for size Small are listed before the first slash, for size Medium between slashes, and for size Large after the second slash. If only one number is given, it applies to all sizes.

MATERIALS

Schachenmayr Merino Extrafine 120; #3 light weight yarn; 100% wool; 131 yd (120 m), 1.75 oz. (50 g) per skein

• 14/16/17 skeins in color of your choice

Circular knitting needles, US 4 (3.5 mm) and US 6 (4.0 mm), each 32 in. (80 cm) long

Cable needle (cn)

GAUGE

In double seed stitch on US 6 (4.0 mm) needles, 22 sts and 34 rows = 4 x 4 in. (10 x 10 cm)

In cable pattern 1 on US 6 (4.0 mm) needles, 58 sts = 8.3 in. (21 cm)

In cable pattern 2 on US 6 (4.0 mm) needles, 18 sts = 3.1 in. (8 cm)

STITCH PATTERN CHARTS B AND C
Page 83

STOCKINETTE STITCH

RS: Knit all sts.
WS: Purl all sts.

RIBBING IN ROWS

RS: Alternate k1, p1.
WS: Work all sts as they appear—knit the knits and purl the purls.

RIBBING IN ROUNDS

All rounds (RS): Alternate k1, p1.

ACCENTED DECREASES

Accented decreases are always worked in RS rows, at both ends of the row as follows: K1, skp, work in pattern to last 3 sts of the row, then k2tog, k1. In WS rows, always purl the first 2 sts and the last 2 sts of the row. In RS rows without decreases, always knit the first 2 sts and the last 2 sts of the row.

DOUBLE SEED STITCH

Row 1: Alternate k1, p1.
Row 2: Knit the knits and purl the purls.

Row 3: Alternate p1, k1.
Row 4: Knit the knits and purl the purls.
Rep Rows 1–4 throughout.

CABLE PATTERN 1

Work from Stitch Pattern Chart B. Only RS rows are shown in the chart; in WS rows, work all sts as they appear (knit the knits and purl the purls), and purl the slipped sts. Work the patt rep (58 sts wide) widthwise across once, and then rep Rows 1–12 heightwise throughout.

CABLE PATTERN 2

Work from Stitch Pattern Chart C. Only RS rows are shown in the chart; in WS rows, work all sts as they appear (knit the knits and purl the purls), and purl the slipped sts. Work the patt rep (18 sts wide) widthwise across once, and then rep Rows 1–12 heightwise throughout.

INSTRUCTIONS

BACK

Using US 4 (3.5 mm) needles, CO 177/189/197 sts, and work 14 rows in ribbing patt; *at the same time*, in the last row, evenly distributed, dec 1/5/5 st(s) (= 176/184/192 sts). Change to US 6 (4.0 mm) needles, and continue in the following pattern: 1 st in St st, 58/62/66 sts in double seed stitch, 58 sts in cable pattern 1, 58/62/66 sts in double seed stitch, 1 st in St st. *At the same time*, for the sloped sides, after having worked 4 rows from end of hem ribbing, work 1 accented decrease at each end of the row (= 174/182/190 sts). Rep accented decreases at both ends of every 4th row 11/17/11 times more, and then alternatingly in every 2nd and every 4th row a total of 18/10/18 times more (= 116/128/132 sts). After this, cont even in established pattern without further decreases. At 21/21.3/21.7 in. (53/54/55 cm) (= 180/184/188 rows) from hem ribbing, BO all sts.

FRONT

Work as the Back, but with neckline shaping. For this, after having worked only 19/19.3/19.7 in. (48/49/50 cm) (= 164/166/168 rows) from end of ribbing, BO the middle 28/30/30 sts, and continue both sides separately. For the rounded neckline, BO sts at the neck edge in every other row as follows: BO 4 sts once, 3 sts twice, 2 sts 3/3/2 times, and 1 st 1/2/4 time(s). At 21/21.3/21.7 in. (53/54/55 cm) (= 180/184/188 rows) from end of ribbing, BO the remaining 27/31/33 sts for each shoulder.

SLEEVES (MAKE 2)

Using US 4 (3.5 mm) needles, CO 51/55/59 sts, and for the cuff, work 14 rows in ribbing patt; *at the same time*, in the last row, evenly distributed, dec 5/3/3 sts (= 46/52/56 sts). Change to US 6 (4.0 mm) needles, and continue in the following pattern: 1 st in St st, 13/16/18 sts in double seed stitch, 18 sts in cable pattern 2, 13/16/18 sts in double seed stitch, 1 st in St st. *At the same time*, for sleeve tapering, after having worked 6/10/10 rows from end of cuff, inc 1 st at each end of the row. Rep these incs in every 6th row 5/0/0 times more, and then in every 8th row 12/15/15 times (= 82/84/88 sts). At 16.1/16.5/16.5 in. (41/42/42 cm) (= 140/142/142 rows) from end of cuff, BO all sts.

FINISHING

Block all pieces to measurements on a soft surface, moisten, and let dry. Close shoulder and side seams from the wrong side, leaving the upper 7.1/7.5/7.9 in. (18/19/20 cm) open for the armholes. Seam the sleeves right sides facing each other and wrong sides facing out, and then sew the sleeves into the armholes from the wrong side.

Using US 4 (3.5 mm) needles, pick up and knit 126/130/134 sts from the neckline edge, join into the round, and work 1.2 in. (3 cm) (= 8 rnds) in ribbing pattern. BO all sts, and weave in ends.

STITCH PATTERN AND COLORWORK CHARTS

COLORWORK CHART A

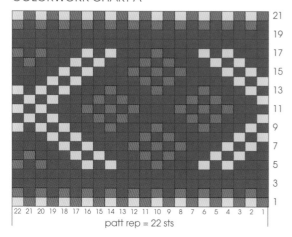

patt rep = 22 sts

KNITTING SYMBOLS

☐ = St st in MC
■ = St st in CC1
■ = St st in CC2

COLORWORK CHART B

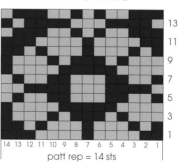

patt rep = 14 sts

KNITTING SYMBOLS

■ = St st in MC
■ = St st in CC

STITCH PATTERN CHART A
Stitch count is a multiple of 10 + 15

patt rep = 10 sts

KNITTING SYMBOLS

■ = knit 1 st
− = purl 1 st
O = make 1 yarn over
◢ = knit 2 sts together
◣ = slip 1, knit 1, pass the slipped st over
▲ = slip 1, knit 2 sts together, pass the slipped st over
☐ = no st, for better overview only

STITCH PATTERN CHART B

cable pattern 1 = 58 sts

STITCH PATTERN CHART C

cable pattern 2 = 18 sts

KNITTING SYMBOLS

■ = knit 1 st
− = purl 1 st
☑ = slip 1 st purlwise with yarn in back of work
= hold 1 st on cn in back of work, knit the next 2 sts, and then knit the st from the cn
= hold 2 sts on cn in front of work, purl the next st, and then knit the 2 sts from the cn
= hold 2 sts on cn in back of work, knit the next 2 sts, and then knit the 2 sts from the cn
= hold 4 sts on cn in back of work, knit the next 4 sts, and then knit the 4 sts from the cn
= hold 4 sts on cn in front of work, knit the next 4 sts, and then knit the 4 sts from the cn

FITTED SHAPE

STOCKINETTE STITCH

RS: Knit all sts.
WS: Purl all sts.

RIBBING IN ROWS

RS: Alternate k1, p1.
WS: Work all sts as they appear—knit the knits and purl the purls.

RIBBING IN ROUNDS

All rounds (RS): Alternate k1, p1.

ACCENTED DECREASES

Accented decreases are always worked in RS rows, at both ends of the row as follows: K1, skp, cont in St st to last 3 sts of the row, then k2tog, k1. In WS rows, always purl the first 2 sts and the last 2 sts of the row. In RS rows without decreases, always knit the first 2 sts and the last 2 sts of the row.

ACCENTED INCREASES

Accented increases are always worked in RS rows, at both ends of the row as follows: K1, inc 1 st from the bar between sts twisted, cont in St st to last st of the row, inc 1 st from the bar between sts twisted, k1. In WS rows, always purl the first 2 sts and the last 2 sts of the row. In RS rows without increases, always knit the first 2 sts and the last 2 sts of the row.

INSTRUCTIONS

BACK

Using US 4 (3.5 mm) needles, CO 115/127/131 sts, and work 14 rows in ribbing patt; *at the same time*, in the last row, evenly distributed, dec 10/10/8 sts (= 105/117/123 sts). Change to US 6 (4.0 mm) needles, and continue in St st. After having worked 2/1.6/1.6 in. (5/4/4 cm) (= 16/12/12 rows) from end of ribbing, for waist shaping, work 1 accented decrease at each end of the row. Rep accented decreases at both ends of the row in every 4th row 8/9/9 times more (= 87/97/103 sts). After having worked 6.7 in. (17 cm) (= 52 rows) from end of ribbing, work 1 accented increase at each end of the row (= 89/99/105 sts). Rep accented increases at both ends of the row in every 4th row 0/4/4 times more and in every 6th row 8/5/5 times more (= 105/117/123 sts). At 21/21.3/21.7 in.

(53/54/55 cm) (= 158/162/166 rows) from hem ribbing, BO all sts.

FRONT

Work as the Back, but with neckline shaping. For this, after having worked only 19/19.3/19.7 in. (48/49/50 cm) (= 144/148/150 rows) from end of hem ribbing, BO the middle 19/23/25 sts, and continue both sides separately. For the rounded neckline, BO sts at the neck edge in every other row as follows: BO 4 sts once, 3 sts 3/3/2 times, 2 sts 1/1/2 time(s), and 1 st 1/1/2 time(s). At 21/21.3/21.7 in. (53/54/55 cm) (= 158/162/166 rows) from end of hem ribbing, BO the remaining 27/31/33 sts for each shoulder.

SLEEVES (MAKE 2)

Using US 4 (3.5 mm) needles, CO 51/55/59 sts, and for the cuff, work 14 rows in ribbing patt; *at the same time*, in the last row, evenly distributed, dec 6/4/4 sts (= 45/51/55 sts). Change to US 6 (4.0 mm) needles, and continue in St st. *At the same time*, for sleeve tapering, after having worked 6/8/8 rows from end of cuff, inc 1 st at each end of the row. Rep these incs in every 6th row 13/10/10 times more and in every 8th row 4/6/6 times more (= 81/85/89 sts). At 16.1/16.5/16.5 in. (41/42/42 cm) (= 124/126/126 rows) from end of cuff, BO all sts.

FINISHING

Block all pieces to measurements on a soft surface, moisten, and let dry. Close shoulder and side seams from the wrong side, leaving the upper 7.1/7.5/7.9 in. (18/19/20 cm) open for the armholes. Seam the sleeves right sides facing each other and wrong sides facing out, and then sew the sleeves into the armholes from the wrong side.

Using US 4 (3.5 mm) needles, pick up and knit 126/130/134 sts from the neckline edge, join into the round, and work 1.2 in. (3 cm) (= 8 rnds) in ribbing pattern. BO all sts, and weave in ends.

SCHEMATIC

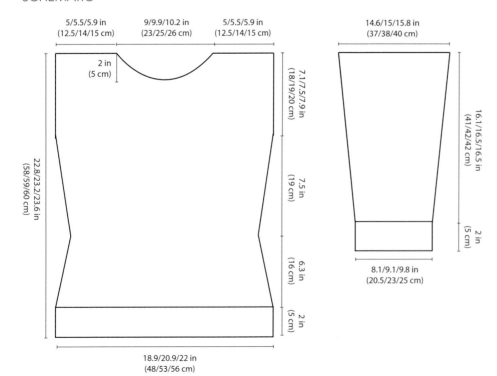

5/5.5/5.9 in (12.5/14/15 cm)
9/9.9/10.2 in (23/25/26 cm)
5/5.5/5.9 in (12.5/14/15 cm)
2 in (5 cm)
7.1/7.5/7.9 in (18/19/20 cm)
22.8/23.2/23.6 in (58/59/60 cm)
18.9/20.9/22 in (48/53/56 cm)

14.6/15/15.8 in (37/38/40 cm)
16.1/16.5/16.5 in (41/42/42 cm)
7.5 in (19 cm)
6.3 in (16 cm)
2 in (5 cm)
2 in (5 cm)
8.1/9.1/9.8 in (20.5/23/25 cm)

SIZES

Small/Medium/Large
(US 6/8, 10/12, 14/16)
Numbers for size Small
are listed before the first
slash, for size Medium
between slashes, and
for size Large after the
second slash. If only
one number is given,
it applies to all sizes.

MATERIALS

Schachenmayr Merino
Extrafine 120; #3 light
weight yarn; 100% wool;
131 yd (120 m), 1.75 oz.
(50 g) per skein

- 10/11/12 skeins #199
  black

Circular knitting nee-
dles, US 4 (3.5 mm) and
US 6 (4.0 mm), each 32
in. (80 cm) long

GAUGE

In stockinette stitch on
US 6 (4.0 mm) needles,
22 sts and 30 rows =
4 x 4 in. (10 x 10 cm)

**STRAIGHT
SLEEVE TOP**

**FITTED
BODY
SHAPE**

FITTED WITH COLORFUL STRIPES

SIZES

Small/Medium/Large (US 6/8, 10/12, 14/16)
Numbers for size Small are listed before the first slash, for size Medium between slashes, and for size Large after the second slash. If only one number is given, it applies to all sizes.

MATERIALS

Schachenmayr Merino Extrafine 120; #3 light weight yarn; 100% wool; 131 yd (120 m), 1.75 oz. (50 g) per skein

- Main color (MC): 4/5/7 skeins in color of your choice
- Contrasting color 1 (CC1): 2/3/4 skeins in color of your choice
- Contrasting color 2 (CC2): 3/4/4 skeins in color of your choice
- Contrasting color 3 (CC3): 1/2/2 skeins in color of your choice
- Contrasting color 4 (CC4): 1/1/2 skeins in color of your choice
- Contrasting color 5 (CC5): 1/1/2 skeins in color of your choice

Circular knitting needles, US 4 (3.5 mm) and US 6 (4.0 mm), each 32 in. (80 cm) long

GAUGE

In stockinette stitch on US 6 (4.0 mm) needles, 22 sts and 30 rows = 4 x 4 in. (10 x 10 cm)

STOCKINETTE STITCH

RS: Knit all sts.
WS: Purl all sts.

RIBBING IN ROWS

RS: Alternate k1, p1.
WS: Work all sts as they appear— knit the knits and purl the purls.

RIBBING IN ROUNDS

All rounds (RS): Alternate k1, p1.

ACCENTED DECREASES

Accented decreases are always worked in RS rows, at both ends of the row as follows: K1, skp, cont in St st to last 3 sts of the row, then k2tog, k1. In WS rows, always purl the first 2 sts and the last 2 sts of the row. In RS rows without decreases, always knit the first 2 sts and the last 2 sts of the row.

ACCENTED INCREASES

Accented increases are always worked in RS rows, at both ends of the row as follows: K1, inc 1 st from the bar between sts twisted, cont in St st to last st of the row, inc 1 st from the bar between sts twisted, k1. In WS rows, always purl the first 2 sts and the last 2 sts of the row. In RS rows without increases, always knit the first 2 sts and the last 2 sts of the row.

STRIPE SEQUENCE A

Alternate 2 rows in MC, 2 rows in CC2.

STRIPE SEQUENCE B

This stripe sequence is worked only once. 18 rows in CC3, 6 rows in CC1, 14 rows in CC4, 6 rows in CC1, 14 rows in MC, 12 rows in CC5, 22 rows in stripe sequence A, 14 rows in CC1, 10 rows in CC2, 10 rows in CC4, 6 rows in CC1.

STRIPE SEQUENCE C

This stripe sequence is worked only once. 18 rows in stripe sequence A, 6 rows in MC, 12 rows in CC5, 22 rows in stripe sequence A, 14 rows in CC1, 10 rows in CC2, 10 rows in CC4, 6 rows in CC1, 14 rows in stripe sequence A, 10 rows in CC4, 6 rows in CC1.

INSTRUCTIONS

BACK

Using US 4 (3.5 mm) needles, CO 115/127/131 sts, and work 14 rows in ribbing patt; *at the same time*, in the last row, evenly distributed, dec 10/10/8 sts (= 105/117/123 sts). Change to US 6 (4.0 mm) needles, and cont in St st in stripe sequence B. After having completed stripe sequence B, cont in St st in stripe sequence A. *At the same time*, shape waist: After having worked 2/1.6/1.6 in. (5/4/4 cm) (= 16/12/12 rows) from end of ribbing, work 1 accented decrease at each end of the row. Rep accented decreases at both ends of the row in every 4th row 8/9/9 times more (= 87/97/103 sts). After having worked 6.7 in. (17 cm) (= 52 rows) from end of ribbing, work 1 accented increase at each end of the row (= 89/99/105 sts). Rep accented increases at both ends of the row in every 4th row 0/4/4 times more and in every 6th row 8/5/5 times more (= 105/117/123

sts). After having worked 21/21.3/21.7 in. (53/54/55 cm) (= 158/162/166 rows) from hem ribbing, BO all sts.

FRONT

Work as the Back, but with neckline shaping. For this, after having worked only 19/19.3/19.7 in. (48/49/50 cm) (= 144/148/150 rows) from end of hem ribbing, BO the middle 19/23/25 sts, and continue both sides separately. For the rounded neckline, BO sts at the neck edge in every other row as follows: BO 4 sts once, 3 sts 3/3/2 times, 2 sts 1/1/2 time(s), and 1 st 1/1/2 time(s). At 21/21.3/21.7 in. (53/54/55 cm) (= 158/162/166 rows) from end of hem ribbing, BO the remaining 27/31/33 sts for each shoulder.

SLEEVES (MAKE 2)

Using US 4 (3.5 mm) needles, CO 51/55/59 sts, and for the cuff, work 14 rows in ribbing patt; *at the same time*, in the last row, evenly distributed, dec 6/4/4 sts (= 45/51/55 sts). Change to US 6 (4.0 mm) needles, and cont in St st in stripe sequence C. After having completed stripe sequence C, cont in St st in stripe sequence A. *At the same time*, for sleeve tapering, after having worked 6/8/8 rows from end of cuff, inc 1 st at each end of the row. Rep these incs in every 6th row 13/10/10 times more and in every 8th row 4/6/6 times more (= 81/85/89 sts). At 16.1/16.5/16.5 in. (41/42/42 cm) (= 124/126/126 rows) from end of cuff, BO all sts.

FINISHING

Block all pieces to measurements on a soft surface, moisten, and let dry. Close shoulder and side seams from the wrong side, leaving the upper 7.1/7.5/7.9 in. (18/19/20 cm) open for the armholes. Seam the sleeves right sides facing each other and wrong sides facing out, and then sew the sleeves into the armholes from the wrong side.

Using US 4 (3.5 mm) needles, pick up and knit 126/130/134 sts from the neckline edge, join into the round, and work 1.2 in. (3 cm) (= 8 rnds) in ribbing pattern. BO all sts, and weave in ends.

FITTED WITH BORDER

SIZES

Small/Medium/Large (US 6/8, 10/12, 14/16)
Numbers for size Small are listed before the first slash, for size Medium between slashes, and for size Large after the second slash. If only one number is given, it applies to all sizes.

MATERIALS

Schachenmayr Merino Extrafine 120; #3 light weight yarn; 100% wool; 131 yd (120 m), 1.75 oz. (50 g) per skein

- Main color (MC): 8/9/11 skeins in color of your choice
- Contrasting color 1 (CC1): 3/3/4 skeins in color of your choice
- Contrasting color 2 (CC2): 1/2/2 skeins in color of your choice

Circular knitting needles, US 4 (3.5 mm) and US 6 (4.0 mm), each 32 in. (80 cm) long

GAUGE

In stockinette stitch on US 6 (4.0 mm) needles, 22 sts and 30 rows = 4 x 4 in. (10 x 10 cm)

COLORWORK CHART A

Page 91

STOCKINETTE STITCH

RS: Knit all sts.
WS: Purl all sts.

RIBBING IN ROWS

RS: Alternate k1, p1.
WS: Work all sts as they appear—knit the knits and purl the purls.

RIBBING IN ROUNDS

All rounds (RS): Alternate k1, p1.

ACCENTED DECREASES

Accented decreases are always worked in RS rows, at both ends of the row as follows: K1, skp, cont in St st to last 3 sts of the row, then k2tog, k1. In WS rows, always purl the first 2 sts and the last 2 sts of the row. In RS rows without decreases, always knit the first 2 sts and the last 2 sts of the row.

ACCENTED INCREASES

Accented increases are always worked in RS rows, at both ends of the row as follows: K1, inc 1 st from the bar between sts twisted, cont in St st to last st of the row, inc 1 st from the bar between sts twisted, k1. In WS rows, always purl the first 2 sts and the last 2 sts of the row. In RS rows without increases, always knit the first 2 sts and the last 2 sts of the row.

BORDER PATTERN

Work in stockinette stitch from Colorwork Chart A. The chart contains both RS and WS rows. Sts are shown as they appear from the RS of the fabric. Begin with the stitch stated in the instructions, work to the end of the patt rep, and then repeat the patt rep widthwise across, ending with the stitch stated in the instructions. Work Rows 1–21 once heightwise.

INSTRUCTIONS

BACK

Using US 4 (3.5 mm) needles, CO 115/127/131 sts, and work 14 rows in ribbing patt; *at the same time*, in the last row, evenly distributed, dec 10/10/8 sts (= 105/117/123 sts). Change to US 6 (4.0 mm) needles, and cont in St st as follows: 2 rows in St st in MC; 21 rows in St st in border patt, beginning with the 2nd/18th/15th st of the patt rep; repeat the patt rep widthwise, ending with the 18th/2nd/5th st of the patt rep; 79 rows in St st in MC; 21 rows in St st in border patt, beginning with the 2nd/18th/15th st of the patt rep; repeat the patt rep widthwise, ending with the 18th/2nd/5th st of the patt rep. After this, work in MC in St st. *At the same time*, after having worked 2/1.6/1.6 in. (5/4/4 cm) (= 16/12/12 rows) from end of ribbing, for waist shaping, work 1 accented decrease at each end of the row. Rep accented decreases at both ends of the row in every 4th row 8/9/9 times more (= 87/97/103 sts). After having worked 6.7 in. (17 cm) (= 52 rows) from end of ribbing, work 1 accented increase at each end of the row (= 89/99/105 sts). Rep accented increases at both ends of the row in every 4th row 0/4/4 times more and in every 6th row 8/5/5 times more (= 105/117/123 sts). At 21/21.3/21.7 in. (53/54/55 cm) (= 158/162/166 rows) from hem ribbing, BO all sts.

FRONT

Work as the Back, but with neckline shaping. For this, after having worked only 19/19.3/19.7 in. (48/49/50 cm) (= 144/148/150 rows) from end of hem ribbing, BO the middle 19/23/25 sts, and continue both sides separately. For the rounded neckline, BO sts at the neck edge in every other row as follows: BO 4 sts once, 3 sts 3/3/2 times, 2 sts 1/1/2 time(s), and 1 st 1/1/2 time(s). At 21/21.3/21.7 in. (53/54/55 cm) (= 158/162/166 rows) from end of hem ribbing, BO the remaining 27/31/33 sts for each shoulder.

SLEEVES (MAKE 2)

Using US 4 (3.5 mm) needles, CO 51/55/59 sts, and for the cuff, work 14 rows in ribbing patt; *at the same time*, in the last row, evenly distributed, dec 6/4/4 sts (= 45/51/55 sts). Change to US 6 (4.0 mm) needles, and continue in St st as follows: 2 rows in St st in MC; 21 rows in St st in border patt, beginning with the 10th/7th/5th st of the patt rep, work the patt rep once, ending with the 10th/13th/15th st of the patt rep. After this, work in MC in St st. For sleeve tapering, after having worked 6/8/8 rows from end of cuff, inc 1 st at each end of the row. Rep these incs in every 6th row 13/10/10 times more and in every 8th row 4/6/6 times more (= 81/85/89 sts). At 16.1/16.5/16.5 in. (41/42/42 cm) (= 124/126/126 rows) from end of cuff, BO all sts.

FINISHING

Block all pieces to measurements on a soft surface, moisten, and let dry. Close shoulder and side seams from the wrong side, leaving the upper 7.1/7.5/7.9 in. (18/19/20 cm) open for the armholes. Seam the sleeves right sides facing each other and wrong sides facing out, and then sew the sleeves into the armholes from the wrong side.

Using US 4 (3.5 mm) needles, pick up and knit 126/130/134 sts from the neckline edge, join into the round, and work 1.2 in. (3 cm) (= 8 rnds) in ribbing pattern. BO all sts, and weave in ends.

FITTED WITH STRANDED PATTERN

SIZES

Small/Medium/Large (US 6/8, 10/12, 14/16)

Numbers for size Small are listed before the first slash, for size Medium between slashes, and for size Large after the second slash. If only one number is given, it applies to all sizes.

MATERIALS

Schachenmayr Merino Extrafine 120; #3 light weight yarn; 100% wool; 131 yd (120 m), 1.75 oz. (50 g) per skein

- Main color (MC): 8/10/11 skeins in color of your choice
- Contrasting color (CC): 6/8/10 skeins in color of your choice

Circular knitting needles, US 4 (3.5 mm) and US 6 (4.0 mm), each 32 in. (80 cm) long

GAUGE

In stranded colorwork pattern on US 6 (4.0 mm) needles, 22 sts and 30 rows = 4 x 4 in. (10 x 10 cm)

COLORWORK CHART B

Page 91

STOCKINETTE STITCH

RS: Knit all sts.

WS: Purl all sts.

RIBBING IN ROWS

RS: Alternate k1, p1.

WS: Work all sts as they appear— knit the knits and purl the purls.

RIBBING IN ROUNDS

All rounds (RS): Alternate k1, p1.

ACCENTED DECREASES

Accented decreases are always worked in RS rows, at both ends of the row as follows: K1, skp, work in pattern to last 3 sts of the row, then k2tog, k1. In WS rows, always purl the first 2 sts and the last 2 sts of the row. In RS rows without decreases, always knit the first 2 sts and the last 2 sts of the row.

ACCENTED INCREASES

Accented increases are always worked in RS rows, at both ends of the row as follows: K1, inc 1 st from the bar between sts twisted, cont in patt to last st of the row, inc 1 st from the bar between sts twisted, k1. In WS rows, always purl the first 2 sts and the last 2 sts of the row. In RS rows without increases, always knit the first 2 sts and the last 2 sts of the row.

STRANDED PATTERN

Work in stockinette stitch from Colorwork Chart B. The chart contains both RS and WS rows. Sts are shown as they appear from the RS of the fabric. Begin with the stitch stated in the instructions, work to the end of the patt rep, and then repeat the patt rep widthwise across, ending with the stitch stated in the instructions. Repeat Rows 1–14 heightwise throughout.

INSTRUCTIONS

BACK

Using US 4 (3.5 mm) needles, CO 115/127/131 sts, and work 14 rows in ribbing patt; *at the same time*, in the last row, evenly distributed, dec 10/10/8 sts (= 105/117/123 sts). Change to US 6 (4.0 mm) needles, and cont in St st in stranded colorwork pattern from Colorwork Chart B, beginning with the 4th/12th/9th st of the chart, and ending with the 10th/2nd/5th st of the chart. *At the same time*, after having worked 2/1.6/1.6 in. (5/4/4 cm) (= 16/12/12 rows) from end of ribbing, for waist shaping, work 1 accented decrease at each end of the row. Rep accented decreases at both ends of the row in every 4th row 8/9/9 times more (= 87/97/103 sts). After having worked 6.7 in. (17 cm) (= 52 rows) from end of ribbing, work 1 accented increase at each end of the row (= 89/99/105 sts). Rep accented increases at both ends of the row in every 4th row 0/4/4 times more and in every 6th row 8/5/5 times more (= 105/117/123 sts). At 21/21.3/21.7 in. (53/54/55 cm) (= 158/162/166 rows) from hem ribbing, BO all sts.

FRONT

Work as the Back, but with neckline shaping. For this, after having worked only 19/19.3/19.7 in. (48/49/50 cm) (= 144/148/150 rows) from end of hem ribbing, BO the middle 19/23/25 sts, and continue both pieces separately. For the rounded neckline, BO sts at the neck edge in every other row as follows: BO 4 sts once, 3 sts 3/3/2 times, 2 sts 1/1/2 time(s), and 1 st 1/1/2 time(s). At 21/21.3/21.7 in. (53/54/55 cm) (= 158/162/166 rows) from end of hem ribbing, BO the remaining 27/31/33 sts for each shoulder.

SLEEVES (MAKE 2)

Using US 4 (3.5 mm) needles, CO 51/55/59 sts, and for the cuff, work 14 rows in ribbing patt; *at the same time*, in the last row, evenly distributed, dec 6/4/4 sts (= 45/51/55 sts). Change to US 6 (4.0 mm) needles, and cont in St st in stranded colorwork pattern from Colorwork Chart B, beginning with the 6th/3rd/1st st of the chart and ending with the 8th/11th/13th st of the chart. *At the same time*, for sleeve tapering, after having worked 6/8/8 rows from end of cuff, inc 1 st at each end of the row. Rep these incs in every 6th row 13/10/10 times more and in every 8th row 4/6/6 times more (= 81/85/89 sts). At 16.1/16.5/16.5 in. (41/42/42 cm) (= 124/126/126 rows) from end of cuff, BO all sts.

FINISHING

Block all pieces to measurements on a soft surface, moisten, and let dry. Close shoulder and side seams from the wrong side, leaving the upper 7.1/7.5/7.9 in. (18/19/20 cm) open for the armholes. Seam the sleeves right sides facing each other and wrong sides facing out, and then sew the sleeves into the armholes from the wrong side.

Using US 4 (3.5 mm) needles, pick up and knit 126/130/134 sts from the neckline edge, join into the round, and work 1.2 in. (3 cm) (= 8 rnds) in ribbing pattern. BO all sts, and weave in ends.

FITTED WITH LACE PATTERN

SIZES

Small/Medium/Large (US 6/8, 10/12, 14/16)
Numbers for size Small are listed before the first slash, for size Medium between slashes, and for size Large after the second slash. If only one number is given, it applies to all sizes.

MATERIALS

Schachenmayr Merino Extrafine 120; #3 light weight yarn; 100% wool; 131 yd (120 m), 1.75 oz. (50 g) per skein
• 10/11/13 skeins in color of your choice
Circular knitting needles, US 4 (3.5 mm) and US 6 (4.0 mm), each 32 in. (80 cm) long

GAUGE

In lace pattern on US 6 (4.0 mm) needles, 20 sts and 28 rows = 4 x 4 in. (10 x 10 cm)

STITCH PATTERN CHART A

Page 91

STOCKINETTE STITCH

RS: Knit all sts.
WS: Purl all sts.

RIBBING IN ROWS

RS: Alternate k1, p1.
WS: Work all sts as they appear—knit the knits and purl the purls.

RIBBING IN ROUNDS

All rounds (RS): Alternate k1, p1.

ACCENTED DECREASES

Accented decreases are always worked in RS rows, at both ends of the row as follows: K1, skp, work in pattern to last 3 sts of the row, then k2tog, k1. In WS rows, always purl the first 2 sts and the last 2 sts of the row. In RS rows without decreases, always knit the first 2 sts and the last 2 sts of the row.

ACCENTED INCREASES

Accented increases are always worked in RS rows, at both ends of the row as follows: K1, inc 1 st from the bar between sts twisted, cont in patt to last st of the row, inc 1 st from the bar between sts twisted, k1. In WS rows, always purl the first 2 sts and the last 2 sts of the row. In RS rows without in-

creases, always knit the first 2 sts and the last 2 sts of the row.

LACE PATTERN

Work from Stitch Pattern Chart A. Only RS rows are shown in the chart; in WS rows, work all sts as they appear, and purl the yarn overs. Begin with the sts before the patt rep, repeat the patt rep widthwise across, and end with the sts after the patt rep. Repeat Rows 1–12 of the chart heightwise throughout.

INSTRUCTIONS

BACK

Using US 4 (3.5 mm) needles, CO 115/127/131 sts, and for hem ribbing, work 14 rows in ribbing patt; *at the same time*, in the last row, evenly distributed, dec 20/22/16 sts (= 95/105/115 sts). Change to US 6 (4.0 mm) needles, and cont in lace pattern. *At the same time*, after having worked 2/1.6/1.6 in. (5/4/4 cm) (= 14/12/12 rows) from end of ribbing, for waist shaping, work 1 accented decrease at each end of the row. Rep accented decreases at each end of the row in every other row 0/0/2 times more and in every 4th row 7 times more (= 79/89/95 sts). After having worked 6.7 in. (17 cm) (= 46 rows) from end of ribbing, work 1 accented increase at each end of the row. Rep accented increases at both ends of the row in every 4th row 0/0/4 times more, in every 6th row 7/5/5 times more, and in every 8th row 0/2/0 times more (= 95/105/115 sts). At 21/21.3/21.7 in. (53/54/55 cm) (= 148/152/154 rows) from hem ribbing, BO all sts.

FRONT

Work as the Back, but with neckline shaping. For this, after having worked only 19/19.3/19.7 in. (48/49/50 cm) (= 134/138/140 rows) from end of ribbing, BO the middle 21/21/29 sts, and continue both sides separately. For the rounded neckline, BO sts at the neck edge in every other row as follows: BO

3 sts 2/3/2 times, 2 sts 3/2/3 times, and 1 st once. At 21/21.3/21.7 in. (53/54/55 cm) (= 148/152/154 rows) from end of ribbing, BO the remaining 24/28/30 sts for each shoulder.

SLEEVES (MAKE 2)

Using US 4 (3.5 mm) needles, CO 51/55/59 sts, and for the cuff, work 14 rows in ribbing patt; *at the same time*, in the last row, evenly distributed, dec 6/8/10 sts (= 45/47/49 sts). Change to US 6 (4.0 mm) needles, and cont in lace pattern as follows: 0/1/2 st(s) in St st, 45 sts in lace pattern, 0/1/2 st(s) in St st. *At the same time*, for sleeve tapering, after having worked 6 rows from end of cuff, inc 1 st at each end of the row. Rep these incs in every 6th row 0/3/4 times more and in every 8th row 12/11/10 times more (= 71/77/79 sts). At 16.1/16.5/16.5 in. (41/42/42 cm) (= 114/118/118 rows) from end of cuff, BO all sts.

Please note: As soon as you have 49 sts on the needles, the first 2 and the last 2 sts will always be worked in St st. Increases at both ends of the row will then always be worked after or before these 2 sts, and the sts gained from increasing are incorporated into the lace pattern.

FINISHING

Block all pieces to measurements on a soft surface, moisten, and let dry. Close shoulder and side seams from the wrong side, leaving the upper 7.1/7.5/7.9 in. (18/19/20 cm) open for the armholes. Seam the sleeves right sides facing each other and wrong sides facing out, and then sew the sleeves into the armholes from the wrong side.

Using US 4 (3.5 mm) needles, pick up and knit 126/130/134 sts from the neckline edge, join into the round, and work 1.2 in. (3 cm) (= 8 rnds) in ribbing pattern. BO all sts, and weave in ends.

FITTED WITH CABLE PATTERN

SIZES

Small/Medium/Large (US 6/8, 10/12, 14/16)
Numbers for size Small are listed before the first slash, for size Medium between slashes, and for size Large after the second slash. If only one number is given, it applies to all sizes.

MATERIALS

Schachenmayr Merino Extrafine 120; #3 light weight yarn; 100% wool; 131 yd (120 m), 1.75 oz. (50 g) per skein
• 12/14/16 skeins in color of your choice
Circular knitting needles, US 4 (3.5 mm) and US 6 (4.0 mm), each 32 in. (80 cm) long
Cable needle (cn)

GAUGE

In double seed stitch on US 6 (4.0 mm) needles, 22 sts and 34 rows = 4 x 4 in. (10 x 10 cm)

In cable pattern 1 on US 6 (4.0 mm) needles, 58 sts = 8.3 in. (21 cm)

In cable pattern 2 on US 6 (4.0 mm) needles, 18 sts = 3.1 in. (8 cm)

STITCH PATTERN CHARTS B AND C

Page 91

STOCKINETTE STITCH

RS: Knit all sts.
WS: Purl all sts.

RIBBING IN ROWS

RS: Alternate k1, p1.
WS: Work all sts as they appear—knit the knits and purl the purls.

RIBBING IN ROUNDS

All rounds (RS): Alternate k1, p1.

ACCENTED DECREASES

Accented decreases are always worked in RS rows, at both ends of the row as follows: K1, skp, work in pattern to last 3 sts of the row, then k2tog, k1. In WS rows, always purl the first 2 sts and the last 2 sts of the row. In RS rows without decreases, always knit the first 2 sts and the last 2 sts of the row.

ACCENTED INCREASES

Accented increases are always worked in RS rows, at both ends of the row as follows: K1, inc 1 st from the bar between sts twisted, cont in St st to last st of the row, inc 1 st from the bar between sts twisted, k1. In WS rows, always purl the first 2 sts and the last 2 sts of the row. In RS rows without increases, always knit the first 2 sts and the last 2 sts of the row.

DOUBLE SEED STITCH

Row 1: Alternate k1, p1.
Row 2: Knit the knits and purl the purls.
Row 3: Alternate p1, k1.
Row 4: Knit the knits and purl the purls.
Rep Rows 1–4 throughout.

CABLE PATTERN 1

Work from Stitch Pattern Chart B. Only RS rows are shown in the chart; in WS rows, work all sts as they appear (knit the knits and purl the purls), and purl the slipped sts. Work the patt rep (58 sts wide) widthwise across once, and then rep Rows 1–12 heightwise throughout.

CABLE PATTERN 2

Work from Stitch Pattern Chart C. Only RS rows are shown in the chart; in WS rows, work all sts as they appear (knit the knits and purl the purls), and purl the slipped sts. Work the patt rep (18 sts wide) widthwise across once, and then rep Rows 1–12 heightwise throughout.

INSTRUCTIONS

BACK

Using US 4 (3.5 mm) needles, CO 115/127/131 sts, and work 14 rows in ribbing patt; *at the same time*, in the last row, evenly distributed, inc 1 st (= 116/128/132 sts). Change to US 6 (4.0 mm) needles, and continue in the following pattern: 1 st in St st, 28/34/36 sts in double seed stitch, 58 sts in cable pattern from Stitch Pattern Chart B, 28/34/36 sts in double seed stitch, 1 st in St st. *At the same time*, after having worked 2/1.6/1.6 in. (5/4/4 cm) (= 18/14/14 rows) from end of ribbing, for waist shaping, work 1 accented decrease at each end of the row. Rep accented decreases in every 4th row 6/7/1 time(s) more and in every 6th row 2/2/6 times more (= 98/108/116 sts). After having worked 6.7 in. (17 cm) (= 58 rows) from end of ribbing, work 1 accented increase at each end of the row. Rep accented increases in every 6th row 5/9/3 times, and in every 8th row 3/0/4 times more (= 116/128/132 sts). At 21/21.3/21.7 in. (53/54/55 cm) (= 180/184/188 rows) from hem ribbing, BO all sts.

FRONT

Work as the Back, but with neckline shaping. For this, after having worked only 19/19.3/19.7 in. (48/49/50 cm) (= 164/166/168 rows) from end of ribbing, BO the middle 28/30/30 sts, and continue both sides separately. For the rounded neckline, BO sts at the neck edge in every other row as follows: BO 4 sts once, 3 sts twice, 2 sts 3/3/2 times, and 1 st 1/2/4 time(s). At 21/21.3/21.7 in. (53/54/55 cm) (= 180/184/188 rows) from end of ribbing, BO the remaining 27/31/33 sts for each shoulder.

SLEEVES (MAKE 2)

Using US 4 (3.5 mm) needles, CO 51/55/59 sts, and for the cuff, work 14 rows in ribbing patt; *at the same time*, in the last row, evenly distributed, dec 5/3/3 sts (= 46/52/56 sts). Change to US 6 (4.0 mm) needles, and continue in the following pattern: 1 st in St st, 13/16/18 sts in double seed stitch, 18 sts in cable pattern 2, 13/16/18 sts in double seed stitch, 1 st in St st. *At the same time*, for sleeve tapering, after having worked 6/10/10 rows from end of cuff, inc 1 st at each end of the row. Rep these incs in every 6th row 5/0/0 times more and in every 8th row 12/15/15 times more (= 82/84/88 sts). At 16.1/16.5/16.5 in. (41/42/42 cm) (= 140/142/142 rows) from end of cuff, BO all sts.

FINISHING

Block all pieces to measurements on a soft surface, moisten, and let dry. Close shoulder and side seams from the wrong side, leaving the upper 7.1/7.5/7.9 in.

(18/19/20 cm) open for the armholes. Seam the sleeves right sides facing each other and wrong sides facing out, and then sew the sleeves into the armholes from the wrong side.

Using US 4 (3.5 mm) needles, pick up and knit 126/130/134 sts from the neckline edge, join into the round, and work 1.2 in. (3 cm) (= 8 rnds) in ribbing pattern. BO all sts, and weave in ends.

COLORWORK AND STITCH PATTERN CHARTS

COLORWORK CHART A

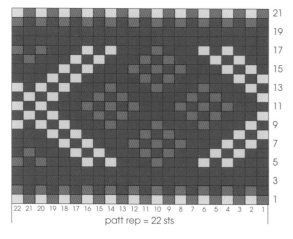

21
19
17
15
13
11
9
7
5
3
1

22 21 20 19 18 17 16 15 14 13 12 11 10 9 8 7 6 5 4 3 2 1
patt rep = 22 sts

KNITTING SYMBOLS

□ = St st in MC
■ = St st in CC1
▨ = St st in CC2

COLORWORK CHART B

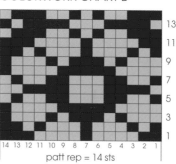

13
11
9
7
5
3
1

14 13 12 11 10 9 8 7 6 5 4 3 2 1
patt rep = 14 sts

KNITTING SYMBOLS

□ = St st in MC
■ = St st in CC

STITCH PATTERN CHART A
Stitch count is a multiple of 10 + 15

11
9
7
5
3
1

patt rep = 10 sts

KNITTING SYMBOLS

■ = knit 1 st
− = purl 1 st
○ = make 1 yarn over
◤ = knit 2 sts together
◣ = slip 1, knit 1, pass the slipped st over
▲ = slip 1, knit 2 sts together, pass the slipped st over
□ = no st, for better overview only

STITCH PATTERN CHART B

11
9
7
5
3
1

cable pattern 1 = 58 sts

STITCH PATTERN CHART C

11
9
7
5
3
1

cable pattern 2 = 18 sts

KNITTING SYMBOLS

■ = knit 1 st
− = purl 1 st
ΩI = slip 1 st purlwise with yarn in back of work
■■◢ = hold 1 st on cn in back of work, knit the next 2 sts, and then knit the st from the cn
◥■■ = hold 2 sts on cn in front of work, purl the next st, and then knit the 2 sts from the cn

■■◢■ = hold 2 sts on cn in back of work, knit the next 2 sts, and then knit the 2 sts from the cn
■■■■◢■■■ = hold 4 sts on cn in back of work, knit the next 4 sts, and then knit the 4 sts from the cn
■■■■◥■■■ = hold 4 sts on cn in front of work, knit the next 4 sts, and then knit the 4 sts from the cn

SCHEMATICS
STRAIGHT BODY

CREWNECK AND SLEEVE WITH STRAIGHT TOP

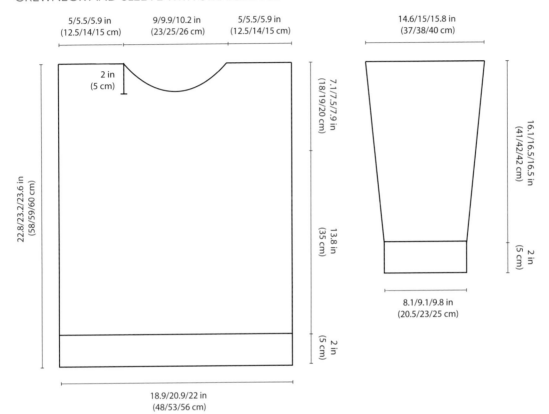

5/5.5/5.9 in
(12.5/14/15 cm)

9/9.9/10.2 in
(23/25/26 cm)

5/5.5/5.9 in
(12.5/14/15 cm)

14.6/15/15.8 in
(37/38/40 cm)

2 in
(5 cm)

7.1/7.5/7.9 in
(18/19/20 cm)

16.1/16.5/16.5 in
(41/42/42 cm)

2 in
(5 cm)

22.8/23.2/23.6 in
(58/59/60 cm)

13.8 in
(35 cm)

2 in
(5 cm)

8.1/9.1/9.8 in
(20.5/23/25 cm)

18.9/20.9/22 in
(48/53/56 cm)

V-NECK AND SLEEVE WITH STRAIGHT TOP

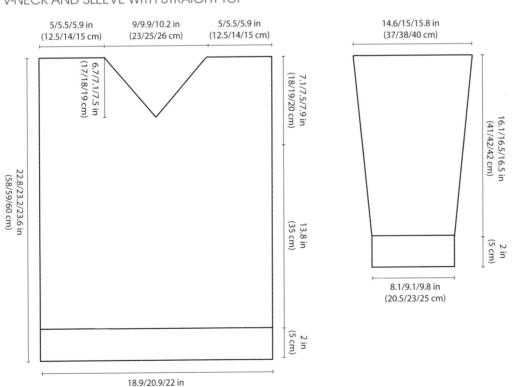

5/5.5/5.9 in
(12.5/14/15 cm)

9/9.9/10.2 in
(23/25/26 cm)

5/5.5/5.9 in
(12.5/14/15 cm)

14.6/15/15.8 in
(37/38/40 cm)

6.7/7.1/7.5 in
(17/18/19 cm)

7.1/7.5/7.9 in
(18/19/20 cm)

16.1/16.5/16.5 in
(41/42/42 cm)

2 in
(5 cm)

22.8/23.2/23.6 in
(58/59/60 cm)

13.8 in
(35 cm)

2 in
(5 cm)

8.1/9.1/9.8 in
(20.5/23/25 cm)

2 in
(5 cm)

18.9/20.9/22 in
(48/53/56 cm)

To make it easier for you to combine all individual building blocks into your own sweater, all applicable schematics have been collected for you on the following pages. Now you can mix and match to your heart's content to find your own favorite combination.

CREWNECK AND SLEEVE WITH SLEEVE CAP

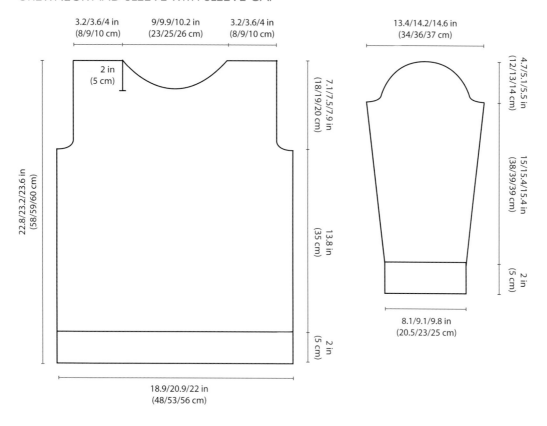

V-NECK AND SLEEVE WITH SLEEVE CAP

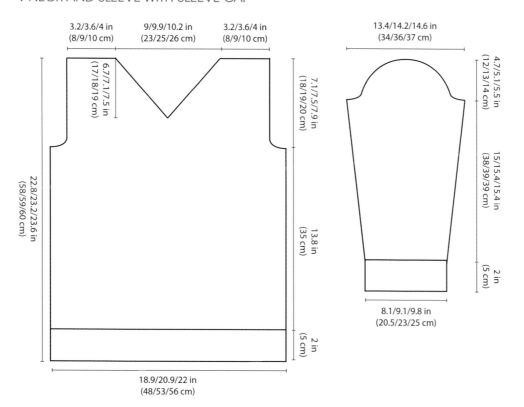

CREWNECK AND RAGLAN SLEEVES

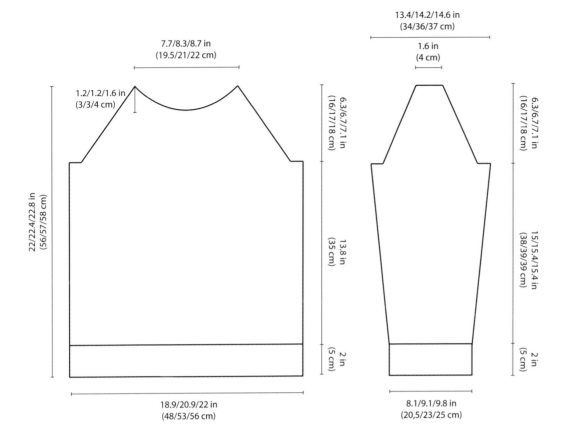

7.7/8.3/8.7 in
(19.5/21/22 cm)

13.4/14.2/14.6 in
(34/36/37 cm)

1.2/1.2/1.6 in
(3/3/4 cm)

1.6 in
(4 cm)

6.3/6.7/7.1 in
(16/17/18 cm)

6.3/6.7/7.1 in
(16/17/18 cm)

22/22.4/22.8 in
(56/57/58 cm)

13.8 in
(35 cm)

15/15.4/15.4 in
(38/39/39 cm)

2 in
(5 cm)

2 in
(5 cm)

18.9/20.9/22 in
(48/53/56 cm)

8.1/9.1/9.8 in
(20,5/23/25 cm)

V-NECK AND RAGLAN SLEEVES

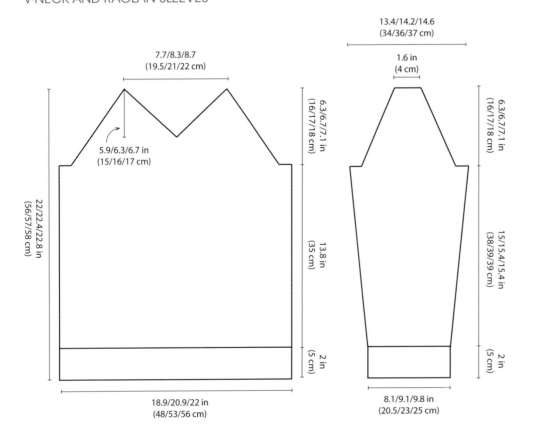

7.7/8.3/8.7 in
(19.5/21/22 cm)

13.4/14.2/14.6
(34/36/37 cm)

1.6 in
(4 cm)

6.3/6.7/7.1 in
(16/17/18 cm)

6.3/6.7/7.1 in
(16/17/18 cm)

5.9/6.3/6.7 in
(15/16/17 cm)

22/22.4/22.8 in
(56/57/58 cm)

13.8 in
(35 cm)

15/15.4/15.4 in
(38/39/39 cm)

2 in
(5 cm)

2 in
(5 cm)

18.9/20.9/22 in
(48/53/56 cm)

8.1/9.1/9.8 in
(20.5/23/25 cm)

A-LINE SHAPED BODY

CREWNECK AND SLEEVE WITH STRAIGHT TOP

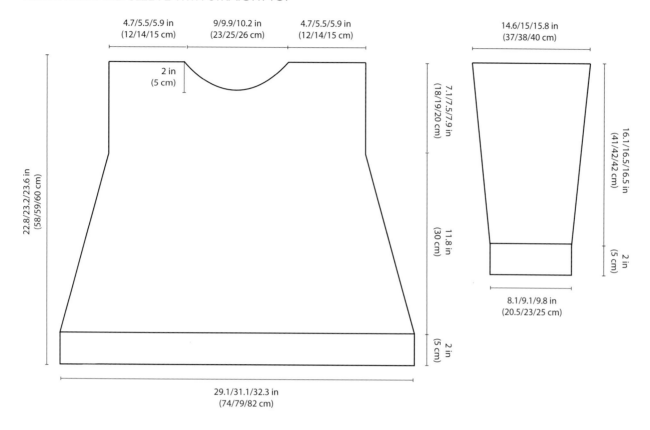

V-NECK AND SLEEVE WITH STRAIGHT TOP

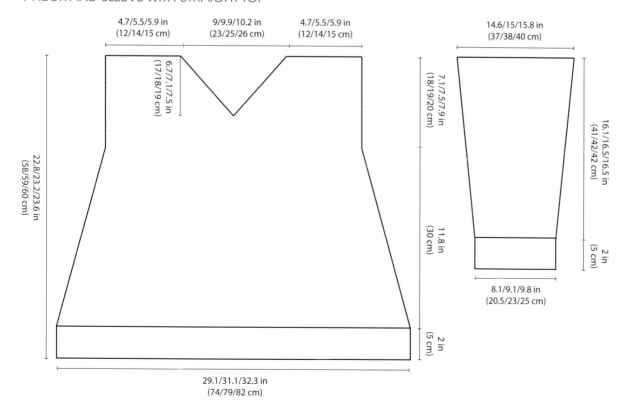

CREWNECK AND SLEEVE WITH SLEEVE CAP

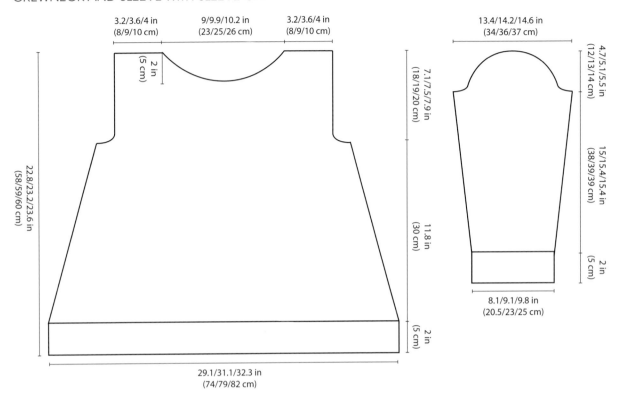

V-NECK AND SLEEVE WITH SLEEVE CAP

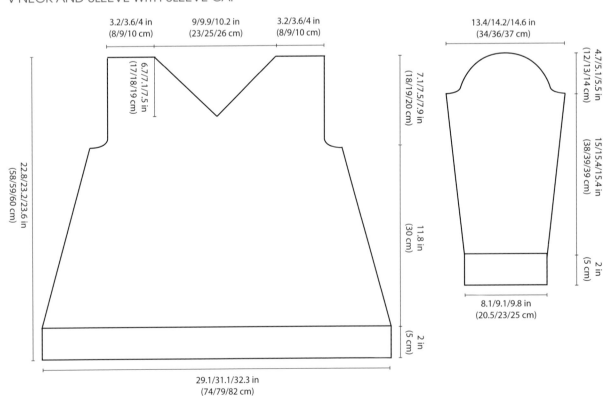

CREWNECK AND RAGLAN SLEEVES

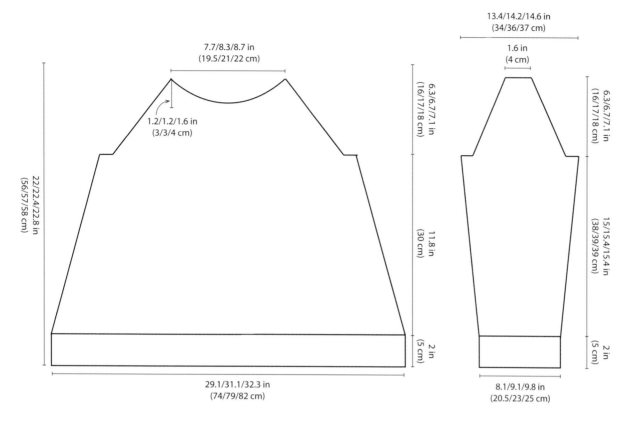

V-NECK AND RAGLAN SLEEVES

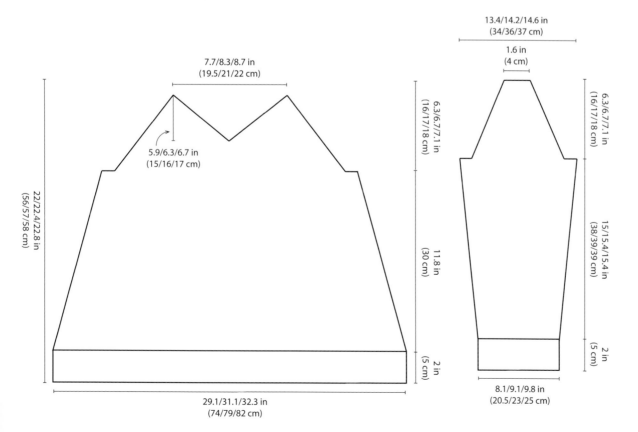

FITTED BODY

CREWNECK AND SLEEVE WITH STRAIGHT TOP

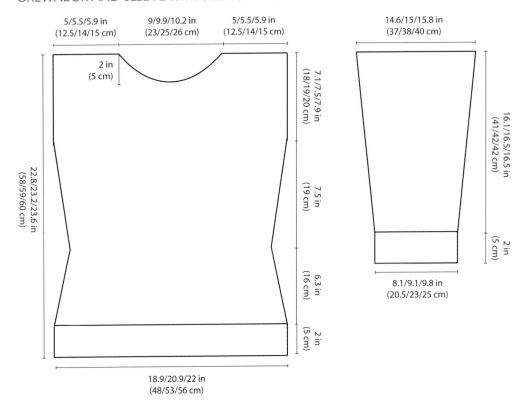

5/5.5/5.9 in
(12.5/14/15 cm)

9/9.9/10.2 in
(23/25/26 cm)

5/5.5/5.9 in
(12.5/14/15 cm)

2 in
(5 cm)

7.1/7.5/7.9 in
(18/19/20 cm)

7.5 in
(19 cm)

6.3 in
(16 cm)

2 in
(5 cm)

22.8/23.2/23.6 in
(58/59/60 cm)

18.9/20.9/22 in
(48/53/56 cm)

14.6/15/15.8 in
(37/38/40 cm)

16.1/16.5/16.5 in
(41/42/42 cm)

2 in
(5 cm)

8.1/9.1/9.8 in
(20.5/23/25 cm)

V-NECK AND SLEEVE WITH STRAIGHT TOP

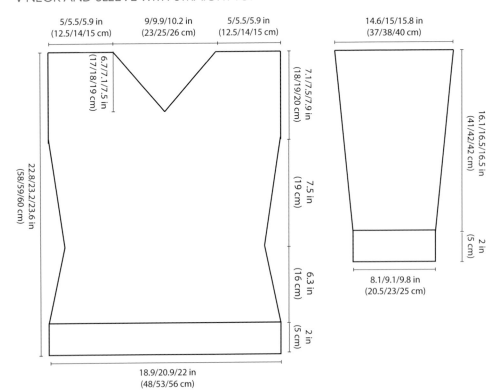

5/5.5/5.9 in
(12.5/14/15 cm)

9/9.9/10.2 in
(23/25/26 cm)

5/5.5/5.9 in
(12.5/14/15 cm)

6.7/7.1/7.5 in
(17/18/19 cm)

7.1/7.5/7.9 in
(18/19/20 cm)

7.5 in
(19 cm)

6.3 in
(16 cm)

2 in
(5 cm)

22.8/23.2/23.6 in
(58/59/60 cm)

18.9/20.9/22 in
(48/53/56 cm)

14.6/15/15.8 in
(37/38/40 cm)

16.1/16.5/16.5 in
(41/42/42 cm)

2 in
(5 cm)

8.1/9.1/9.8 in
(20.5/23/25 cm)

CREWNECK AND SLEEVE WITH SLEEVE CAP

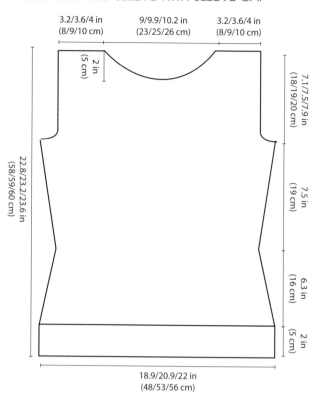

3.2/3.6/4 in
(8/9/10 cm)

9/9.9/10.2 in
(23/25/26 cm)

3.2/3.6/4 in
(8/9/10 cm)

2 in
(5 cm)

22.8/23.2/23.6 in
(58/59/60 cm)

7.1/7.5/7.9 in
(18/19/20 cm)

7.5 in
(19 cm)

6.3 in
(16 cm)

2 in
(5 cm)

18.9/20.9/22 in
(48/53/56 cm)

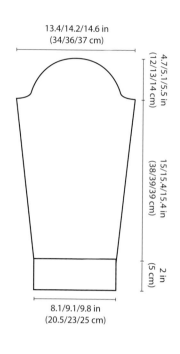

13.4/14.2/14.6 in
(34/36/37 cm)

4.7/5.1/5.5 in
(12/13/14 cm)

15/15.4/15.4 in
(38/39/39 cm)

2 in
(5 cm)

8.1/9.1/9.8 in
(20.5/23/25 cm)

V-NECK AND SLEEVE WITH SLEEVE CAP

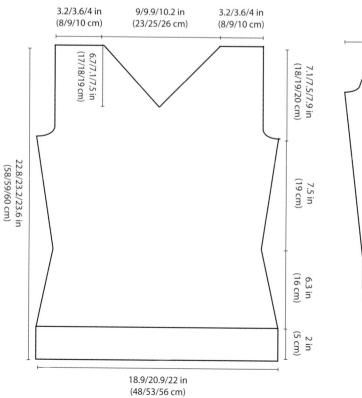

3.2/3.6/4 in
(8/9/10 cm)

9/9.9/10.2 in
(23/25/26 cm)

3.2/3.6/4 in
(8/9/10 cm)

6.7/7.1/7.5 in
(17/18/19 cm)

22.8/23.2/23.6 in
(58/59/60 cm)

7.1/7.5/7.9 in
(18/19/20 cm)

7.5 in
(19 cm)

6.3 in
(16 cm)

2 in
(5 cm)

18.9/20.9/22 in
(48/53/56 cm)

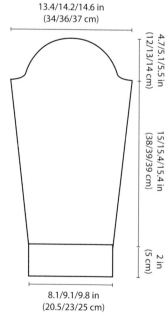

13.4/14.2/14.6 in
(34/36/37 cm)

4.7/5.1/5.5 in
(12/13/14 cm)

15/15.4/15.4 in
(38/39/39 cm)

2 in
(5 cm)

8.1/9.1/9.8 in
(20.5/23/25 cm)

CREWNECK AND RAGLAN SLEEVES

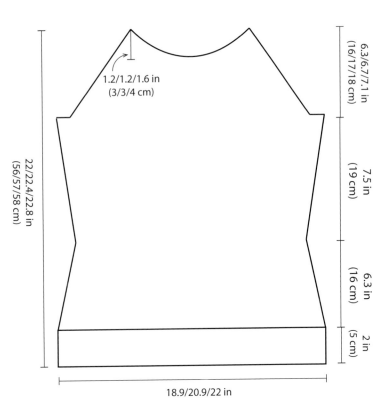

1.2/1.2/1.6 in
(3/3/4 cm)

6.3/6.7/7.1 in
(16/17/18 cm)

7.5 in
(19 cm)

6.3 in
(16 cm)

2 in
(5 cm)

22/22.4/22.8 in
(56/57/58 cm)

18.9/20.9/22 in

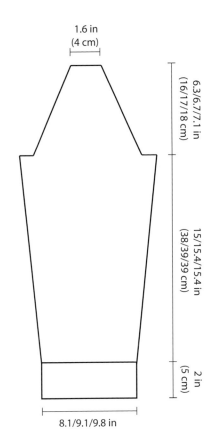

1.6 in
(4 cm)

6.3/6.7/7.1 in
(16/17/18 cm)

15/15.4/15.4 in
(38/39/39 cm)

2 in
(5 cm)

8.1/9.1/9.8 in

V-NECK AND RAGLAN SLEEVES

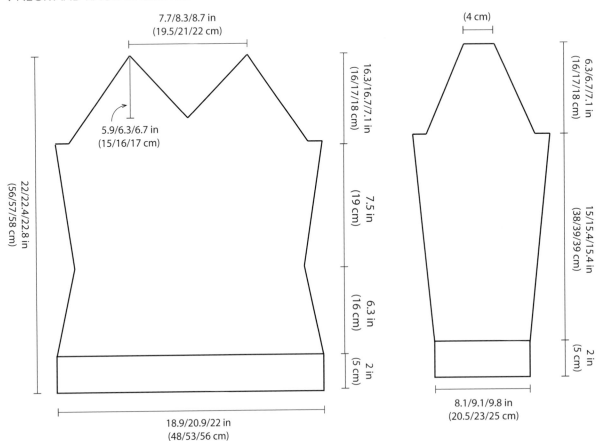

7.7/8.3/8.7 in
(19.5/21/22 cm)

5.9/6.3/6.7 in
(15/16/17 cm)

16.3/16.7/7.1 in
(16/17/18 cm)

7.5 in
(19 cm)

6.3 in
(16 cm)

2 in
(5 cm)

22/22.4/22.8 in
(56/57/58 cm)

18.9/20.9/22 in
(48/53/56 cm)

(4 cm)

6.3/6.7/7.1 in
(16/17/18 cm)

15/15.4/15.4 in
(38/39/39 cm)

2 in
(5 cm)

8.1/9.1/9.8 in
(20.5/23/25 cm)

OVERSIZED BODY

Please note: All sweaters with oversized fit in this book have drop shoulders and long sleeves, which means that options with sleeve cap or raglan sleeve are not possible for this sweater shape.

CREWNECK AND SLEEVE WITH DROP (STRAIGHT) SHOULDER

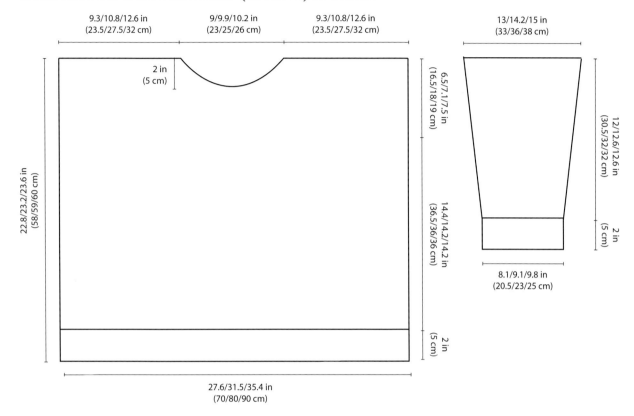

9.3/10.8/12.6 in (23.5/27.5/32 cm)

9/9.9/10.2 in (23/25/26 cm)

9.3/10.8/12.6 in (23.5/27.5/32 cm)

2 in (5 cm)

22.8/23.2/23.6 in (58/59/60 cm)

2 in (5 cm)

27.6/31.5/35.4 in (70/80/90 cm)

13/14.2/15 in (33/36/38 cm)

6.5/7.1/7.5 in (16.5/18/19 cm)

12/12.6/12.6 in (30.5/32/32 cm)

14.4/14.2/14.2 in (36.5/36/36 cm)

2 in (5 cm)

8.1/9.1/9.8 in (20.5/23/25 cm)

V-NECK AND SLEEVE WITH DROP (STRAIGHT) SHOULDER

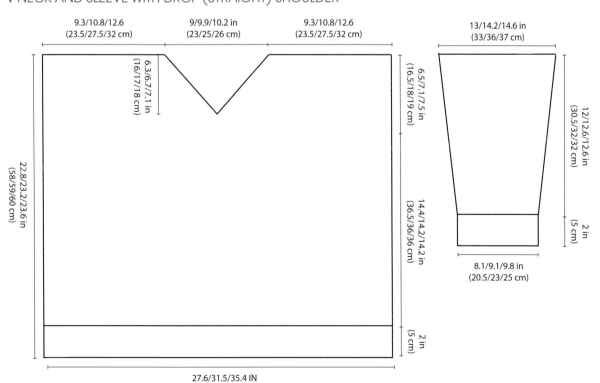

9.3/10.8/12.6 (23.5/27.5/32 cm)

9/9.9/10.2 in (23/25/26 cm)

9.3/10.8/12.6 (23.5/27.5/32 cm)

6.3/6.7/7.1 in (16/17/18 cm)

22.8/23.2/23.6 in (58/59/60 cm)

2 in (5 cm)

27.6/31.5/35.4 IN (70/80/90 cm)

13/14.2/14.6 in (33/36/37 cm)

6.5/7.1/7.5 in (16.5/18/19 cm)

12/12.6/12.6 in (30.5/32/32 cm)

14.4/14.2/14.2 in (36.5/36/36 cm)

2 in (5 cm)

8.1/9.1/9.8 in (20.5/23/25 cm)

SLEEVE LENGTHS

STRAIGHT SLEEVE SHAPE

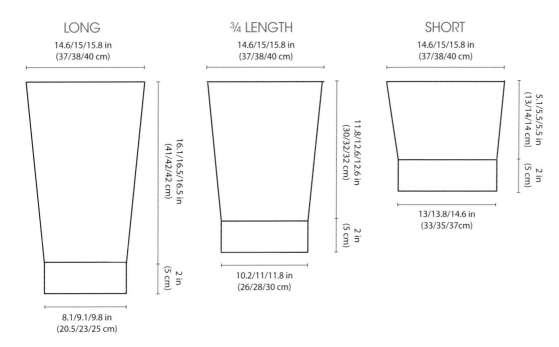

LONG
14.6/15/15.8 in
(37/38/40 cm)

16.1/16.5/16.5 in
(41/42/42 cm)

2 in
(5 cm)

8.1/9.1/9.8 in
(20.5/23/25 cm)

¾ LENGTH
14.6/15/15.8 in
(37/38/40 cm)

11.8/12.6/12.6 in
(30/32/32 cm)

2 in
(5 cm)

10.2/11/11.8 in
(26/28/30 cm)

SHORT
14.6/15/15.8 in
(37/38/40 cm)

5.1/5.5/5.5 in
(13/14/14 cm)

2 in
(5 cm)

13/13.8/14.6 in
(33/35/37cm)

SLEEVE WITH SLEEVE CAP

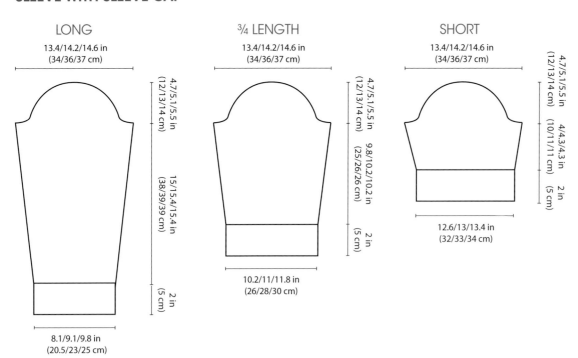

LONG
13.4/14.2/14.6 in
(34/36/37 cm)

4.7/5.1/5.5 in
(12/13/14 cm)

15/15.4/15.4 in
(38/39/39 cm)

2 in
(5 cm)

8.1/9.1/9.8 in
(20.5/23/25 cm)

¾ LENGTH
13.4/14.2/14.6 in
(34/36/37 cm)

4.7/5.1/5.5 in
(12/13/14 cm)

9.8/10.2/10.2 in
(25/26/26 cm)

2 in
(5 cm)

10.2/11/11.8 in
(26/28/30 cm)

SHORT
13.4/14.2/14.6 in
(34/36/37 cm)

4.7/5.1/5.5 in
(12/13/14 cm)

4/4.3/4.3 in
(10/11/11 cm)

2 in
(5 cm)

12.6/13/13.4 in
(32/33/34 cm)

RAGLAN SLEEVE

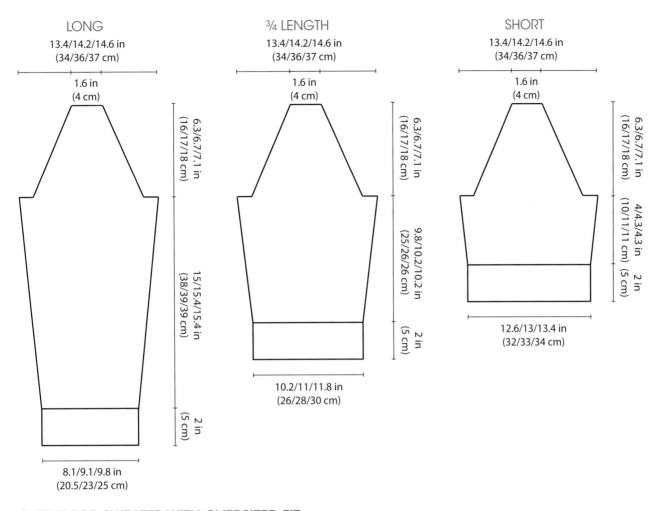

LONG

13.4/14.2/14.6 in
(34/36/37 cm)

1.6 in
(4 cm)

6.3/6.7/7.1 in
(16/17/18 cm)

15/15.4/15.4 in
(38/39/39 cm)

2 in
(5 cm)

8.1/9.1/9.8 in
(20.5/23/25 cm)

¾ LENGTH

13.4/14.2/14.6 in
(34/36/37 cm)

1.6 in
(4 cm)

6.3/6.7/7.1 in
(16/17/18 cm)

9.8/10.2/10.2 in
(25/26/26 cm)

2 in
(5 cm)

10.2/11/11.8 in
(26/28/30 cm)

SHORT

13.4/14.2/14.6 in
(34/36/37 cm)

1.6 in
(4 cm)

6.3/6.7/7.1 in
(16/17/18 cm)

4/4.3/4.3 in
(10/11/11 cm)

2 in
(5 cm)

12.6/13/13.4 in
(32/33/34 cm)

SLEEVE FOR SWEATER WITH OVERSIZED FIT

LONG

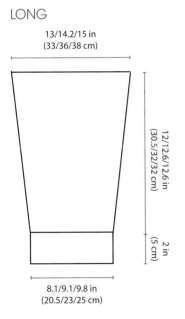

13/14.2/15 in
(33/36/38 cm)

12/12.6/12.6 in
(30.5/32/32 cm)

2 in
(5 cm)

8.1/9.1/9.8 in
(20.5/23/25 cm)

STITCH PATTERN LIBRARY

It goes without saying that no restrictions are placed on you when choosing your favorite stitch pattern. On the following pages, I will show you alternate stitch pattern options for all Basic Sweaters, which you can use without having to make any further adjustments. If you, for instance, have decided on a Basic Sweater with lace pattern, you can switch out any one of the four lace patterns suggested here. For cable sweaters, accordingly choose one of the four cable patterns. The stitch count for the Basic Sweater you've picked does not need to be adjusted—you just need to exchange the stitch pattern or colorwork charts.

However, it is important that the gauge exactly matches the one stated in the pattern. For this reason, it might be necessary to work alternate stitch patterns using a smaller or larger needle size to achieve the correct measurements.

KNIT-PURL PATTERNS

These stitch patterns can be used as alternate patterns for all Basic Sweaters in stockinette stitch if stitch counts match (adjust as necessary). Also, be sure you meet the following gauge (adjust needle size if necessary).

GAUGE
In the respective knit-purl pattern on US 6 (4.0 mm) needles, 22 sts and 30 rows = 4 x 4 in. (10 x 10 cm)

KNIT-PURL PATTERN 1

(odd stitch count)
Row 1 (RS): Knit all sts through the back loop.
Row 2: *K1, p1-tbl, rep from * to last st of row, then k1.
Row 3: *P1, k1-tbl, rep from * to last st of row, then p1.
Row 4: Work as Row 2.
Row 5: Knit all sts through the back loop.
Row 6: *P1-tbl, k1, rep from * to last st of row, then p1-tbl.
Row 7: *K1-tbl, p1, rep from * to last st of row, then k1-tbl.
Row 8: Work as Row 6.
Rep Rows 1–8 throughout.

KNIT-PURL PATTERN 2

(works for any stitch count)

Rows 1–5: Work in stockinette stitch. (RS: knit, WS: purl)

Row 6 (WS): Knit all stitches.

Rows 7–11: Work in stockinette stitch.

Rows 12–14: Work in reverse stockinette. (RS: purl, WS: knit)

Rep Rows 1–14 throughout.

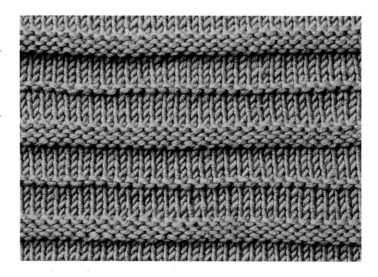

KNIT-PURL PATTERN 3

(stitch count is a multiple of 3)

Row 1: Knit all stitches.

Row 2 (and all other WS rows): Knit the knits and purl the purls.

Row 3: Knit all stitches.

Row 5: K1, *p1, k2, rep from * to last 2 sts, then p1, k1.

Row 7: Work as Row 5.

Row 9: *P2, k1, rep from * throughout.

Row 11: Work as Row 9.

Rep Rows 1–12 throughout.

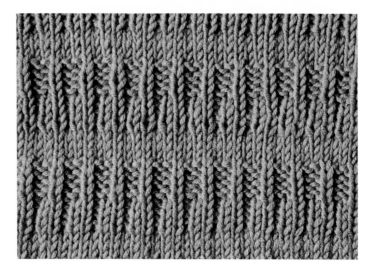

KNIT-PURL PATTERN 4

(odd stitch count)

Row 1: K1, *alternate p1, k1, rep from * throughout.

Row 2: Purl all stitches.

Rep Rows 1 and 2 throughout.

STRANDED COLORWORK PATTERNS

These stitch patterns can be used for all Basic Sweaters with stranded colorwork pattern if stitch counts match—just make sure to always distribute the pattern starting in the middle of the row. The marked center stitch always has to end up in the middle of the knitted piece. The following gauge applies to all patterns (adjust needle size if necessary).

GAUGE
In stranded colorwork pattern on US 6 (4.0 mm) needles, 22 sts and 30 rows = 4 x 4 in. (10 x 10 cm)

KNITTING SYMBOLS
■ = St st in MC
□ = St st in CC

STRANDED PATTERN 1
Work in stockinette stitch in stranded colorwork pattern from the following colorwork chart. The chart contains both RS and WS rows. Sts are shown as they appear from the RS of the fabric. Distribute the pattern starting in the middle of the row, with the marked center stitch exactly in the middle. Repeat the patt rep (10 sts widthwise and 10 rows heightwise) throughout.

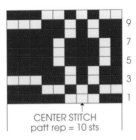

CENTER STITCH
patt rep = 10 sts

STRANDED PATTERN 2
Work in stockinette stitch in stranded colorwork pattern from the following colorwork chart. The chart contains both RS and WS rows. Sts are shown as they appear from the RS of the fabric. Distribute the pattern starting in the middle of the row, with the marked center stitch exactly in the middle. Repeat the patt rep (8 sts widthwise and 8 rows heightwise) throughout.

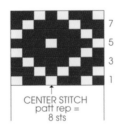

CENTER STITCH
patt rep = 8 sts

STRANDED PATTERN 3

Work in stockinette stitch in stranded colorwork pattern from the following colorwork chart. The chart contains both RS and WS rows. Sts are shown as they appear from the RS of the fabric. Distribute the pattern starting in the middle of the row, with the marked center stitch exactly in the middle. Repeat the patt rep (22 sts widthwise and 16 rows heightwise) throughout.

STRANDED PATTERN 4

Work in stockinette stitch in stranded colorwork pattern from the following colorwork chart. The chart contains both RS and WS rows. Sts are shown as they appear from the RS of the fabric. Distribute the pattern starting in the middle of the row, with the marked center stitch exactly in the middle. Repeat the patt rep (12 sts widthwise and 22 rows heightwise) throughout.

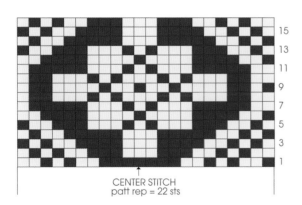

CENTER STITCH
patt rep = 22 sts

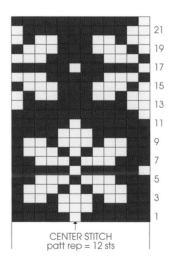

CENTER STITCH
patt rep = 12 sts

LACE PATTERNS

These stitch patterns can be used for all Basic Sweaters with lace pattern if stitch counts match (adjust if necessary). The following gauge applies to all patterns (adjust needle size if necessary).

GAUGE

In lace pattern on US 6 (4.0 mm) needles, 20 sts and 28 rows = 4 x 4 in. (10 x 10 cm)

KNITTING SYMBOLS

■	= knit 1 st
−	= purl 1 st
O	= make 1 yarn over

◢	= knit 2 sts together
◣	= slip 1, knit 1, pass the slipped st over
▲	= slip 1, knit 2 sts together, pass the slipped st over
☐	= no st, for better overview only

LACE PATTERN 1

Work from the following chart. Only RS rows are shown in the chart; in WS rows, work all sts as they appear, and purl the yarn overs. Begin with the sts before the patt rep, repeat the patt rep widthwise across, and end with the sts after the patt rep. Rep Rows 1–10 heightwise throughout.

LACE PATTERN 2

Work from the following chart. Only RS rows are shown in the chart; in WS rows, work all sts as they appear, and purl the yarn overs. Begin with the sts before the patt rep, repeat the patt rep widthwise across, and end with the sts after the patt rep. Rep Rows 1–16 heightwise throughout.

patt rep = 10 sts

patt rep = 10 sts

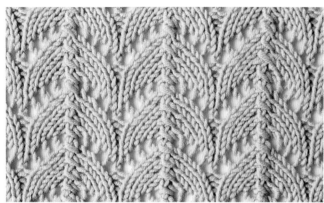

LACE PATTERN 3

Work from the following chart. Only RS rows are shown in the chart; in WS rows, work all sts as they appear, and purl the yarn overs. Begin with the sts before the patt rep, repeat the patt rep widthwise across, and end with the sts after the patt rep. Rep Rows 1–28 heightwise throughout.

LACE PATTERN 4

Work from the following chart. Only RS rows are shown in the chart; in WS rows, work all sts as they appear, and purl the yarn overs. Begin with the sts before the patt rep, repeat the patt rep widthwise across, and end with the sts after the patt rep. Rep Rows 1–8 heightwise throughout.

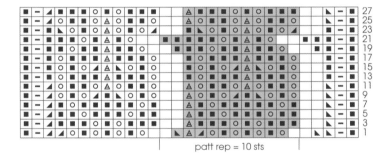

patt rep = 10 sts

patt rep = 10 sts

CABLE PATTERNS

These stitch patterns can be used for Basic Sweater 6 with cable pattern—replacing the 58 sts of cable pattern 1 with one of the alternatives below. The following gauge applies to all cable patterns (adjust needle size if necessary).

GAUGE

In cable pattern on US 6 (4.0 mm) needles, 58 sts = 8.3 in. (21 cm)

CABLE PATTERN 1

cable pattern = 58 sts

CABLE PATTERN 2

cable pattern = 58 sts

CABLE PATTERN 3

cable pattern = 58 sts

CABLE PATTERN 4

cable pattern = 58 sts

KNITTING SYMBOLS

■ = knit 1 st

– = purl 1 st

◧ = slip 1 st knitwise, with yarn in back of work

◆ = knit 1 st through the back loop

= hold 2 sts on cn in front of work, purl the next st, and then knit the sts from the cn

= hold 1 st on cn in back of work, knit the next 2 sts, and then purl the st from the cn

= hold 2 sts on cn in front of work, knit the next st, and then knit the sts from the cn

= hold 2 sts on cn in front of work, knit the next 2 sts, and then knit the sts from the cn

= hold 2 sts on cn in back of work, knit the next 2 sts, and then knit the sts from the cn

= hold 2 sts on cn in back of work, knit the next 2 sts, and then purl the sts from the cn

= hold 2 sts on cn in front of work, purl the next 2 sts, and then knit the sts from the cn

= hold 3 sts on cn in back of work, knit the next 3 sts, and then knit the sts from the cn

= hold 3 sts on cn in front of work, knit the next 3 sts, and then knit the sts from the cn

CABLE PATTERN 1

Work from chart. Only RS rows are shown in the chart; in WS rows, work all sts as they appear and purl the slipped stitches. Work the patt rep (58 sts wide) once widthwise; rep Rows 1–24 heightwise throughout.

CABLE PATTERN 2

Work from chart. Only RS rows are shown in the chart; in WS rows, work all sts as they appear. Work the patt rep (58 sts wide) once widthwise; rep Rows 1–16 heightwise throughout.

CABLE PATTERN 3

Work from chart. Only RS rows are shown in the chart; in WS rows, work all sts as they appear. Work the patt rep (58 sts wide) once widthwise; rep Rows 1–12 heightwise throughout.

CABLE PATTERN 4

Work from chart. Only RS rows are shown in the chart; in WS rows, work all sts as they appear, and purl the slipped stitches. Work the patt rep (58 sts wide) once widthwise; rep Rows 1–24 heightwise throughout.

ADJUSTING KNITTED GARMENTS

This book already contains a multitude of options for adjusting your dream sweater to your personal preferences. If you have still more ideas about possible modifications, the following section offers instructions for individual adjustments to length, width, and stitch patterns.

LENGTH

Of course it is possible to change the length of your sweater by inserting additional rows. If you decide to do this, please note the following rules:

Always insert additional rows before beginning the armhole, because otherwise the sleeves would no longer fit into the armhole.

Always adjust the number of additional rows to the stitch pattern used. This way, you make sure that the armholes begin exactly in the spot where they should as per instructions. For stockinette sweaters without patterning, the number of rows worked additionally doesn't matter. For sweaters with patterns, the following applies:

- For Basic Sweaters with stripes, either insert an additional stripe or make existing stripes wider. Armholes need to start in the same row of the stripe as stated in the instructions.
- For Basic Sweaters with border, insert additional rows only after completion of the border.
- For Basic Sweaters with stranded colorwork, increase the number of rows by one or more complete pattern repeats heightwise.
- For Basic Sweaters with lace pattern, increase the number of rows by one or more complete pattern repeats heightwise.
- For Basic Sweaters with cable pattern, it is the same: increase the number of rows by one or more complete pattern repeats heightwise.

For the different Body shapes, there are additional rules to follow:

- For the fitted Basic Sweater, insert additional rows before beginning the waist decreases. This ensures that the waist will later be at the correct level.
- For the Basic Sweater in A-line, insert additional rows immediately after the hems and cuffs. Add these rows before starting the decreases. If you want to add a lot of extra rows, you should work one or more additional decreases. You will need to have accordingly more stitches after the hems and cuffs. For every additional A-line decrease, you need to have 2 stitches more on the needles.

Of course, the same principles apply if you want to make your sweater shorter instead of longer.

WIDTH

The width of your sweater can be adjusted, too. However, I only recommend doing this for sweaters with drop shoulders. Otherwise, it could happen that the armholes are no longer in the correct spot. For stockinette sweaters, you can just cast on any number of additional stitches. However, keep in mind that this might require you to shorten the sleeves later, since the shoulder will be dropped more than stated in the pattern. For pattern stitches, if at all possible, always add stitches in increments that allow you to work one additional pattern repeat widthwise. When this is not feasible, the pattern has to be adjusted on the sides—make sure the center stitch of the pattern repeat is always located exactly in the middle of the row.

STITCH PATTERN

Although in this book I already present a large number of alternate stitch patterns, you can use other patterns of your own choice as well. For this, it is important that the gauge of your stitch pattern exactly matches the gauge of the pattern listed in the instructions. Otherwise, measurements would be off later on! If the count of your stitch pattern is different from the one in the pattern, here, too, you have to distribute the pattern repeats from the middle, and make sure that the center stitch of the pattern repeat ends up exactly in the middle of the row. This way, the pattern gets equally distributed, and the edges on both sides of the knitted piece have the same pattern.

I hope that these adjustment suggestions inspire your creativity even more!

FITTED WITH LACE PATTERN AND NUPP HEM AND CUFFS

Instructions on page 122

V-NECK WITH RIBBED NECKBAND

ARMHOLE WITH SLEEVE CAP

¾ SLEEVE

FITTED SHAPE

HEM AND CUFFS IN NUPP PATTERN

WITH THREE-COLOR LACE PATTERN

Pictured on page 118

BUILDING BLOCK PARTS

BODY SHAPE	Straight
BACK	Basic Sweater 5
FRONT	Basic Sweater 5
SLEEVE	Basic Sweater 5
ARMHOLE	Straight
SLEEVE LENGTH	Long
NECKLINE	Boatneck
HEMS AND CUFFS	Ribbed hem and cuffs
SPECIAL FEATURES	This design features seed stitch strips between color blocks and in the upper part of the sweater. The Front is worked without neckline shaping, creating a boatneck.

SIZES

Small/Medium/Large (US 6/8, 10/12, 14/16)

Numbers for size Small are listed before the first slash, for size Medium between slashes, and for size Large after the second slash. If only one number is given, it applies to all sizes.

MATERIALS

Schachenmayr Merino Extrafine 120; #3 light weight yarn; 100% wool; 131 yd (120 m), 1.75 oz. (50 g) per skein

- Main color (MC): 4/5/6 skeins #101 white
- Contrasting color 1 (CC1): 2/2/3 skeins #168 dark blue
- Contrasting color 2 (CC2): 2/2/3 skeins #165 medium blue
- Contrasting color 3 (CC3): 2/2/3 skeins #152 light blue

Circular knitting needles, US 4 (3.5 mm) and US 6 (4.0 mm), each 32 in. (80 cm) long

GAUGE

In lace pattern on US 6 (4.0 mm) needles, 20 sts and 28 rows = 4 x 4 in. (10 x 10 cm)

In seed stitch on US 6 (4.0 mm) needles, 22 sts and 32 rows = 4 x 4 in. (10 x 10 cm)

STOCKINETTE STITCH

RS: Knit all sts.
WS: Purl all sts.

SEED STITCH

For odd stitch counts, in RS and WS rows, alternate k1, p1.

RIBBING IN ROWS

RS: Alternate k1, p1.
WS: Work all sts as they appear—knit the knits and purl the purls.

RIBBING IN ROUNDS

All rounds (RS): Alternate k1, p1.

LACE PATTERN

Work from Stitch Pattern Chart A. Only RS rows are shown in the chart; in WS rows, work all sts as they appear, and purl the yarn overs. Begin with the sts before the patt rep, repeat the patt rep widthwise across, and end with the sts after the patt rep. Repeat Rows 1–12 of the chart heightwise throughout.

INSTRUCTIONS

BACK

Using US 4 (3.5 mm) needles and MC (white), CO 115/127/131 sts, and for hem ribbing, work 14 rows in ribbing patt; *at the same time*, in the last row, evenly distributed, dec 20/22/16 sts (= 95/105/115 sts). Change to US 6 (4.0 mm) needles, and cont as follows: 36 rows in lace pattern in CC1 (dark blue), knit 1 row in MC; 5 rows in seed stitch in MC; 36 rows in lace pattern in CC2 (medium blue), again beginning with Row 1 of the chart; knit 1 row in MC; 5 rows in seed stitch in MC; 36 rows in lace pattern in CC3 (light blue), again beginning with Row 1 of the chart; and in the last row, evenly distributed, inc 10/10/6 sts (= 105/115/121 sts). Knit 1 RS row in MC, and then cont in seed stitch in MC. At 21/21.3/21.7 in. (53/54/55 cm) (= 148/152/154 rows) from hem ribbing, BO all sts.

STITCH PATTERN CHART A

Stitch count is a multiple of 10 + 15.

patt rep = 10 sts

KNITTING SYMBOLS

■ = knit 1 st
− = purl 1 st
○ = make 1 yarn over

◢ = knit 2 sts together
◣ = slip 1, knit 1, pass the slipped st over

▲ = slip 1, knit 2 sts together, pass the slipped st over
☐ = no st, for better overview only

FRONT

Work as the Back.

SLEEVES (MAKE 2)

Using US 4 (3.5 mm) needles and MC, CO 51/55/59 sts, and for the cuff, work 14 rows in ribbing patt; *at the same time*, in the last row, evenly distributed, dec 6/8/10 sts (= 45/47/49 sts). Change to US 6 (4.0 mm) needles, and cont in lace pattern in CC1 as follows: 0/1/2 st(s) in St st, 45 sts in lace pattern, 0/1/2 st(s) in St st. After having worked 28 rows in CC1, cont as follows: knit 1 row in MC; 5 rows in seed stitch in MC; 28 rows in lace pattern in CC2, again beginning with Row 1 of the chart; knit 1 row in MC; 5 rows in seed stitch in MC; 28 rows in lace pattern in CC3, again beginning with Row 1 of the chart.

At the same time, for sleeve tapering, after having worked 6 rows from end of cuff, inc 1 st at each end of the row. Rep these incs in every 6th row 0/3/4 times more and in every 8th row 11/8/8 times more (= 69/71/75 sts).

Please note: As soon as you have 49 sts on the needles, the first 2 and the last 2 sts will always be worked in St. st. Increases at both ends of the row will then always be worked after or before these 2 sts, and the sts gained from increasing are incorporated into the lace pattern. For the lace pattern strips in CC2 and CC3, the stitch pattern is adjusted from the middle out, the first 2 and the last 2 sts continue to be worked in stockinette.

After having completed the last lace pattern strip, knit 1 RS row in MC, increasing 8 sts evenly distributed (= 77/79/83 sts). Continue in seed stitch in MC. For further sleeve tapering, inc 1 st in every 8th row 2 times (= 81/83/87 sts). At 16.1/16.5/16.5 in. (41/42/42 cm) (= 120/124/124 rows) from hem ribbing, BO all sts.

FINISHING

Block all pieces to measurements on a soft surface, moisten, and let dry. Close the shoulder seams over a length of 5/5.5/5.9 in. (12.5/14/15 cm) right sides facing each other, leaving the middle 9/9.9/10.2 in. (23/25/26 cm) open for the neckline. Close the side seams wrong sides facing out, leaving the upper 7.1/7.5/7.9 in. (18/19/20 cm) open for the armholes. Seam the sleeves right sides facing each other and wrong sides facing out, and, finally, sew the sleeves into the armholes from the wrong side.

SCHEMATIC

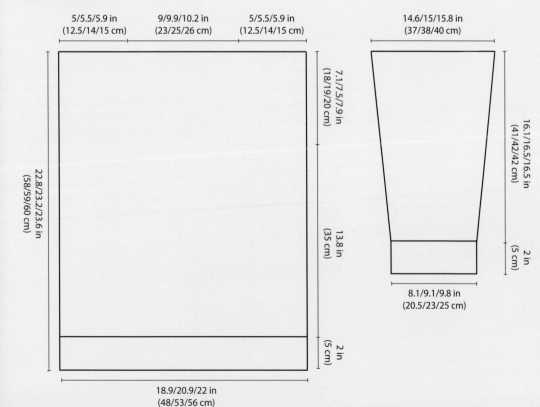

FITTED WITH LACE PATTERN AND NUPP HEM AND CUFFS

Pictured on page 119

BUILDING BLOCK PARTS

BODY SHAPE	Fitted
BACK	Basic Sweater 5
FRONT	Basic Sweater 5
SLEEVE	Basic Sweater 5
ARMHOLE	Sleeve cap
SLEEVE LENGTH	¾ length
NECKLINE	V-neck with ribbed neckband
HEMS AND CUFFS	Hem and cuffs in nupp pattern

SIZES

Small/Medium/Large (US 6/8, 10/12, 14/16)
Numbers for size Small are listed before the first slash, for size Medium between slashes, and for size Large after the second slash. If only one number is given, it applies to all sizes.

MATERIALS

Schachenmayr Merino Extrafine 120; #3 light weight yarn; 100% wool; 131 yd (120 m), 1.75 oz. (50 g) per skein
• 10/12/13 skeins #133 burgundy
Circular knitting needles, US 4 (3.5 mm) and US 6 (4.0 mm), each 32 in. (80 cm) long

GAUGE

In nupp pattern on US 4 (3.5 mm) needles, 21 sts and 29 rows = 4 x 4 in. (10 x 10 cm)
In lace pattern on US 6 (4.0 mm) needles, 20 sts and 28 rows = 4 x 4 in. (10 x 10 cm)

STOCKINETTE STITCH

RS: Knit all sts.
WS: Purl all sts.

RIBBING IN ROWS

RS: Alternate k1, p1.
WS: Work all sts as they appear—knit the knits and purl the purls.

RIBBING IN ROUNDS

All rounds (RS): Alternate k1, p1.

NUPP PATTERN

Work from Stitch Pattern Chart D. Only RS rows are shown in the chart; in WS rows, purl all sts and yarn overs. Repeat the patt rep widthwise across, ending with the 2 sts after the patt rep.

LACE PATTERN

Work from Stitch Pattern Chart A. Only RS rows are shown in the chart; in WS rows, work all sts as they appear, and purl the yarn overs. Begin with the sts before the patt rep, repeat the patt rep widthwise across, and end with the

sts after the patt rep. Repeat Rows 1–12 of the chart heightwise throughout.

ACCENTED DECREASES

Accented decreases are always worked in RS rows, at both ends of the row as follows: K1, skp, work in pattern to last 3 sts of the row, then k2tog, k1. In WS rows, always purl the first 2 sts and the last 2 sts of the row. In RS rows without decreases, always knit the first 2 sts and the last 2 sts of the row.

ACCENTED INCREASES

Accented increases are always worked in RS rows as follows: K1, inc 1 st from the bar between sts twisted, cont in patt to last st of the row, inc 1 st from the bar between sts twisted, k1. In WS rows, always purl the first 2 sts and the last 2 sts of the row. In RS rows without increases, always knit the first 2 sts and the last 2 sts of the row.

INSTRUCTIONS

BACK

Using US 4 (3.5 mm) needles, CO 101/112/123 sts, and work as follows: 4 rows garter st, 16 rows in nupp pattern, 4 rows garter st; *at the same time*, in the last row, evenly distributed, dec 6/7/8 sts (= 95/105/115 sts). Change to US 6 (4.0 mm) needles, and cont in lace pattern.

STITCH PATTERN CHART A
Stitch count is a multiple of 10 + 15

patt rep = 10 sts

STITCH PATTERN CHART D
Stitch count is a multiple of 11 + 2

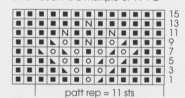

patt rep = 11 sts

KNITTING SYMBOLS

■ = knit 1 st
– = purl 1 st
○ = make 1 yarn over
◢ = knit 2 sts together

◣ = slip 1, knit 1, pass the slipped st over
▲ = slip 1, knit 2 sts together, pass the slipped st over
☐ = no st, for better overview only

N = 1 nupp (= work k1, p1, k1, p1, k1 all into the next st, turn work, purl the 5 nupp sts, turn work again one after another, pass the 2nd, 3rd, 4th and 5th st over the first one)

After having worked 2/1.6/1.6 in. (5/4/4 cm) (= 14/12/12 rows) from end of ribbing, for waist shaping, work 1 accented decrease at each end of the row. Rep accented decreases at each end of the row in every other row 0/0/2 times more and in every 4th row 7 times more (= 79/89/95 sts). After having worked 6.7 in. (17 cm) (= 46 rows) from end of ribbing, work 1 accented increase at each end of the row. Rep accented increases at both ends of the row in every 4th row 0/0/4 times more, in every 6th row 7/5/5 times more, and in every 8th row 0/2/0 times more (= 95/105/115 sts).

For armhole shaping, after having worked 13.8 in. (35 cm) (= 98 rows) from end of ribbing, BO 3/4/5 sts at each end of the row. After this, in every other row, BO another 2 sts twice and 1 st 1/2/1 time(s). At 21/21.3/21.7 in. (53/54/55 cm) (= 148/152/154 rows) from end of ribbing, BO the remaining 79/85/95 sts.

FRONT

Work as the Back, but with V-neck. For this, after having worked 14.2/14.6/13.8 in. (36/37/35 cm) (= 100/102/98 rows) from end of ribbing, BO the center stitch and continue both sides separately. For the sloped neckline, at the neck edge, in every RS row, work accented decrease of 1 st each 23/24/27 times more. At 21/21.3/21.7 in. (53/54/55 cm) (= 148/152/154 rows) from end of ribbing, BO the remaining 16/18/20 sts.

SLEEVES (MAKE 2)

Using US 4 (3.5 mm) needles, CO 57/57/68 sts, and work as follows: 4 rows garter st, 16 rows in nupp pattern, 4 rows garter st; *at the same time*, in the last row, evenly distributed, dec 2/0/9 sts (= 55/57/59 sts). Change to US 6 (4.0 mm) needles, and cont in lace pattern as follows: 0/1/2 st(s) in St st, 55 sts in lace pattern from Stitch Pattern Chart A, 0/1/2 st(s) in St st. For sleeve tapering, after having worked 8/8/6 rows from end of cuff, inc 1 st at each end of the row. Rep these incs in every 6th row 0/0/6 times more and in every 8th row 6/8/3 times more (= 69/75/79 sts).

For the sleeve cap, after having worked 9.9/10.2/10.2 in. (25/26/26 cm) (= 70/72/72 rows) from end of cuff, BO sts at both ends of the row as follows: BO 3/4/5 sts each once; then, in every other row, 2 sts twice, 1 st 9/10/12 times, 2 sts 4/4/3 times, and 3 sts once. At sleeve cap height of 4.7/5.1/5.5 in. (12/13/14 cm) (= 34/36/38 rows), BO the remaining 15/17/19 sts.

Please note: The first 2 and the last 2 sts will always be worked in St st. Increases at both ends of the row will then always be worked after or before these 2 sts, and the sts gained from increasing are incorporated into the lace pattern.

FINISHING

Block all pieces to measurements on a soft surface, moisten, and let dry. Close shoulder, side, and sleeve seams from the wrong side, and then sew the sleeves into the armholes from the wrong side.

Using US 4 (3.5 mm) needles, beginning at the left shoulder, pick up and knit 156/162/168 sts around the V-neck neckline edge as follows: 52/54/56 sts to 1 st before the deepest point of the V-neck, 1 st from the tip of the V-neck, 52/54/56 sts up to the right shoulder, and 51/53/55 sts along the Back neckline. Join into the round, and work ribbing as follows:

Rnd 1: Work in ribbing pattern.
Rnd 2: Work in ribbing to 1 st before the tip of the V-neck, work cdd over 3 sts (= slip 2 sts together knitwise, knit the next st, and pass the slipped sts over the knitted one), and then cont in ribbing to end of rnd.
Rnd 3: Knit the knits and purl the purls.
Rep Rnds 2 and 3 twice more, and then BO all sts.

Weave in ends.

SCHEMATIC

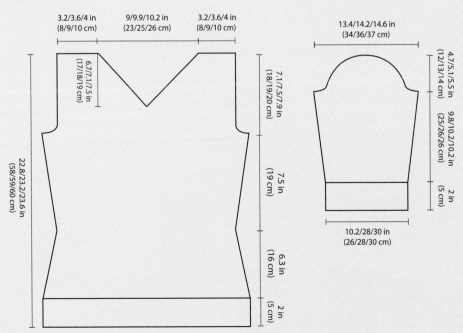

3.2/3.6/4 in (8/9/10 cm) 9/9.9/10.2 in (23/25/26 cm) 3.2/3.6/4 in (8/9/10 cm)

6.7/7.1/7.5 in (17/18/19 cm)

22.8/23.2/23.6 in (58/59/60 cm)

18.9/20.9/22 in (48/53/56 cm)

13.4/14.2/14.6 in (34/36/37 cm)

7.1/7.5/7.9 in (18/19/20 cm)

4.7/5.1/5.5 in (12/13/14 cm)

9.8/10.2/10.2 in (25/26/26 cm)

7.5 in (19 cm)

6.3 in (16 cm)

2 in (5 cm)

2 in (5 cm)

10.2/28/30 in (26/28/30 cm)

CREWNECK
WITH MOCK
TURTLENECK

RAGLAN WITH STRANDED COLORWORK AND MOCK TURTLENECK

Instructions on page 126

ARMHOLE WITH
RAGLAN SHAPING

STRAIGHT
BODY

LONG
SLEEVE

HEM AND
CUFFS IN
STRANDED
PATTERN

STRIPED V-NECK CARDIGAN

Instructions on page 128

V-NECK WITH RIBBED NECKBAND

ARMHOLE WITH SLEEVE CAP

LONG SLEEVE

STRAIGHT BODY

RIBBED HEM AND CUFFS

RAGLAN WITH STRANDED COLORWORK AND MOCK TURTLENECK

Pictured on page 124

BUILDING BLOCK PARTS

BODY SHAPE	Straight
BACK	Basic Sweater 4
FRONT	Basic Sweater 4
SLEEVES	Basic Sweater 1
ARMHOLE	Raglan
SLEEVE LENGTH	Long
NECKLINE	Crewneck with mock turtleneck
HEMS AND CUFFS	Hem and cuffs in stranded pattern

SIZES

Small/Medium/Large (US 6/8, 10/12, 14/16)
Numbers for size Small are listed before the first slash, for size Medium between slashes, and for size Large after the second slash. If only one number is given, it applies to all sizes.

MATERIALS

Schachenmayr Merino Extrafine 120; #3 light weight yarn; 100% wool; 131 yd (120 m), 1.75 oz. (50 g) per skein
- Main color (MC): 8/10/11 skeins #199 black
- Contrasting color (CC): 7/8/9 skeins #121 yellow

Circular knitting needles, US 4 (3.5 mm) and US 6 (4.0 mm), each 32 in. (80 cm) long

GAUGE

In stranded colorwork pattern C on US 6 (4.0 mm) needles, 22 sts and 30 rows = 4 x 4 in. (10 x 10 cm)

In stranded colorwork pattern A on US 6 (4.0 mm) needles, 22 sts and 30 rows = 4 x 4 in. (10 x 10 cm)

STOCKINETTE STITCH

RS: Knit all sts.
WS: Purl all sts.

GARTER STITCH IN ROWS

All rows (RS and WS): Knit all sts.

GARTER STITCH IN ROUNDS

Knit all sts in odd-numbered rnds, purl all sts in even-numbered rnds.

STRANDED PATTERN A

Work in stockinette in stranded colorwork pattern from Colorwork Chart C (in rows). The chart contains both RS and WS rows. Sts are shown as they appear from the RS of the fabric. Repeat the patt rep (6 sts wide) widthwise across, ending with the 3 sts after the patt rep. Work Rows 1–6 of the chart twice heightwise.

STRANDED PATTERN B

Work from Colorwork Chart C (in rounds). The chart shows all rounds as viewed from the RS of the fabric. Repeat the patt rep (6 sts wide) widthwise across. Work Rows 1–6 of the chart twice heightwise.

STRANDED PATTERN C

Work in stockinette stitch in stranded colorwork pattern from Colorwork Chart B. The chart contains both RS and WS rows. Sts are shown as they appear from the RS of the fabric. Begin with the stitch stated in the instructions, work to the end of the patt rep, and then repeat the patt rep widthwise across, ending with the stitch stated in the instructions. Repeat Rows 1–14 heightwise throughout.

ACCENTED DECREASES ON THE FRONT AND BACK

Accented decreases are always worked in RS rows in CC as follows: K1, skp, work in stranded colorwork pattern to last 3 sts of the row, then in CC k2tog, k1. In WS rows, always purl the first 2 sts and the last 2 sts in CC. In RS rows without decreases, always knit the first 2 sts and the last 2 sts in CC.

ACCENTED DECREASES ON THE SLEEVE

Accented decreases are worked the same as for the Front and Back, but all sts are always worked in MC here.

COLORWORK CHART B

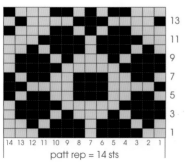

patt rep = 14 sts

COLORWORK CHART C (IN ROWS)

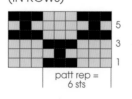

patt rep = 6 sts

COLORWORK CHART C (IN ROUNDS)

patt rep = 6 sts

KNITTING SYMBOLS

■ = St st in MC (black)
□ = St st in CC (yellow)

RAGLAN WITH CABLE PATTERN AND TURTLENECK

Instructions on page 134

ROUND NECKLINE WITH TURTLENECK

ARMHOLE WITH RAGLAN SHAPING

LONG SLEEVE

STRAIGHT BODY

RIBBED HEM AND CUFFS

RAGLAN WITH LACE SLEEVES, HEM, AND CUFFS

Pictured on page 130

BUILDING BLOCK PARTS

BODY SHAPE	Straight
BACK	Basic Sweater 1
FRONT	Basic Sweater 1
SLEEVE	Basic Sweater 5
ARMHOLE	Raglan
SLEEVE LENGTH	Long
NECKLINE	Round neckline with rolled edge
HEMS AND CUFFS	Hem and cuffs in lace pattern

SIZES

Small/Medium/Large (US 6/8, 10/12, 14/16)

Numbers for size Small are listed before the first slash, for size Medium between slashes, and for size Large after the second slash. If only one number is given, it applies to all sizes.

MATERIALS

Schachenmayr Merino Extrafine 120; #3 light weight yarn; 100% wool; 131 yd (120 m), 1.75 oz. (50 g) per skein

- 10/11/13 skeins #131 Cherry

Circular knitting needles, US 4 (3.5 mm) and US 6 (4.0 mm), each 32 in. (80 cm) long

GAUGE

In stockinette stitch on US 6 (4.0 mm) needles, 22 sts and 30 rows = 4 x 4 in. (10 x 10 cm)

In lace pattern A on US 4 (3.5 mm) needles, 21 sts and 32 rows = 4 x 4 in. (10 x 10 cm)

In lace pattern B on US 6 (4.0 mm) needles, 20 sts and 28 rows = 4 x 4 in. (10 x 10 cm)

STOCKINETTE STITCH IN ROWS

RS: Knit all sts.

WS: Purl all sts.

STOCKINETTE STITCH IN ROUNDS

All rounds (RS): Knit all stitches.

LACE PATTERN A

Work from Stitch Pattern Chart E. Only RS rows are shown in the chart; in WS rows, purl all sts and yarn overs. Begin

with the 7 sts before the patt rep, repeat the patt rep widthwise, and end with the 6 sts after the patt rep. Work Rows 1–16 once heightwise.

LACE PATTERN B

Work from Stitch Pattern Chart A. Only RS rows are shown in the chart; in WS rows, work all sts as they appear, and purl the yarn overs. Begin with the sts before the patt rep, repeat the patt rep widthwise across, and end with the sts after the patt rep. Repeat Rows 1–12 of the chart heightwise throughout.

ACCENTED DECREASES

Accented decreases are always worked in RS rows, at both ends of the row as follows: K1, skp, work in pattern to last 3 sts of the row, then k2tog, k1. In WS rows, always purl the first 2 sts and the last 2 sts of the row. In RS rows without decreases, always knit the first 2 sts and the last 2 sts of the row.

STITCH PATTERN CHART A
Stitch count is a multiple of 10 + 15

patt rep = 10 sts

STITCH PATTERN CHART E
Stitch count is a multiple of 10 + 13

patt rep = 10 sts

KNITTING SYMBOLS

- ■ = knit 1 st
- − = purl 1 st
- ○ = make 1 yarn over
- ◢ = knit 2 sts together
- ◣ = slip 1, knit 1, pass the slipped st over
- ▲ = slip 1, knit 2 sts together, pass the slipped st over
- ☐ = no st, for better overview only

INSTRUCTIONS

BACK

Using US 4 (3.5 mm) needles, CO 103/113/123 sts, and for hem ribbing, work 16 rows in lace pattern A; *at the same time*, in the last row, evenly distributed, inc 2/4/0 sts (= 105/117/123 sts). Change to US 6 (4.0 mm) needles, and continue in St st.

For raglan shaping, after having worked 13.8 in. (35 cm) (= 104 rows) from end of ribbing, BO at both ends of the row as follows: BO 6/7/8 sts once; then, in every other row, 3 sts once, and then 2 sts once. Then, at both ends of the row, work accented decrease of 1 st each in every other row 16/21/22 times, and then work accented decrease of 1 st at each end of the row in every 4th row 3/1/1 time(s) more. At 20/20.5/21 in. (51/52/53 cm) (= 154/156/158 rows) from end of ribbing, BO the remaining 45/49/51 sts.

FRONT

Work as the Back, but with neckline shaping. For this, after having worked only 19/19.3/19.7 in. (48/49/50 cm) (= 144/148/150 rows) from end of hem ribbing, BO the middle 19/23/25 sts, and continue both sides separately. For the rounded neckline, BO sts at the neck edge in every other row as follows: 4 sts once, 3 sts 1/2/1 time(s), 2 sts 2/1/2 time(s), and 1 st 1/0/1 time(s). At 20/20.5/21 in. (51/52/53 cm) (= 154/156/158 rows) from end of ribbing, break the working yarn, leaving a not-too-short end, and pull the tail through the last stitch.

SLEEVES (MAKE 2)

Using US 4 (3.5 mm) needles, CO 43/53/53 sts, and for the cuff, work 16 rows in lace pattern A; *at the same time*, in the last row, evenly distributed, inc 2 sts/dec 6 sts/dec 4 sts (= 45/47/49 sts). Change to US 6 (4.0 mm) needles,

and cont in lace pattern B as follows: 0/1/2 st(s) in St st, 45 sts in lace pattern from Stitch Pattern Chart A, 0/1/2 st(s) in St st. For sleeve tapering, after having worked 6 rows from end of cuff, inc 1 st at each end of the row. Rep these incs in every 6th row 0/4/9 times more and in every 8th row 11/9/5 times more (= 69/75/79 sts).

For raglan shaping, after having worked 15/15.4/15.4 in. (38/39/39 cm) (= 106/110/110 rows) from end of cuff, BO at both ends of the row as follows: BO 6/7/8 sts once; then, in every other row, 3 sts once, and then 2 sts once. Then work accented decrease of 1 st at each end of the row in every other row 19/21/22 times. At raglan height 6.3/6.7/7.1 in. (16/17/18 cm) (= 44/48/52 rows), BO the remaining 9 sts.

FINISHING

Block all pieces to measurements on a soft surface, moisten, and let dry. Right sides facing each other and wrong sides facing out, sew the sleeves to the Front and Back along the raglan lines. Close side and sleeve seams from the wrong side.

Using US 4 (3.5 mm) needles, pick up and knit 126/130/134 sts from the neckline edge, join into the round, and purl 1 rnd. Then work 16 rnds in St st. BO all sts, and weave in ends.

SCHEMATIC

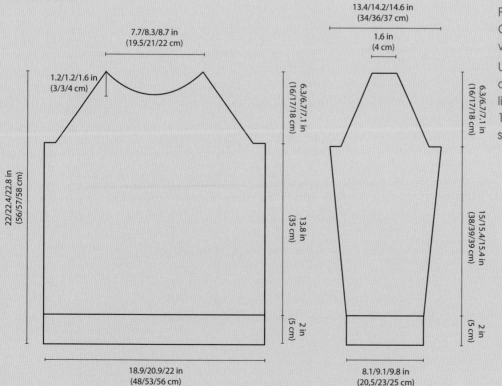

7.7/8.3/8.7 in
(19.5/21/22 cm)

1.2/1.2/1.6 in
(3/3/4 cm)

22/22.4/22.8 in
(56/57/58 cm)

18.9/20.9/22 in
(48/53/56 cm)

13.4/14.2/14.6 in
(34/36/37 cm)

1.6 in
(4 cm)

6.3/6.7/7.1 in
(16/17/18 cm)

13.8 in
(35 cm)

2 in
(5 cm)

6.3/6.7/7.1 in
(16/17/18 cm)

15/15.4/15.4 in
(38/39/39 cm)

2 in
(5 cm)

8.1/9.1/9.8 in
(20,5/23/25 cm)

RAGLAN WITH CABLE PATTERN AND TURTLENECK

Pictured on page 131

BUILDING BLOCK PARTS

BODY SHAPE	Straight
BACK	Basic Sweater 6
FRONT	Basic Sweater 6
SLEEVE	Basic Sweater 6
ARMHOLE	Raglan
SLEEVE LENGTH	Long
NECKLINE	Round neckline with turtleneck
HEMS AND CUFFS	Ribbed hem and cuffs

SIZES

Small/Medium/Large (US 6/8, 10/12, 14/16)
Numbers for size Small are listed before the first slash, for size Medium between slashes, and for size Large after the second slash. If only one number is given, it applies to all sizes.

MATERIALS

Schachenmayr Merino Extrafine 120; #3 light weight yarn; 100% wool; 131 yd (120 m), 1.75 oz. (50 g) per skein

• 12/13/15 skeins #102 natural

Circular knitting needles, US 4 (3.5 mm) and US 6 (4.0 mm), each 32 in. (80 cm) long

Cable needle (cn)

GAUGE

In double seed stitch on US 6 (4.0 mm) needles, 22 sts and 34 rows = 4 x 4 in. (10 x 10 cm)

In cable pattern 1 on US 6 (4.0 mm) needles, 58 sts = 8.3 in. (21 cm)

STOCKINETTE STITCH

RS: Knit all sts.
WS: Purl all sts.

RIBBING IN ROWS

RS: Alternate k1, p1.
WS: Work all sts as they appear— knit the knits and purl the purls.

RIBBING IN ROUNDS

All rounds (RS): Alternate k1, p1.

DOUBLE SEED STITCH

Row 1: Alternate k1, p1.
Row 2: Knit the knits and purl the purls.
Row 3: Alternate p1, k1.
Row 4: Knit the knits and purl the purls.
Rep Rows 1–4 throughout.

CABLE PATTERN 1

Work from Stitch Pattern Chart B. Only RS rows are shown in the chart; in WS rows, work all sts as they appear (knit the knits and purl the purls), and purl the slipped sts. Work the patt rep (58 sts wide) widthwise across once, and then rep Rows 1–12 heightwise throughout.

CABLE PATTERN 2

Work from Stitch Pattern Chart C. Only RS rows are shown in the chart; in WS rows, work all sts as they appear (knit the knits and purl the purls), and purl the slipped sts. Work the patt rep (18 sts wide) widthwise across once, and then rep Rows 1–12 heightwise throughout.

ACCENTED DECREASES

Accented decreases are always worked in RS rows, at both ends of the row, as follows: K1, skp, work in pattern to last 3 sts of the row, then k2tog, k1. In WS rows, always purl the first 2 sts and the last 2 sts of the row. In RS rows without decreases, always knit the first 2 sts and the last 2 sts of the row.

SCHEMATIC

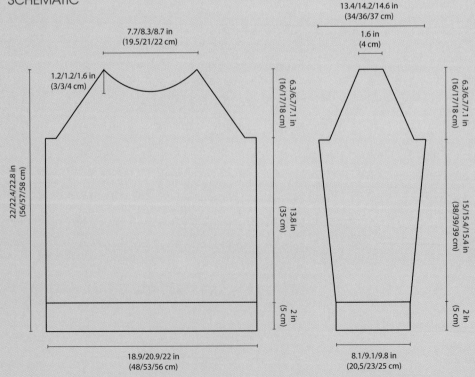

7.7/8.3/8.7 in (19.5/21/22 cm)

1.2/1.2/1.6 in (3/3/4 cm)

22/22.4/22.8 in (56/57/58 cm)

18.9/20.9/22 in (48/53/56 cm)

13.4/14.2/14.6 in (34/36/37 cm)

1.6 in (4 cm)

6.3/6.7/7.1 in (16/17/18 cm)

13.8 in (35 cm)

2 in (5 cm)

6.3/6.7/7.1 in (16/17/18 cm)

15/15.4/15.4 in (38/39/39 cm)

2 in (5 cm)

8.1/9.1/9.8 in (20,5/23/25 cm)

end of cuff, inc 1 st at each end of the row. Rep these incs in every 6th row 7/2/0 times more and in every 8th row 7/11/12 times more (= 75/79/81 sts).

For raglan shaping, after having worked 15/15.4/15.4 in. (38/39/39 cm) (= 116/118/118 rows) from end of ribbing, BO sts at both ends of the row as follows: 6/7/8 sts each once, and then, in every other row, 3 sts once and 2 sts once. Then, at both ends of the row, in every other row, work accented decrease of 1 st each 22/23/23 times, and

then in every 4th row 0/0/1 time(s) more. At raglan height 6.3/6.7/7.1 in. (16/17/18 cm) (= 50/52/54 rows), BO the remaining 9 sts.

FINISHING

Block all pieces to measurements on a soft surface, moisten, and let dry. Right sides facing each other and wrong sides facing out, sew the sleeves to the Front and Back along the raglan lines. Close side and sleeve seams from the wrong side.

Using US 4 (3.5 mm) needles, pick up and knit sts for the button band as follows: along the front edge of right and left Fronts, 118/122/122 sts each, and work ribbing for 1.2 in. (3 cm) (= 8 rows). When working the buttonhole band on the right Front, after only 3 rows of ribbing, incorporate 6 buttonholes as follows: 5/7/7 sts ribbing, * BO 2 sts, 19 sts ribbing, rep from * 4 times more, BO 2 sts, 6/8/8 sts ribbing. In the next WS row, CO the same number of sts over the previously bound-off sts.

Using US 4 (3.5 mm) needles, pick up and knit 125/129/133 sts from the neckline edge (including those of the Front bands), and work ribbing for 1.2 in. (3 cm) (= 8 rows). After having worked 3 rows, atop the other buttonholes, work another buttonhole as follows: 3 sts ribbing, BO 2 sts, cont in ribbing to end of row. In the next row, CO the same number of sts over the previously bound-off sts. BO all sts in pattern, and weave in ends. Sew buttons to the left Front band opposite the buttonholes.

SCHEMATIC

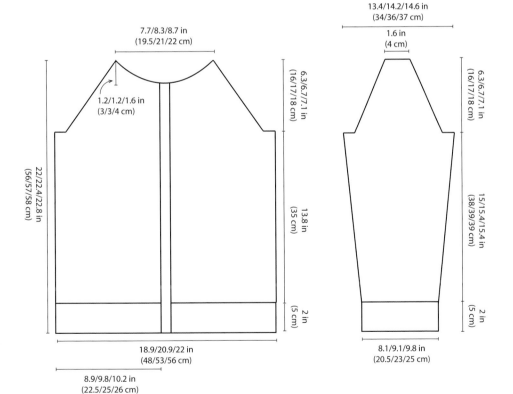

7.7/8.3/8.7 in (19.5/21/22 cm)

1.2/1.2/1.6 in (3/3/4 cm)

6.3/6.7/7.1 in (16/17/18 cm)

22/22.4/22.8 in (56/57/58 cm)

13.8 in (35 cm)

2 in (5 cm)

18.9/20.9/22 in (48/53/56 cm)

8.9/9.8/10.2 in (22.5/25/26 cm)

13.4/14.2/14.6 in (34/36/37 cm)

1.6 in (4 cm)

6.3/6.7/7.1 in (16/17/18 cm)

15/15.4/15.4 in (38/39/39 cm)

2 in (5 cm)

8.1/9.1/9.8 in (20.5/23/25 cm)

ROUND NECKLINE WITH ROLLED EDGE

OVERSIZED WITH STRANDED COLORWORK AND HEM AND CUFFS IN MOSAIC PATTERN

Instructions on page 142

STRAIGHT SLEEVE TOP

LONG SLEEVE

OVERSIZED BODY SHAPE

HEM AND CUFFS IN MOSAIC PATTERN

STRAIGHT WITH MOSAIC HEM AND CUFFS AND SLEEVES IN A LAYERED LOOK

Instructions on page 144

STRAIGHT SLEEVE TOP

STRAIGHT BODY

LONG SLEEVE

HEM AND CUFFS IN MOSAIC PATTERN

ROUND NECKLINE WITH GARTER STITCH NECKBAND

OVERSIZED WITH STRANDED COLORWORK AND HEM AND CUFFS IN MOSAIC PATTERN

Pictured on page 140

BUILDING BLOCK PARTS

BODY SHAPE	Oversized
BACK	Basic Sweater 4
FRONT	Basic Sweater 4
SLEEVE	Basic Sweater 4
ARMHOLE	Straight
SLEEVE LENGTH	Long
NECKLINE	Round neckline with rolled edge
HEMS AND CUFFS	Hem and cuffs in mosaic pattern

SIZES

Small/Medium/Large (US 6/8, 10/12, 14/16)

Numbers for size Small are listed before the first slash, for size Medium between slashes, and for size Large after the second slash. If only one number is given, it applies to all sizes.

MATERIALS

Schachenmayr Merino Extrafine 120; #3 light weight yarn; 100% wool; 131 yd (120 m), 1.75 oz. (50 g) per skein

- Main color (MC): 8/9/11 skeins #169 medium blue
- Contrasting color (CC): 7/8/9 skeins #101 white

Circular knitting needles, US 4 (3.5 mm) and US 6 (4.0 mm), each 40 in. (100 cm) long

GAUGE

In stranded colorwork pattern on US 6 (4.0 mm) needles, 22 sts and 30 rows = 4 x 4 in. (10 x 10 cm)

In mosaic pattern on US 4 (3.5 mm) needles, 22 sts and 30 rows = 4 x 4 in. (10 x 10 cm)

STOCKINETTE STITCH

RS: Knit all sts.
WS: Purl all sts.

COLORWORK CHART B

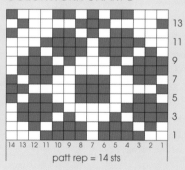

patt rep = 14 sts

KNITTING SYMBOLS

■ = St st in MC (medium blue)
□ = St st in CC (white)

STOCKINETTE STITCH IN ROUNDS

All rounds (RS): Knit all stitches.

RIBBING IN ROWS

RS: Alternate k1, p1.
WS: Work all sts as they appear— knit the knits and purl the purls.

RIBBING IN ROUNDS

All rounds (RS): Alternate k1, p1.

GARTER STITCH

All rows (RS and WS): Knit all sts.

MOSAIC PATTERN

RS rows: *K1 in contrasting color (CC), k1 in main color (MC), rep from * throughout, ending with k1 in CC.
WS rows: *P1 in MC, p1 in CC, rep from * throughout, ending with p1 in MC.

STRANDED PATTERN

Work in stockinette stitch in stranded colorwork pattern from Colorwork Chart B. The chart contains both RS and WS rows. Sts are shown as they appear from the RS of the fabric. Begin with the stitch stated in the instructions, work to the end of the patt rep, and then repeat the patt rep widthwise across, ending with the stitch stated in the instructions. Repeat Rows 1–14 heightwise throughout.

INSTRUCTIONS

BACK

Using US 4 (3.5 mm) needles and CC (white), CO 153/177/197 sts, and work as follows: 4 rows garter st in CC, 10 rows mosaic pattern, 4 rows garter st in CC. Change to US 6 (4.0 mm) needles, and cont in St st in stranded pattern, beginning with the 1st/3rd/7th st of the chart and ending with the 13th/11th/7th st of the chart. At 21/21.3/21.7 in. (53/54/55 cm) (= 158/162/166 rows) from hem ribbing, BO all sts.

FRONT

Work as the Back, but with neckline shaping. For this, after having worked only 19/19.3/19.7 in. (48/49/50 cm) (= 144/148/150 rows) from end of hem ribbing, BO the middle 19/23/25 sts, and continue both sides separately. For the rounded neckline, BO sts at the neck edge in every other row as follows: BO 4 sts once, 3 sts 3/3/2 times, 2 sts 1/1/2 time(s), and 1 st 1/1/2 time(s). At 21/21.3/21.7 in. (53/54/55 cm) (= 158/162/166 rows) from end of ribbing, BO the remaining 51/61/70 sts for each shoulder.

SLEEVES (MAKE 2)

Using US 4 (3.5 mm) needles and CC, CO 45/51/55 sts, and work as follows: 4 rows garter st in CC, 10 rows mosaic pattern, 4 rows garter st in CC. Change to US 6 (4.0 mm) needles, and cont in St st in stranded colorwork pattern, beginning with the 6th/3rd/1st st of the chart and ending with the 8th/11th/13th st of the chart. Incorporate the increased sts into the stitch pattern.

For sleeve tapering, after having worked 6/8/8 rows from end of cuff, inc 1 st at each end of the row. Rep these incs in every 6th row 13/10/10 times more and in every 8th row 0/3/3 times more (= 73/79/83 sts). At 12/12.6/12.6 in. (30.5/32/32 cm) (= 92/98/98 rows) from end of cuff, BO all sts.

FINISHING

Block all pieces to measurements on a soft surface, moisten, and let dry. Close shoulder and side seams from the wrong side, leaving the upper 6.5/7.1/7.5 in. (16.5/18/19 cm) open for the armholes. Seam the sleeves right sides facing each other and wrong sides facing out, and then sew the sleeves into the armholes from the wrong side.

Using US 4 (3.5 mm) needles and CC, pick up and knit 126/130/134 sts from the neckline edge, join into the round, and purl 1 rnd. Then work 16 rnds in St st. BO all sts, and weave in ends.

SCHEMATIC

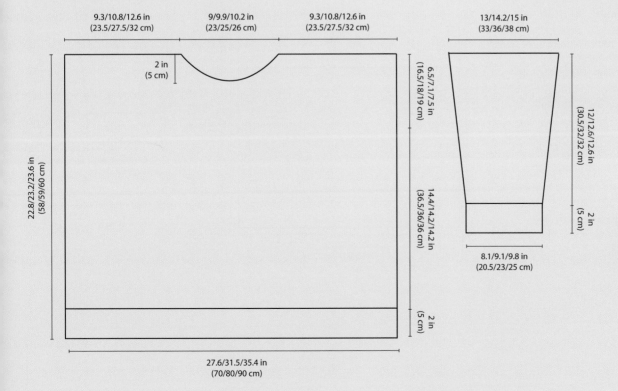

9.3/10.8/12.6 in (23.5/27.5/32 cm)

9/9.9/10.2 in (23/25/26 cm)

9.3/10.8/12.6 in (23.5/27.5/32 cm)

13/14.2/15 in (33/36/38 cm)

2 in (5 cm)

6.5/7.1/7.5 in (16.5/18/19 cm)

12/12.6/12.6 in (30.5/32/32 cm)

22.8/23.2/23.6 in (58/59/60 cm)

14.4/14.2/14.2 in (36.5/36/36 cm)

2 in (5 cm)

2 in (5 cm)

8.1/9.1/9.8 in (20.5/23/25 cm)

27.6/31.5/35.4 in (70/80/90 cm)

STRAIGHT WITH MOSAIC HEM AND CUFFS AND SLEEVES IN A LAYERED LOOK

Pictured on page 141

BUILDING BLOCK PARTS

BODY SHAPE	Straight
BACK	Basic Sweater 1
FRONT	Basic Sweater 1
SLEEVES	Basic Sweater 1
ARMHOLE	Straight
SLEEVE LENGTH	Long
NECKLINE	Crewneck with garter stitch neckband
HEMS AND CUFFS	Hem and cuffs in mosaic pattern
SPECIAL FEATURES	In this sweater, the hem and cuff pattern is additionally incorporated into Front and Back as mosaic border, while the sleeves are worked in a layered look. The neckband is knit in garter stitch.

SIZES

Small/Medium/Large (US 6/8, 10/12, 14/16)

Numbers for size Small are listed before the first slash, for size Medium between slashes, and for size Large after the second slash. If only one number is given, it applies to all sizes.

MATERIALS

Schachenmayr Merino Extrafine 120; #3 light weight yarn; 100% wool; 131 yd (120 m), 1.75 oz. (50 g) per skein

- Main color (MC): 6/8/9 skeins #155 navy
- Contrasting color (CC): 6/7/8 skeins #104 sand heathered

Circular knitting needles, US 4 (3.5 mm) and US 6 (4.0 mm), each 32 in. (80 cm) long

2 spare US 6 circular needles

GAUGE

In stockinette stitch on US 6 (4.0 mm) needles, 22 sts and 30 rows = 4 x 4 in. (10 x 10 cm)

SCHEMATIC

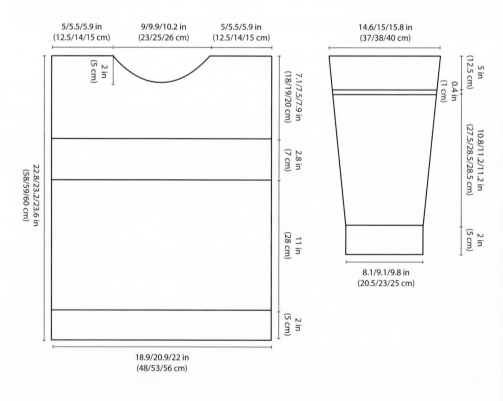

5/5.5/5.9 in (12.5/14/15 cm)

9/9.9/10.2 in (23/25/26 cm)

5/5.5/5.9 in (12.5/14/15 cm)

2 in (5 cm)

7.1/7.5/7.9 in (18/19/20 cm)

2.8 in (7 cm)

22.8/23.2/23.6 in (58/59/60 cm)

11 in (28 cm)

2 in (5 cm)

18.9/20.9/22 in (48/53/56 cm)

14.6/15/15.8 in (37/38/40 cm)

5 in (12.5 cm)

0.4 in (1 cm)

10.8/11.2/11.2 in (27.5/28.5/28.5 cm)

2 in (5 cm)

8.1/9.1/9.8 in (20.5/23/25 cm)

STOCKINETTE STITCH

RS: Knit all sts.
WS: Purl all sts.

GARTER STITCH IN ROWS

All rows (RS and WS): Knit all sts.

GARTER STITCH IN ROUNDS

Knit all sts in odd-numbered rnds,
purl all sts in even-numbered rnds.

MOSAIC PATTERN

RS rows: *K1 in contrasting color (CC),
k1 in main color (MC), rep from *
throughout, ending with k1 in CC.
WS rows: *P1 in MC, p1 in CC, rep from
* throughout, ending with p1 in MC.

INSTRUCTIONS

BACK

Using US 4 (3.5 mm) needles, CO
105/117/123 sts in CC (sand heathered), and for hem ribbing, work as
follows: 4 rows garter st in CC, 10 rows
mosaic pattern, 4 rows garter st in MC
(navy). Change to US 6 (4.0 mm) needles, and cont in St st in CC. After having worked 11 in. (28 cm) (= 84 rows)
from end of ribbing, work a mosaic
border as follows: 4 rows garter st in MC,
10 rows mosaic pattern, 4 rows garter
st in CC. Then cont in St st in MC. After
having worked 21/21.3/21.7 in.
(53/54/55 cm) (= 158/162/166 rows)
from hem ribbing, BO all sts.

FRONT

Work as the Back, but with neckline
shaping. For this, after having worked
only 19/19.3/19.7 in. (48/49/50 cm) (=
144/148/150 rows) from end of hem
ribbing, BO the middle 19/23/25 sts, and
continue both sides separately. For the
rounded neckline, BO sts at the neck
edge in every other row as follows: BO
4 sts once, 3 sts 3/3/2 times, 2 sts 1/1/2
time(s), and 1 st 1/1/2 time(s). At
21/21.3/21.7 in. (53/54/55 cm) (= 158/
162/166 rows) from end of hem ribbing,
BO the remaining 27/31/33 sts for each
shoulder.

SLEEVES (MAKE 2)

For the bottom part of the sleeve, using the smaller needle size and CC,
CO 45/51/55 sts, and work as follows:
4 rows garter st in CC, 10 rows mosaic
pattern, 4 rows garter st in MC.
Change to US 6 (4.0 mm) needles, and
cont in St st in CC.

For sleeve tapering, after having worked
6/8/8 rows from end of cuff, inc 1 st at
each end of the row. Rep these incs in
every 6th row 13/10/10 times more and
in every 8th row 0/3/3 times more (=
73/79/83 sts). After 11.8/12.2/12.2 in.
(30/31/31 cm) (= 90/94/94 rows) from
end of cuff, transfer all sts to a spare
needle for holding.

For the top part of the sleeve, CO
73/79/83 sts in MC, and work 4 rows in
garter st for the upper cuff. Then work

4 rows in St st, and transfer all sts to a
spare needle for holding.

To join the two sleeve parts, now place
the bottom part of the sleeve under
the top part of the sleeve, both pieces
right side up. Then, using MC and a
spare needle, knit 1 st from the top part
of the sleeve together with 1 st from
the bottom part. Cont in MC (navy) in
St st. For further sleeve tapering, after
having worked 6/10/10 rows from end
of upper cuff, inc 1 st at each end of
the row. Rep these incs in every 8th row
3/2/2 times more (= 81/85/89 sts). At
5/4.7/4.7 in. (12.5/12/12 cm) from end
of upper cuff, BO all sts.

FINISHING

Block all pieces to measurements on a
soft surface, moisten, and let dry. Close
shoulder and side seams from the
wrong side, leaving the upper
7.1/7.5/7.9 in. (18/19/20 cm) open for
the armholes. Seam the sleeves right
sides facing each other and wrong
sides facing out, and then sew the
sleeves into the armholes from the
wrong side.

For the neckband, using MC, pick up
and knit 126/130/134 sts from the neckline edge, join into the round, and work
garter st for 1.2 in. (3 cm) (= 12 rnds). BO
all sts, and weave in ends.

ROUND
NECKLINE
WITH ROLLED
EDGE

STRAIGHT
WITH
SLEEVE
CAP AND
STRIPES
Instructions on page 148

ARMHOLE
WITH SLEEVE
CAP

STRAIGHT
BODY

LONG
SLEEVE

HEM AND
CUFFS IN
CABLE
PATTERN

ROUND
NECKLINE
WITH ROLLED
EDGE

LONG
SLEEVE

STRAIGHT
ARMHOLE

TWO
COLORED
WITH
ROLLED
EDGES

Instructions on page 150

STRAIGHT
BODY

ROLLED EDGES

STRAIGHT WITH SLEEVE CAP AND STRIPES

Pictured on page 146

BUILDING BLOCK PARTS

BODY SHAPE	Straight
BACK	Basic Sweater 2
FRONT	Basic Sweater 2
SLEEVE	Basic Sweater 2
ARMHOLE	Sleeve cap
SLEEVE LENGTH	Long
NECKLINE	Round neckline with rolled edge
HEMS AND CUFFS	Hem and cuffs in cable pattern
SPECIAL FEATURES	In this sweater, only stripe sequence A of Basic Sweater 2 is used.

SIZES

Small/Medium/Large (US 6/8, 10/12, 14/16)

Numbers for size Small are listed before the first slash, for size Medium between slashes, and for size Large after the second slash. If only one number is given, it applies to all sizes.

MATERIALS

Schachenmayr Merino Extrafine 120; #3 light weight yarn; 100% wool; 131 yd (120 m), 1.75 oz. (50 g) per skein

- Main color (MC): 8/9/11 skeins #198 dark gray heathered
- Contrasting color (CC): 4/5/6 skeins #175 lemon

Circular knitting needles, US 4 (3.5 mm) and US 6 (4.0 mm), each 32 in. (80 cm) long

Cable needle (cn)

GAUGE

In cable pattern on US 4 (3.5 mm) needles, 24 sts and 32 rows = 4 x 4 in. (10 x 10 cm)

In stockinette stitch on US 6 (4.0 mm) needles, 22 sts and 30 rows = 4 x 4 in. (10 x 10 cm)

STOCKINETTE STITCH IN ROWS

RS: Knit all sts.
WS: Purl all sts.

STOCKINETTE STITCH IN ROUNDS

All rounds (RS): Knit all stitches.

CABLE PATTERN

Row 1 (RS): *P2, k2, p2, k4, rep from * to last 6 sts of row, ending with p2, k2, p2.

Row 2 (WS): Knit the knits and purl the purls.

Row 3 (RS): *P2, k2, p2, hold 2 sts on cn in back of work, k2, then k2 from cn, rep from * to last 6 sts of row, ending with p2, k2, p2.

Row 4 (WS): Knit the knits and purl the purls.

Rep Rows 1–4 throughout.

STRIPE SEQUENCE A

Alternate 2 rows in CC (lemon), 2 rows in MC (dark gray heathered).

INSTRUCTIONS

BACK

Using US 4 (3.5 mm) needles and MC (dark gray heathered), CO 116/126/136 sts, and for hem ribbing, work 16 rows in cable pattern; in the last WS row, evenly distributed, dec 11/9/13 sts (= 105/117/123 sts). Change to US 6 (4.0 mm) needles, and cont in MC in St st. After having worked 11/10.6/10.6 in. (28/27/27 cm) (= 86/82/82 rows) from end of ribbing, work 44/52/52 rows in St st in stripe sequence A, and then cont in CC (lemon) in St st.

At the same time, for armhole shaping, after having worked 13.8 in. (35 cm) (= 104 rows) from end of ribbing, BO 3/4/5 sts at each end of the row once; then, in every other row, BO another 2 sts twice and 1 st 2/2/0 times. At 21/21.3/21.7 in. (53/54/55 cm) (= 158/162/166 rows) from hem ribbing, BO all sts.

FRONT

Work as the Back, but with neckline shaping. For this, after having worked 19/19.3/19.7 in. (48/49/50 cm) (= 144/148/150 rows) from end of hem ribbing, BO the middle 19/23/25 sts, and continue both sides separately. For the rounded neckline, BO sts at the neck edge in every other row as follows: BO 4 sts once, 3 sts 3/3/2 times, 2 sts 1/1/2 time(s), and 1 st 1/1/2 time(s). At 21/21.3/21.7 in. (53/54/55 cm) (= 158/162/166 rows) from end of ribbing, BO the remaining 18/21/24 sts for each shoulder.

SLEEVES (MAKE 2)

Using US 4 (3.5 mm) needles, CO 46/56/66 sts, and work 16 rows in cable pattern; *at the same time*, in the last row, evenly distributed, dec 1/5/11 st(s) (= 45/51/55 sts). Change to US 6 (4.0 mm) needles, and cont in MC in St st. For sleeve tapering, after having worked 6/8/8 rows from end of cuff, inc 1 st at each end of the row. Rep these incs in every 6th row 7/2/0 times more and in every 8th row 7/11/12 times more (= 75/79/81 sts).

After having worked 12.6/13/13 in. (32/33/33 cm) (= 98/100/100 rows) from end of ribbing, work 44/52/52 rows in St st in stripe sequence A, and then cont in CC in St st.

At the same time, for sleeve cap shaping, at a height of 15/15.4/15.4 in. (38/39/39 cm) (= 116/118/118 rows) from end of ribbing, BO 3/4/5 sts at each end of the row once, and then in every other row as follows: BO 2 sts twice, 1 st 10/12/14 times, 2 sts 5/4/3 times, and 3 sts once. At sleeve cap height of 4.7/5.1/5.5 in. (12/13/14 cm) (= 38/40/42 rows), BO the remaining 15/17/17 sts.

FINISHING

Block all pieces to measurements on a soft surface, moisten, and let dry.

Close sleeve, shoulder, and side seams from the wrong side, and then sew the sleeves into the armholes from the wrong side.

Using US 4 (3.5 mm) needles, pick up and knit 126/130/134 sts from the neckline edge, join into the round, and purl 1 rnd. Then work 16 rnds in St st. BO all sts, and weave in ends.

SCHEMATIC

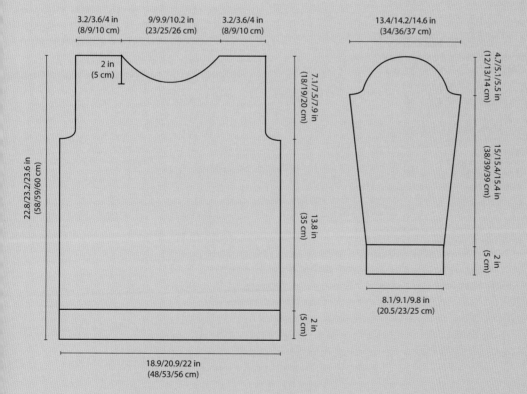

TWO COLORED WITH ROLLED EDGES

Pictured on page 147

BUILDING BLOCK PARTS

BODY SHAPE	Straight
BACK	Basic Sweater 1
FRONT	Basic Sweater 1
SLEEVE	Basic Sweater 1
ARMHOLE	Straight
SLEEVE LENGTH	Long
NECKLINE	Round neckline with rolled edge
HEMS AND CUFFS	Rolled edge
SPECIAL FEATURES	Basic Sweater 1 is here worked in two colors—to ensure equal width of the two-color panels, Front and Back are both one stitch wider than the Basic Sweater.

SIZES

Small/Medium/Large (US 6/8, 10/12, 14/16)

Numbers for size Small are listed before the first slash, for size Medium between slashes, and for size Large after the second slash. If only one number is given, it applies to all sizes.

MATERIALS

Schachenmayr Merino Extrafine 120; #3 light weight yarn; 100% wool; 131 yd (120 m), 1.75 oz. (50 g) per skein

- Main color (MC): 6/7/8 skeins #146 plum
- Contrasting color (CC): 5/6/7 skeins #190 light gray heathered

Circular knitting needles, US 4 (3.5 mm) and US 6 (4.0 mm), each 32 in. (80 cm) long

GAUGE

In stockinette stitch on US 6 (4.0 mm) needles, 22 sts and 30 rows = 4 x 4 in. (10 x 10 cm)

STOCKINETTE STITCH IN ROWS

RS: Knit all sts.
WS: Purl all sts.

STOCKINETTE STITCH IN ROUNDS

All rounds (RS): Knit all stitches.

INSTRUCTIONS

BACK

Using US 4 (3.5 mm) needles, first CO 53/59/62 sts in CC (light gray heathered), and then CO 53/59/62 sts more in MC (plum). In this same color segmentation, for the rolled edge, work 13 rows in St st, and then knit 1 WS row. Change to US 6 (4.0 mm) needles, and cont in same color segmentation. When changing colors, cross strands in back of work to avoid unsightly holes in the color change spots. At 21/21.3/21.7 in. (53/54/55 cm) (= 158/162/166 rows) from hem ribbing, BO all sts.

FRONT

Work as the Back, but in opposite color segmentation, and with neckline shaping. Accordingly, first CO 53/59/62 sts in MC and after this, 53/59/62 sts in CC, and cont in this reverse color placement.

For the neckline, after having worked 19/19.3/19.7 in. (48/49/50 cm) (= 144/148/150 rows) from end of ribbing, BO the middle 20/24/25 sts, and continue both sides separately. For the rounded neckline, BO sts at the neck edge in every other row as follows: BO 4 sts once, 3 sts 3/3/2 times, 2 sts 1/1/2 time(s), and 1 st 1/1/2 time(s). At

21/21.3/21.7 in. (53/54/55 cm) (= 158/162/166 rows) from end of hem ribbing, BO the remaining 27/31/33 sts for each shoulder.

RIGHT SLEEVE

Using US 4 (3.5 mm) needles and MC, CO 45/51/55 sts, and for the rolled edge, work 13 rows in St st. Then knit 1 WS row. Change to US 6 (4.0 mm) needles, and continue in St st. For sleeve tapering, after having worked 6/8/8 rows from end of cuff, inc 1 st at each

end of the row. Rep these incs in every 6th row 13/10/10 times more and in every 8th row 4/6/6 times more (= 81/85/89 sts). At 16.1/16.5/16.5 in. (41/42/42 cm) (= 124/126/126 rows) from end of cuff, BO all sts.

Work the second sleeve the same way, but in CC.

FINISHING

Block all pieces to measurements on a soft surface, moisten, and let dry. Close

shoulder and side seams from the wrong side, leaving the upper 7.1/7.5/7.9 in. (18/19/20 cm) open for armhole. Seam the sleeves right sides facing each other and wrong sides facing out. Right sides facing each other and wrong sides facing out, sew each sleeve to the color-matched side of the sweater.

Using US 4 (3.5 mm) needles and MC, pick up and knit 126/130/134 sts from the neckline edge, join into the round, and purl 1 rnd. Then work 16 rnds in St st. BO all sts, and weave in ends.

SCHEMATIC

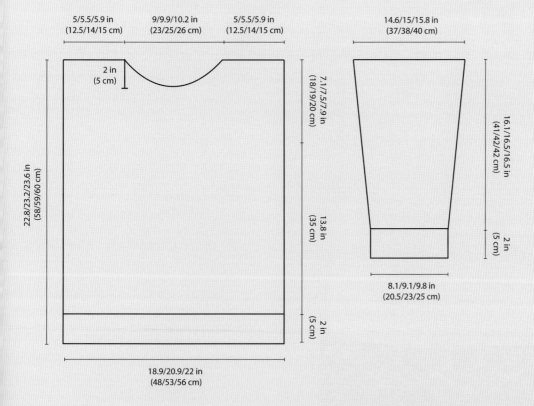

5/5.5/5.9 in (12.5/14/15 cm)
9/9.9/10.2 in (23/25/26 cm)
5/5.5/5.9 in (12.5/14/15 cm)
14.6/15/15.8 in (37/38/40 cm)

2 in (5 cm)

7.1/7.5/7.9 in (18/19/20 cm)

16.1/16.5/16.5 in (41/42/42 cm)

22.8/23.2/23.6 in (58/59/60 cm)

13.8 in (35 cm)

2 in (5 cm)

2 in (5 cm)

8.1/9.1/9.8 in (20.5/23/25 cm)

18.9/20.9/22 in (48/53/56 cm)

ROUND NECKLINE WITH NECKBAND IN STRANDED COLORWORK PATTERN

FITTED WITH SLEEVE CAP AND HEM AND CUFFS IN STRANDED COLORWORK

Instructions on page 154

ARMHOLE WITH SLEEVE CAP

TAILORED FIT

LONG SLEEVE

HEM AND CUFFS WITH STRANDED COLORWORK PATTERN

OVERSIZED WITH CABLES AND ELONGATED BACK

Instructions on page 156

ROUND NECKLINE WITH RIBBED NECKBAND

STRAIGHT SLEEVE TOP

OVERSIZED BODY SHAPE

LONG SLEEVE

RIBBED HEM AND CUFFS

FITTED WITH SLEEVE CAP AND HEM AND CUFFS IN STRANDED COLORWORK

Pictured on page 152

BUILDING BLOCK PARTS

BODY SHAPE	Fitted
BACK	Basic Sweater 1
FRONT	Basic Sweater 1
SLEEVE	Basic Sweater 1
ARMHOLE	Sleeve with sleeve cap
SLEEVE LENGTH	Long
NECKLINE	Round neckline with neckband in stranded colorwork pattern
HEM AND CUFFS	Hem and cuffs in stranded colorwork pattern
SPECIAL FEATURES	In this sweater, hem and cuffs feature a colorwork play: garter stitch rows on the neckband are worked in main color instead of in contrasting color.

SIZES

Small/Medium/Large (US 6/8, 10/12, 14/16)

Numbers for size Small are listed before the first slash, for size Medium between slashes, and for size Large after the second slash. If only one number is given, it applies to all sizes.

MATERIALS

Schachenmayr Merino Extrafine 120; #3 light weight yarn; 100% wool; 131 yd (120 m), 1.75 oz. (50 g) per skein

- Main color (MC): 8/9/10 skeins #175 lemon
- Contrasting color (CC): 3/3/4 skeins #199 black

Circular knitting needles, US 4 (3.5 mm) and US 6 (4.0 mm), each 32 in. (80 cm) long

GAUGE

In stranded colorwork pattern on US 6 (4.0 mm) needles, 22 sts and 30 rows = 4 x 4 in. (10 x 10 cm)

In stockinette stitch on US 6 (4.0 mm) needles, 22 sts and 30 rows = 4 x 4 in. (10 x 10 cm)

STOCKINETTE STITCH IN ROWS

RS: Knit all sts.
WS: Purl all sts.

STOCKINETTE STITCH IN ROUNDS

All rounds (RS): Knit all stitches.

GARTER STITCH IN ROWS

All rows (RS and WS): Knit all sts.

GARTER STITCH IN ROUNDS

Knit all sts in odd-numbered rnds, purl all sts in even-numbered rnds.

STRANDED PATTERN IN ROWS

Work in stockinette in stranded colorwork pattern from Colorwork Chart C. The chart contains both RS and WS rows. Sts are shown as they appear from the RS of the fabric. Repeat the patt rep (6 sts wide) widthwise across, ending with the 3 sts after the patt rep. Work Rows 1–6 of the chart twice heightwise.

STRANDED PATTERN IN ROUNDS

Work in stockinette in stranded colorwork pattern from Colorwork Chart C. The chart shows all rounds as stitches appear on the right side of the fabric. Repeat the patt rep (6 sts wide) widthwise across; ignore the 3 sts after the patt rep, as these are not worked. Work Rnds 1–6 of the chart twice heightwise.

ACCENTED DECREASES

Accented decreases are always worked in RS rows as follows: K1, skp, cont in St st to last 3 sts of the row, then k2tog, k1. In WS rows, always purl the first 2 sts and the last 2 sts of the row. In RS rows without decreases, always knit the first 2 sts and the last 2 sts of the row.

ACCENTED INCREASES

Accented increases are always worked in RS rows as follows: K1, inc 1 st from the bar between sts twisted, cont in St st to last st of the row, inc 1 st from the bar between sts twisted, k1. In WS rows, always purl the first 2 sts and the last 2 sts of the row. In RS rows without increases, always knit the first 2 sts and the last 2 sts of the row.

COLORWORK CHART C

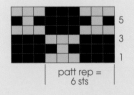

patt rep = 6 sts

KNITTING SYMBOLS

☐ = St st in MC (lemon)
■ = St st in CC (black)

INSTRUCTIONS

BACK

Using US 4 (3.5 mm) needles and CC (black), CO 105/117/123 sts, and work as follows: 4 rows garter st in CC, 12 rows in stranded pattern, 4 rows garter st in CC. Change to US 6 (4.0 mm) needles, and cont in MC (lemon) in St st.

After having worked 2/1.6/1.6 in. (5/4/4 cm) (= 16/12/12 rows) from end of ribbing, for waist shaping, work 1 accented decrease at each end of the row. Rep accented decreases at each end of the row in every 4th row 8/9/9 times more (= 87/97/103 sts). After having worked 6.7 in. (17 cm) (= 52 rows) from end of ribbing, work 1 accented increase at each end of the row (= 89/99/105 sts). Rep accented increases at both ends of the row in every 4th row 0/4/4 times more and in every 6th row 8/5/5 times more (= 105/117/123 sts).

For armhole shaping, after having worked 13.8 in. (35 cm) (= 104 rows) from end of ribbing, BO 3/4/5 sts at each end of the row once, and then in every other row another 2 sts twice and 1 st 2/2/0 times. At 21/21.3/21.7 in. (53/54/55 cm) (= 158/162/166 rows) from hem ribbing, BO all sts.

FRONT

Work as the Back, but with neckline shaping. For this, after having worked only 19/19.3/19.7 in. (48/49/50 cm) (= 144/148/150 rows) from end of hem ribbing, BO the middle 19/23/25 sts, and continue both sides separately. For the rounded neckline, BO sts at the neck edge in every other row as follows: BO 4 sts once, 3 sts 3/3/2 times, 2 sts 1/1/2 time(s), and 1 st 1/1/2 time(s). At 21/21.3/21.7 in. (53/54/55 cm) (= 158/162/166 rows) from end of ribbing, BO the remaining 18/21/24 sts for each shoulder.

SLEEVES (MAKE 2)

Using US 4 (3.5 mm) needles and CC, CO 45/51/57 sts, and work as follows: 4 rows garter st in CC, 12 rows in stranded pattern, 4 rows garter st in CC; in the last WS row, evenly distributed, dec 0/0/2 sts (= 45/51/55 sts). After this, cont in MC in St st. For sleeve tapering, after having worked 6/8/8 rows from end of cuff, inc 1 st at each end of the row. Rep these incs in every 6th row 7/2/0 times more and in every 8th row 7/11/12 times more (= 75/79/81 sts).

For the sleeve cap, at a height of 15/15.4/15.4 in. (38/39/39 cm) (= 116/118/118 rows) from end of cuff, BO sts at both ends of the row as follows: BO 3/4/5 sts once; then, in every other row, 2 sts twice, 1 st 10/12/14 times, 2 sts 5/4/3 times, and 3 sts once. At sleeve cap height of 4.7/5.1/5.5 in. (12/13/14 cm) (= 38/40/42 rows), BO the remaining 15/17/17 sts.

FINISHING

Block all pieces to measurements on a soft surface, moisten, and let dry. Close sleeve, shoulder, and side seams from the wrong side, and then sew the sleeves into the armholes from the wrong side.

Using US 4 (3.5 mm) needles and MC, pick up and knit 120/126/132 sts from the neckline edge, join into the round, and work as follows: 4 rnds in MC in garter st, 12 rnds in stranded colorwork pattern, 4 rnds in MC in garter st. BO all sts, and weave in ends.

SCHEMATIC

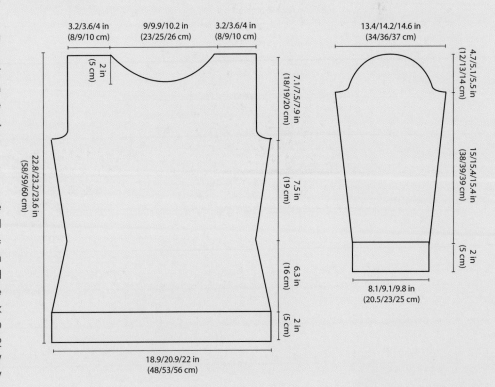

OVERSIZED WITH CABLES AND ELONGATED BACK

Pictured on page 153

BUILDING BLOCK PARTS

BODY SHAPE	Oversized
BACK	Basic Sweater 1
FRONT	Basic Sweater 6
SLEEVE	Basic Sweater 1
ARMHOLE	Straight
SLEEVE LENGTH	Long
NECKLINE	Round neckline with ribbed neckband
HEMS AND CUFFS	Ribbed hem and cuffs
SPECIAL FEATURES	This sweater features a Back that is 2 in. (5 cm) longer than the Front.

SIZES

Small/Medium/Large (US 6/8, 10/12, 14/16)

Numbers for size Small are listed before the first slash, for size Medium between slashes, and for size Large after the second slash. If only one number is given, it applies to all sizes.

MATERIALS

Schachenmayr Merino Extrafine 120; #3 light weight yarn; 100% wool; 131 yd (120 m), 1.75 oz. (50 g) per skein

- 13/14/15 skeins #114 wood heathered

Circular knitting needles, US 4 (3.5 mm) and US 6 (4.0 mm), each 40 in. (100 cm) long

Cable needle (cn)

GAUGE

In stockinette stitch on US 6 (4.0 mm) needles, 22 sts and 30 rows = 4 x 4 in. (10 x 10 cm)

In double seed stitch on US 6 (4.0 mm) needles, 22 sts and 34 rows = 4 x 4 in. (10 x 10 cm)

In cable pattern 1 on US 6 (4.0 mm) needles, 58 sts = 8.3 in. (21 cm)

STOCKINETTE STITCH

RS: Knit all sts.
WS: Purl all sts.

RIBBING IN ROWS

RS: Alternate k1, p1.
WS: Work all sts as they appear— knit the knits and purl the purls.

RIBBING IN ROUNDS

All rounds (RS): Alternate k1, p1.

DOUBLE SEED STITCH

Row 1: Alternate k1, p1.

Row 2: Knit the knits and purl the purls.
Row 3: Alternate p1, k1.
Row 4: Knit the knits and purl the purls.
Rep Rows 1–4 throughout.

CABLE PATTERN 1

Work from Stitch Pattern Chart B. Only RS rows are shown in the chart; in WS rows, work all sts as they appear (knit the knits and purl the purls), and purl the slipped sts. Work the patt rep (58 sts wide) widthwise across once, and then rep Rows 1–12 heightwise throughout.

INSTRUCTIONS

BACK

Using US 4 (3.5 mm) needles, CO 167/191/215 sts, and for hem ribbing,

STITCH PATTERN CHART B

cable pattern 1 = 58 sts

KNITTING SYMBOLS

■ = knit 1 st

– = purl 1 st

al = slip 1 st purlwise with yarn in back of work

= hold 1 st on cn in back of work, knit the next 2 sts, and then knit the st from the cn

= hold 2 sts on cn in front of work, purl the next st, and then knit the 2 sts from the cn

= hold 2 sts on cn in back of work, knit the next 2 sts, and then knit the 2 sts from the cn

= hold 4 sts on cn in back of work, knit the next 4 sts, and then knit the 4 sts from the cn

= hold 4 sts on cn in front of work, knit the next 4 sts, and then knit the 4 sts from the cn

work 14 rows in ribbing patt; *at the same time*, in the last row, evenly distributed, dec 14/14/18 sts (= 153/177/197 sts). Change to US 6 (4.0 mm) needles, and continue in St st. After 22.8/23.2/23.6 in. (58/59/60 cm) (= 174/176/180 rows) from hem ribbing, BO all sts.

FRONT

Using US 4 (3.5 mm) needles, CO 167/191/215 sts, and for hem ribbing, work 14 rows in ribbing patt; *at the same time*, in the last row, evenly distributed, dec 3/3/7 sts (= 164/188/208 sts). Change to US 6 (4.0 mm) needles, and continue in the following pattern: 1 st in St st, 52/64/74 sts in double seed stitch, 58 sts in cable pattern, 52/64/74 sts in double seed stitch, 1 st in St st.

For the neckline, after having worked 19/19.3/19.7 in. (48/49/50 cm) (= 162/164/168 rows) from end of ribbing,

BO the middle 28/30/30 sts, and continue both sides separately. For the rounded neckline, BO sts at the neck edge in every other row as follows: BO 4 sts once, 3 sts twice, 2 sts 3/3/2 times, and 1 st 1/2/4 time(s). At 21/21.3/21.7 in. (53/54/55 cm) (= 180/184/188 rows) from end of ribbing, BO the remaining 51/61/71 sts for each shoulder.

SLEEVES (MAKE 2)

Using US 4 (3.5 mm) needles, CO 51/55/59 sts, and work 14 rows in ribbing patt; *at the same time*, in the last row, evenly distributed, dec 6/4/4 sts (= 45/51/55 sts). Change to US 6 (4.0 mm) needles, and continue in St st. For sleeve tapering, after having worked 6/8/8 rows from end of cuff, inc 1 st at each end of the row. Rep these incs in every 6th row 13/10/10 times more and in every 8th row 0/3/3 times more (=

73/79/83 sts). At 12/12.6/12.6 in. (30.5/32/32 cm) (= 92/98/98 rows) from end of cuff, BO all sts.

FINISHING

Block all pieces to measurements on a soft surface, moisten, and let dry. Close shoulder and side seams from the wrong side, seaming the Front to the Back leaving the upper 6.5/7.1/7.5 in. (16.5/18/19 cm) open for the armholes and not attaching the Back hem. Seam the sleeves right sides facing each other and wrong sides facing out, and then sew the sleeves into the armholes from the wrong side.

Using US 4 (3.5 mm) needles, pick up and knit 126/130/134 sts from the neckline edge, join into the round, and work 1.2 in. (3 cm) (= 8 rnds) in ribbing pattern. BO all sts in pattern, and weave in ends.

SCHEMATIC

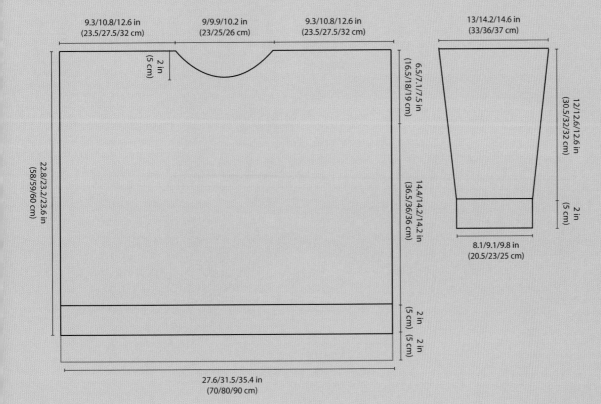

9.3/10.8/12.6 in (23.5/27.5/32 cm)

9/9.9/10.2 in (23/25/26 cm)

9.3/10.8/12.6 in (23.5/27.5/32 cm)

13/14.2/14.6 in (33/36/37 cm)

2 in (5 cm)

6.5/7.1/7.5 in (16.5/18/19 cm)

12/12.6/12.6 in (30.5/32/32 cm)

22.8/23.2/23.6 in (58/59/60 cm)

14.4/14.2/14.2 in (36.5/36/36 cm)

2 in (5 cm)

2 in (5 cm)

2 in (5 cm)

8.1/9.1/9.8 in (20.5/23/25 cm)

27.6/31.5/35.4 in (70/80/90 cm)

V-NECK
WITH RIBBED
NECKBAND

OVERSIZED
WITH STRIPES
AND V-NECK

Instructions on page 160

STRAIGHT
SLEEVE TOP

LONG
SLEEVE

STRAIGHT
BODY

RIBBED HEM
AND CUFFS

WITH TWO-COLOR STRIPES AND NUPP PATTERN HEM AND CUFFS

Instructions on page 162

ROUND
NECKLINE
WITH ROLLED
EDGE

ARMHOLE
WITH SLEEVE
CAP

LONG
SLEEVE

STRAIGHT
BODY

HEM AND
CUFFS
IN NUPP
PATTERN

OVERSIZED WITH STRIPES AND V-NECK

Pictured on page 158

BUILDING BLOCK PARTS

BODY SHAPE	Oversized
BACK	Basic Sweater 2
FRONT	Basic Sweater 2
SLEEVE	Basic Sweater 1
ARMHOLE	Straight
SLEEVE LENGTH	Long
NECKLINE	V-neck with ribbed neckband
HEMS AND CUFFS	Ribbed hem and cuffs
SPECIAL FEATURES	This design features the stripe sequence of Basic Sweater 2, but using only 5 instead of the original 6 colors. The sleeves are worked in one color.

SIZES

Small/Medium/Large (US 6/8, 10/12, 14/16)
Numbers for size Small are listed before the first slash, for size Medium between slashes, and for size Large after the second slash. If only one number is given, it applies to all sizes.

MATERIALS

Schachenmayr Merino Extrafine 120; #3 light weight yarn; 100% wool; 131 yd (120 m), 1.75 oz. (50 g) per skein

- Main color (MC): 5/6/7 skeins #176 ocean green
- Contrasting color 1 (CC1): 2/2/3 skeins #166 ocean blue heathered
- Contrasting color 2 (CC2): 1/1/2 skeins #103 linen
- Contrasting color 3 (CC3): 2/2/2 skeins #155 navy
- Contrasting color 4 (CC4): 2/2/3 skeins #167 mint

Circular knitting needles, US 4 (3.5 mm) and US 6 (4.0 mm), each 40 in. (100 cm) long

GAUGE

In stockinette stitch on US 6 (4.0 mm) needles, 22 sts and 30 rows = 4 x 4 in. (10 x 10 cm)

STOCKINETTE STITCH

RS: Knit all sts.
WS: Purl all sts.

RIBBING IN ROWS

RS: Alternate k1, p1.
WS: Work all sts as they appear—knit the knits and purl the purls.

RIBBING IN ROUNDS

All rounds (RS): Alternate k1, p1.

STRIPE SEQUENCE A

Alternate 2 rows in MC (ocean green), 2 rows in CC2 (linen).

STRIPE SEQUENCE B

This stripe sequence is worked only once.
18 rows in CC3, 6 rows in CC1, 14 rows in CC4, 6 rows in CC1, 14 rows in MC, 12 rows in CC3, 22 rows in stripe sequence A, 14 rows in CC1, 10 rows in CC2, 10 rows in CC4, 6 rows in CC1.

ACCENTED DECREASES

Accented decreases are always worked in RS rows as follows: K1, skp, cont in St st to last 3 sts of the row, then k2tog, k1. In WS rows, always purl the first 2 sts and the last 2 sts of the row. In RS rows without decreases, always knit the first 2 sts and the last 2 sts of the row.

INSTRUCTIONS

BACK

Using US 4 (3.5 mm) needles and MC (ocean green), CO 167/191/215 sts, and for hem ribbing, work 14 rows in ribbing patt; *at the same time,* in the last row, evenly distributed, dec 14/14/18 sts (= 153/177/197 sts). Change to US 6 (4.0 mm) needles, and cont in St st in stripe sequence B. After having completed stripe sequence B, finish the Back in stripe sequence A. At 21/21.3/21.7 in. (53/54/55 cm) (= 158/162/166 rows) from hem ribbing, BO all sts.

FRONT

Work as the Back, but with V-neck. For this, after having worked only 13.8/13.8/14.2 in. (35/35/36 cm) (= 106/106/108 rows) from end of ribbing, BO 1 st in the middle, and continue both sides separately. For the sloped neckline, at the neck edge, in every RS row, work accented decrease of 1 st 25/27/28 times. At 21/21.3/21.7 in. (53/54/55 cm) (= 158/162/166 rows) from end of ribbing, BO the remaining 51/61/70 sts for each shoulder.

SLEEVES (MAKE 2)

Using US 4 (3.5 mm) needles and MC, CO 51/55/59 sts, and work 14 rows in ribbing patt; *at the same time*, in the last row, evenly distributed, dec 6/4/4 sts (= 45/51/55 sts). Change to US 6 (4.0 mm) needles, and continue in St st. For sleeve tapering, after having worked 6/8/8 rows from end of cuff, inc 1 st at each end of the row. Rep these incs in every 6th row 13/10/10 times more and in every 8th row 0/3/3 times more (= 73/79/83 sts). At 12/12.6/12.6 in. (30.5/32/32 cm) (= 92/98/98 rows) from end of cuff, BO all sts.

FINISHING

Block all pieces to measurements on a soft surface, moisten, and let dry. Close shoulder and side seams from the wrong side, leaving the upper 6.5/7.1/7.5 in. (16.5/18/19 cm) open for the armholes. Seam the sleeves right sides facing each other and wrong sides facing out, and then sew the sleeves into the armholes from the wrong side.

Beginning at the left shoulder, pick up and knit 156/162/168 sts around the neckline edge as follows: 52/54/56 sts to 1 st before the deepest point of the V-neck, 1 st from the tip of the V-neck, 52/54/56 sts up to the right shoulder, and 51/53/55 sts along the Back neckline. Join into the round, and work ribbing as follows:

Rnd 1: Work in ribbing pattern.
Rnd 2: Work in ribbing to 1 st before the tip of the V-neck, work cdd over 3 sts (= slip 2 sts together knitwise, knit the next st, and pass the slipped sts over the knitted one), cont in ribbing to end of rnd.
Rnd 3: Knit the knits and purl the purls.
Rep Rnds 2 and 3 twice more, and then BO all sts.
Weave in ends.

SCHEMATIC

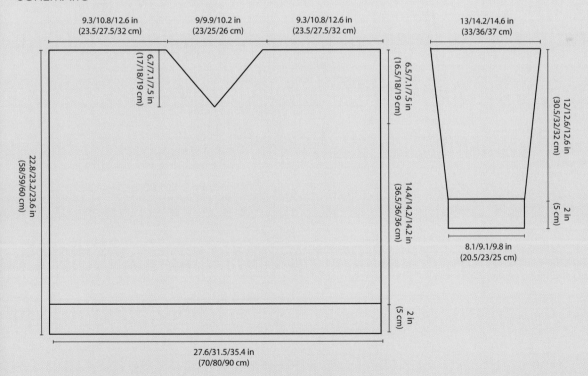

WITH TWO-COLOR STRIPES AND NUPP PATTERN HEM AND CUFFS

Pictured on page 159

BUILDING BLOCK PARTS

BODY SHAPE	Straight
BACK	Basic Sweater 2
FRONT	Basic Sweater 2
SLEEVE	Basic Sweater 2
ARMHOLE	Sleeve cap
SLEEVE LENGTH	Long
NECKLINE	Round neckline with rolled edge
HEMS AND CUFFS	Hem and cuffs in nupp pattern
SPECIAL FEATURES	This design features the stripe sequence of Basic Sweater 2, but using only 2 instead of the original 6 colors.

SIZES

Small/Medium/Large (US 6/8, 10/12, 14/16)

Numbers for size Small are listed before the first slash, for size Medium between slashes, and for size Large after the second slash. If only one number is given, it applies to all sizes.

MATERIALS

Schachenmayr Merino Extrafine 120; #3 light weight yarn; 100% wool; 131 yd (120 m), 1.75 oz. (50 g) per skein

- Main color (MC): 6/7/9 skeins #129 rose pink
- Contrasting color (CC): 5/6/7 skeins #102 natural

Circular knitting needles, US 4 (3.5 mm) and US 6 (4.0 mm), each 32 in. (80 cm) long

GAUGE

In stockinette stitch on US 6 (4.0 mm) needles, 22 sts and 30 rows = 4 x 4 in. (10 x 10 cm)

In nupp pattern on US 4 (3.5 mm) needles, 21 sts and 29 rows = 4 x 4 in. (10 x 10 cm)

STOCKINETTE STITCH IN ROWS

RS: Knit all sts.

WS: Purl all sts.

STOCKINETTE STITCH IN ROUNDS

All rounds (RS): Knit all stitches.

GARTER STITCH

All rows (RS and WS): Knit all sts.

NUPP PATTERN

Work from Stitch Pattern Chart D. Only RS rows are shown in the chart; in WS rows, purl all sts and yarn overs. Repeat the patt rep widthwise across, ending with the 2 sts after the patt rep.

STRIPE SEQUENCE A

Alternate 2 rows in MC, 2 rows in CC.

STRIPE SEQUENCE B

This stripe sequence is worked only once.
18 rows in CC, 6 rows in MC, 14 rows in CC, 6 rows in MC, 14 rows in CC, 12 rows in MC, 22 rows in stripe sequence A, 14 rows in MC, 10 rows in CC, 10 rows in MC, 6 rows in CC.

STRIPE SEQUENCE C

This stripe sequence is worked only once.
18 rows in stripe sequence A, 6 rows in MC, 12 rows in CC, 22 rows in stripe sequence A, 14 rows in MC, 10 rows in CC, 10 rows in MC, 6 rows in CC, 16 rows in stripe sequence A, 4 rows in MC, 10 rows in CC, 10 rows in MC, 6 rows in CC.

STITCH PATTERN CHART D
Stitch count is a multiple of 11 + 2

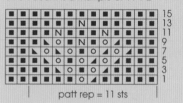

patt rep = 11 sts

KNITTING SYMBOLS

■ = knit 1 st

− = purl 1 st

○ = make 1 yarn over

◢ = knit 2 sts together

◣ = slip 1, knit 1, pass the slipped st over

◭ = slip 1, knit 2 sts together, pass the slipped st over

☐ = no st, for better overview only

N = 1 nupp (= work k1, p1, k1, p1, k1 all into the next st, turn work, purl the 5 nupp sts, turn work again one after another, pass the 2nd, 3rd, 4th and 5th st over the first one)

INSTRUCTIONS

BACK

Using US 4 (3.5 mm) needles and MC (rose pink), CO 101/112/123 sts, and work as follows: 4 rows garter st, 16 rows in nupp pattern, 4 rows garter st; *at the same time*, in the last row, evenly distributed, inc 4/5/0 sts (= 105/117/123 sts). Change to US 6 (4.0 mm) needles, and cont in St st in stripe sequence B. After having completed stripe sequence B, finish the piece in stripe sequence A.

For armhole shaping, after having worked 13.8 in. (35 cm) (= 104 rows) from end of ribbing, BO 3/4/5 sts at

each end of the row once; then, in every other row, BO another 2 sts twice and 1 st 2/2/0 times. At 21/21.3/21.7 in. (53/54/55 cm) (= 158/162/166 rows) from end of ribbing, BO the remaining 87/97/105 sts.

FRONT

Work as the Back, but with neckline shaping. For this, after having worked only 19/19.3/19.7 in. (48/49/50 cm) (= 144/148/150 rows) from end of hem ribbing, BO the middle 19/23/25 sts, and continue both sides separately. For the rounded neckline, BO sts at the neck edge in every other row as follows: BO 4 sts once, 3 sts 3/3/2 times, 2 sts 1/1/2

time(s), and 1 st 1/1/2 time(s). At 21/21.3/21.7 in. (53/54/55 cm) (158/162/166 rows) from end of ribbing, BO the remaining 18/21/24 sts for each shoulder.

SLEEVES (MAKE 2)

Using US 4 (3.5 mm) needles and MC, CO 46/46/57 sts, and work as follows: 4 rows garter st, 16 rows in nupp pattern, 4 rows garter st; *at the same time*, in the last row, evenly distributed, dec 1 st/inc 5 sts/dec 2 sts (= 45/51/55 sts). Change to US 6 (4.0 mm) needles, and cont in St st in stripe sequence C, and then finish the sleeve in stripe sequence A.

For sleeve tapering, after having worked 6/8/8 rows from end of cuff, inc 1 st at each end of the row. Rep these incs in every 6th row 7/2/0 times more and in every 8th row 7/11/12 times more (= 75/79/81 sts).

For the sleeve cap, at a height of 15/15.4/15.4 in. (38/39/39 cm) (= 116/118/118 rows) from end of cuff, BO 3/4/5 sts at each end of the row. After this, BO sts at both ends of the row in every other row as follows: BO 2 sts twice, 1 st 10/12/14 times, 2 sts 5/4/3 times, and 3 sts once. At sleeve cap height of 4.7/5.1/5.5 in. (12/13/14 cm) (= 38/40/42 rows), BO the remaining 15/17/17 sts.

FINISHING

Block all pieces to measurements on a soft surface, moisten, and let dry. Close sleeve, shoulder, and side seams from the wrong side, and then sew the sleeves into the armholes from the wrong side.

Using US 4 (3.5 mm) needles and MC, pick up and knit 126/130/134 sts from the neckline edge, join into the round, and purl 1 rnd. Then work 16 rnds in St st. BO all sts, and weave in ends.

SCHEMATIC

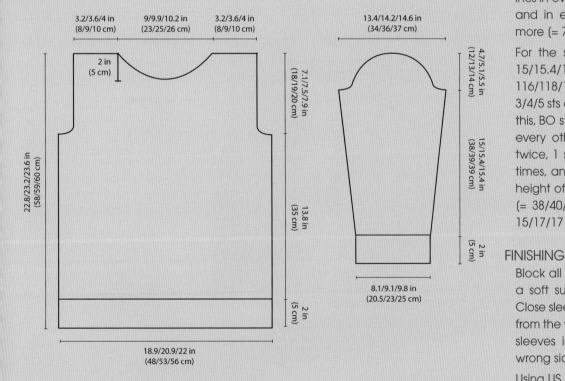

3.2/3.6/4 in (8/9/10 cm) 9/9.9/10.2 in (23/25/26 cm) 3.2/3.6/4 in (8/9/10 cm)

2 in (5 cm)

7.1/7.5/7.9 in (18/19/20 cm)

22.8/23.2/23.6 in (58/59/60 cm)

13.8 in (35 cm)

2 in (5 cm)

18.9/20.9/22 in (48/53/56 cm)

13.4/14.2/14.6 in (34/36/37 cm)

4.7/5.1/5.5 in (12/13/14 cm)

15/15.4/15.4 in (38/39/39 cm)

2 in (5 cm)

8.1/9.1/9.8 in (20.5/23/25 cm)

ROUND
NECKLINE
WITH RIBBED
NECKBAND

WITH
SECTIONS IN
STRANDED
COLORWORK
AND LACE

Instructions on page 166

ARMHOLE WITH
SLEEVE CAP

¾ SLEEVE

HEM AND
CUFFS IN
LACE PATTERN

STRAIGHT
BODY

OVERSIZED AS PONCHO WITH CABLE PATTERN

Instructions on page 168

ROUND NECKLINE WITH TURTLENECK

NO SLEEVES

STRAIGHT SLEEVE TOP

OVERSIZED BODY SHAPE

RIBBED HEM AND CUFFS

WITH SECTIONS IN STRANDED COLORWORK AND LACE

Pictured on page 164

BUILDING BLOCK PARTS

BODY SHAPE	Straight
BACK	Bottom part Basic Sweater 5, top part Basic Sweater 4
FRONT	Bottom part Basic Sweater 5, top part Basic Sweater 4
SLEEVE	Bottom part Basic Sweater 5, top part Basic Sweater 4
ARMHOLE	Sleeve cap
SLEEVE LENGTH	¾ length
NECKLINE	Round neckline with ribbed neckband
HEMS AND CUFFS	Hem and cuffs in lace pattern
SPECIAL FEATURES	In this sweater, a lace pattern is combined with stranded colorwork—both sections divided by a narrow garter stitch stripe.

SIZES

Small/Medium/Large (US 6/8, 10/12, 14/16)

Numbers for size Small are listed before the first slash, for size Medium between slashes, and for size Large after the second slash. If only one number is given, it applies to all sizes.

MATERIALS

Schachenmayr Merino Extrafine 120; #3 light weight yarn; 100% wool; 131 yd (120 m), 1.75 oz. (50 g) per skein

- Main color (MC): 8/9/10 skeins #142 red
- Contrasting Color (CC): 3/4/5 skeins #104 sand heathered

Circular knitting needles, US 4 (3.5 mm) and US 6 (4.0 mm), each 32 in. (80 cm) long

GAUGE

In lace pattern B on US 6 (4.0 mm) needles, 20 sts and 28 rows = 4 x 4 in. (10 x 10 cm)

In stranded colorwork pattern on US 6 (4.0 mm) needles, 22 sts and 30 rows = 4 x 4 in. (10 x 10 cm)

STOCKINETTE STITCH

RS: Knit all sts.
WS: Purl all sts.

GARTER STITCH

All rows (RS and WS): Knit all sts.

RIBBING IN ROUNDS

All rounds (RS): Alternate k1, p1.

LACE PATTERN A

Work from Stitch Pattern Chart E. Only RS rows are shown in the chart; in WS rows, purl all sts and yarn overs. Begin with the 7 sts before the patt rep, repeat the patt rep widthwise, and end with the 6 sts after the patt rep. Work Rows 1–16 once heightwise.

LACE PATTERN B

Work from Stitch Pattern Chart A. Only RS rows are shown in the chart; in WS rows, work all sts as they appear, and purl the yarn overs. Begin with the sts before the patt rep, repeat the patt rep widthwise across, and end with the sts after the patt rep. Repeat Rows 1–12 of the chart heightwise throughout.

STRANDED PATTERN

Work in stockinette stitch in stranded colorwork pattern from Colorwork Chart B. The chart contains both RS and WS rows. Sts are shown as they appear from the RS of the fabric. Begin with the stitch stated in the instructions, work to the end of the patt rep, and then repeat the patt rep widthwise across, ending with the stitch stated in the instructions. Repeat Rows 1–14 heightwise throughout.

INSTRUCTIONS

BACK

Using US 4 (3.5 mm) needles and MC (red), CO 103/113/123 sts, and for hem, work 16 rows in lace pattern A; *at the same time*, in the last row, evenly distributed, dec 8 sts (= 95/105/115 sts). Change to US 6 (4.0 mm) needles, and work in lace pattern B for 21.4 in. (31.5 cm) (= 88 rows); *at the same time*, in the last row, evenly distributed, inc 10/12/8 sts (= 105/117/123 sts).

In CC (sand heathered), first work 6 rows garter st, and then cont in St st in stranded colorwork pattern, beginning with the 4th/12th/9th st of the chart and ending with the 10th/2nd/5th st of the chart.

For armhole shaping, after having worked 4 rows in stranded colorwork pattern, BO 3/4/5 sts at each end of the row once; then, in every other row, BO another 2 sts twice and 1 st 2/2/0 times. At 21/21.3/21.7 in. (53/54/55 cm) (= 152/156/160 rows) from hem ribbing, BO all sts.

FRONT

Work as the Back, but with neckline shaping. For this, after having worked only 5.5/5.9/6.5 in. (14/15/16.5 cm) (= 42/46/50 rows) in stranded colorwork pattern, BO the middle 19/23/25 sts, and continue both sides separately. For the rounded neckline, BO sts at the neck edge in every other row as follows: BO 4 sts once, 3 sts 3/3/2 times, 2 sts 1/1/2 time(s), and 1 st 1/1/2 time(s). At 21/21.3/21.7 in. (53/54/55 cm) (= 152/156/160 rows) from end of ribbing, BO the remaining 18/21/24 sts for each shoulder.

SLEEVES (MAKE 2)

Using US 4 (3.5 mm) needles and MC, CO 63/63/73 sts, and for the cuff, work

SCHEMATIC

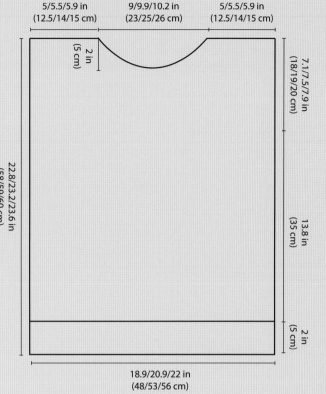

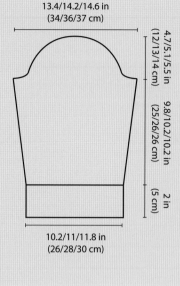

16 rows in lace pattern A, in the last WS row, evenly distributed, dec 8/6/14 sts (= 55/57/59 sts). Change to US 6 (4.0 mm) needles, and work 9 in. (23 cm) (= 64 rows) in lace pattern B as follows: 0/1/2 st(s) in St st, 55 sts in lace pattern from Stitch Pattern Chart A, 0/1/2 st(s) in St st.

Please note: As soon as there are 59 sts on the needles in lace pattern B, the first 2 and the last 2 sts will always be worked in St st. Increases at both ends of the row will then always be worked after or before these 2 sts, and the sts gained from increasing are incorporated into the lace pattern.

For sleeve tapering, after having worked 8/8/6 rows from end of cuff, inc 1 st at each end of the row. Rep these incs in every 6th row 0/0/6 times more and in every 8th row 6/8/3 times more (= 67/73/77 sts). After having worked 9 in. (23 cm) (= 63 rows) from end of ribbing, in a WS row, evenly distributed, inc 8/6/4 sts (= 75/79/81 sts).

In CC, first work 6 rows garter st, and then cont in St st in stranded colorwork pattern, beginning with the 12th/10th/9th st of the chart and ending with the 2nd/4th/5th st of the chart.

For the sleeve cap, after having worked 4 rows in stranded colorwork pattern, BO 3/4/5 sts at each end of the row once, and then in every other row as follows: BO 2 sts twice, 1 st 10/12/14 times, 2 sts 5/4/3 times, and 3 sts once. At armhole height of 4.7/5.1/5.5 in. (12/13/14 cm) (= 40/42/46 rows), BO the remaining 15/17/17 sts.

FINISHING

Block all pieces to measurements on a soft surface, moisten, and let dry. Close sleeve, shoulder, and side seams from the wrong side, and then sew the sleeves into the armholes from the wrong side.

Using US 4 (3.5 mm) needles and CC, pick up and knit 126/130/134 sts from the neckline edge, join into the round, and work 1.2 in. (3 cm) (= 8 rnds) in ribbing pattern. BO all sts, and weave in ends.

COLORWORK CHART B

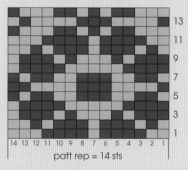

patt rep = 14 sts

KNITTING SYMBOLS

■ = St st in MC (red)
☐ = St st in CC (sand heathered)

STITCH PATTERN CHART A
Stitch count is a multiple of 10 + 15

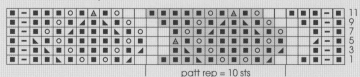

patt rep = 10 sts

STITCH PATTERN CHART E
Stitch count is a multiple of 10 + 13

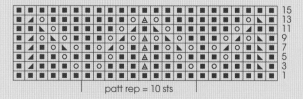

patt rep = 10 sts

KNITTING SYMBOLS

■ = knit 1 st

− = purl 1 st

○ = make 1 yarn over

◢ = knit 2 sts together

◣ = slip 1, knit 1, pass the slipped st over

▲ = slip 1, knit 2 sts together, pass the slipped st over

☐ = no st, for better overview only

OVERSIZED AS PONCHO WITH CABLE PATTERN

Pictured on page 165

BUILDING BLOCK PARTS

BODY SHAPE	Oversized
BACK	Basic Sweater 6
FRONT	Basic Sweater 6
SLEEVE	n/a—has no sleeves
ARMHOLE	Straight
SLEEVE LENGTH	n/a—has no sleeves
NECKLINE	Round neckline with turtleneck
HEMS AND CUFFS	Ribbed hem and cuffs
SPECIAL FEATURES	In this design, the sleeves are omitted altogether, and the oversized sweater is turned into a poncho by adding a 1.2 in. (3 cm) wide button band.

STOCKINETTE STITCH

RS: Knit all sts.
WS: Purl all sts.

RIBBING IN ROWS

RS: Alternate k1, p1.
WS: Work all sts as they appear—knit the knits and purl the purls.

RIBBING IN ROUNDS

All rounds (RS): Alternate k1, p1.

SIZES

Small/Medium/Large (US 6/8, 10/12, 14/16)

Numbers for size Small are listed before the first slash, for size Medium between slashes, and for size Large after the second slash. If only one number is given, it applies to all sizes.

MATERIALS

Schachenmayr Merino Extrafine 120; #3 light weight yarn; 100% wool; 131 yd (120 m), 1.75 oz. (50 g) per skein

• 14/15/17 skeins #198 dark gray heathered

Circular knitting needles, US 4 (3.5 mm) and US 6 (4.0 mm), each 40 in. (100 cm) long

Cable needle (cn)

6 dark gray buttons, approx. 0.9 in. (22 mm)

GAUGE

In double seed stitch on US 6 (4.0 mm) needles, 22 sts and 34 rows = 4 x 4 in. (10 x 10 cm)

In cable pattern 1 on US 6 (4.0 mm) needles, 58 sts = 8.3 in. (21 cm)

SCHEMATIC

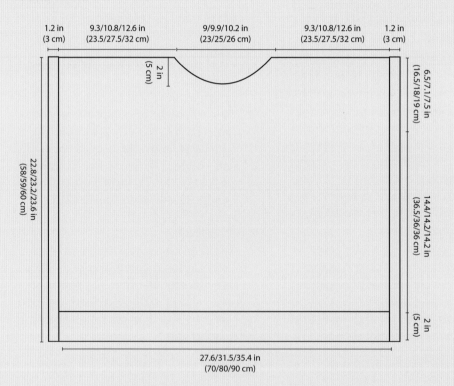

DOUBLE SEED STITCH

Row 1: Alternate k1, p1.
Row 2: Knit the knits and purl the purls.
Row 3: Alternate p1, k1.
Row 4: Knit the knits and purl the purls.
Rep Rows 1–4 throughout.

CABLE PATTERN 1

Work from Stitch Pattern Chart B. Only RS rows are shown in the chart; in WS rows, work all sts as they appear (knit the knits and purl the purls), and purl the slipped sts. Work the patt rep (58 sts wide) widthwise across once, and then rep Rows 1–12 heightwise throughout.

INSTRUCTIONS

BACK

Using US 4 (3.5 mm) needles, CO 167/191/215 sts, and for hem ribbing, work 14 rows in ribbing patt; *at the same time*, in the last row, evenly distributed, dec 3/3/7 sts (= 164/188/208 sts). Change to US 6 (4.0 mm) needles, and continue in the following pattern: 1 st in St st, 52/64/74 sts in double seed stitch, 58 sts in cable pattern from Stitch Pattern Chart B, 52/64/74 sts in double seed stitch, 1 st in St st. At 21/21.3/21.7 in. (53/54/55 cm) (= 180/184/188 rows) from hem ribbing, BO all sts.

FRONT

Work as the Back, but with neckline shaping. For this, after having worked 19/19.3/19.7 in. (48/49/50 cm) (= 164/166/168 rows) from end of ribbing, BO the middle 28/30/30 sts, and continue both sides separately. For the rounded neckline, BO sts at the neck edge in every other row as follows: BO 4 sts once, 3 sts twice, 2 sts 3/3/2 times, and 1 st 1/2/4 time(s). At 21/21.3/21.7 in. (53/54/55 cm) (= 180/184/188 rows) from end of ribbing, BO the remaining 51/61/71 sts for each shoulder.

FINISHING

Block all pieces to measurements on a soft surface, moisten, and let dry. Close the shoulder seams right sides facing each other and wrong sides out. For the side band on the left edge, with right side facing out and starting at the bottom of the front edge of the garment, pick up and knit a total of 281/285/289 sts along the left edge of the Front and Back, and then work 3 rows in ribbing patt.

In the next RS row, work 3 buttonholes as follows: 61/63/65 sts ribbing, *BO 2 sts, 19 sts ribbing; rep from * once, BO 2 sts, and then cont in ribbing to end of row. In the next WS row, CO the same number of sts over the previously bound-off sts. Work 3 rows more in ribbing patt, then in a WS row, BO all sts.

Work the side band for the right edge as a mirror image of the left side—that is, work buttonholes as follows: 176/178/180 sts ribbing, *BO 2 sts, 19 sts ribbing, rep from * once, BO 2 sts, and then cont in ribbing to end of row.

Using US 4 (3.5 mm) needles, pick up and knit 126/130/134 sts from the neckline edge, join into the round, and, for the turtleneck, work in ribbing patt for 9.5 in. (24 cm) (= 72 rnds). BO all sts in pattern, and weave in ends. Sew buttons opposite the buttonholes to the inside of the side band.

STITCH PATTERN CHART B

cable pattern 1 = 58 sts

KNITTING SYMBOLS

☐ = knit 1 st

☐ = purl 1 st

☐ = slip 1 st purlwise with yarn in back of work

= hold 1 st on cn in back of work, knit the next 2 sts, and then purl the 1 st from the cn

= hold 2 sts on cn in front of work, purl the next st, and then knit the 2 sts from the cn

= hold 2 sts on cn in back of work, knit the next 2 sts, and then knit the 2 sts from the cn

= hold 4 sts on cn in back of work, knit the next 4 sts, and then knit the 4 sts from the cn

= hold 4 sts on cn in front of work, knit the next 4 sts, and then knit the 4 sts from the cn

CARDIGAN WITH POCKETS AND STRANDED COLORWORK PATTERN

BUILDING BLOCK PARTS

BODY SHAPE	Straight
BACK	Combination of Basic Sweaters 1 and 4
FRONT	Combination of Basic Sweaters 1 and 4
SLEEVE	Combination of Basic Sweaters 1 and 4
ARMHOLE	Straight
SLEEVE LENGTH	Long
NECKLINE	V-neck
HEMS AND CUFFS	Ribbed hem and cuffs
SPECIAL FEATURES	For this sweater, the Front of the basic sweater is simply divided into two halves—minus a few stitches, which will later be replaced by a 1.2 in. (3 cm) wide button band. Additionally, the cardigan gets two pockets.

SIZES

Small/Medium/Large (US 6/8, 10/12, 14/16)

Numbers for size Small are listed before the first slash, for size Medium between slashes, and for size Large after the second slash. If only one number is given, it applies to all sizes.

MATERIALS

Schachenmayr Merino Extrafine 120; #3 light weight yarn; 100% wool; 131 yd (120 m), 1.75 oz. (50 g) per skein

- Main color (MC): 7/9/11 skeins #150 marine blue
- Contrasting color (CC): 3/4/5 skeins #101 white

Circular knitting needles, US 4 (3.5 mm) and US 6 (4.0 mm), each 32 in. (80 cm) long

2 spare needles

5 buttons, approx. 0.8 in. (20 mm)

GAUGE

In stranded colorwork pattern on US 6 (4.0 mm) needles, 22 sts and 30 rows = 4 x 4 in. (10 x 10 cm)

In stockinette stitch on US 6 (4.0 mm) needles, 22 sts and 30 rows = 4 x 4 in. (10 x 10 cm)

RIBBING IN ROWS

RS: Alternate k1, p1.

WS: Work all sts as they appear—knit the knits and purl the purls.

STOCKINETTE STITCH

RS: Knit all sts.

WS: Purl all sts.

COLORWORK CHART B

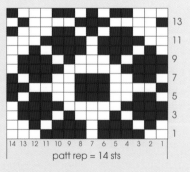

patt rep = 14 sts

KNITTING SYMBOLS

■ = St st in MC (marine blue)
□ = St st in CC (white)

STRANDED PATTERN

Work in stockinette stitch in stranded colorwork pattern from Colorwork Chart B. The chart contains both RS and WS rows. Sts are shown as they appear from the RS of the fabric. Begin with the stitch stated in the instructions, work to the end of the patt rep, and then repeat the patt rep widthwise across, ending with the stitch stated in the instructions. Repeat Rows 1–14 heightwise throughout.

STRIPE SEQUENCE

Alternate 2 rows in MC, 2 rows in CC.

ACCENTED DECREASES

Accented decreases are always worked in RS rows as follows:

At the right edge of the piece: K1, skp, cont in St st. (In WS rows, purl the last 2 sts.)

At the left edge of the piece: K to last 3 sts, then k2tog, k1. (In WS rows, purl the first 2 sts.)

ROUND NECKLINE WITH RIBBED NECKBAND

STRAIGHT SLEEVE TOP

LONG SLEEVE

STRAIGHT BODY

RIBBED HEM AND CUFFS

INSTRUCTIONS

BACK

Using US 4 (3.5 mm) needles and MC (navy), CO 115/127/131 sts and work 14 rows in ribbing patt; *at the same time,* in the last row, evenly distributed, dec 10/10/8 sts (= 105/117/123 sts). Change to US 6 (4.0 mm) needles, and cont in St st in stranded pattern, beginning with the 4th/12th/9th st of the chart, and ending with the 10th/2nd/5th st of the chart. After having worked 6.7 in. (17 cm) (= 52 rows) from end of hem, continue in St st as follows: 2 rows in CC (white), 2 rows in MC, 2 rows in CC, and then cont in St st in MC. At 21/21.3/21.7 in. (53/54/55 cm) (= 158/162/166 rows) from hem ribbing, BO all sts.

POCKET LINING (MAKE 2)

Using US 6 (4.0 mm) needles and MC, CO 33 sts and cont in St st in stripe sequence. After having worked 5.7 in. (14.5 cm) (= 44 rows) from cast-on edge, transfer all sts to a spare needle for holding.

LEFT FRONT

Using US 4 (3.5 mm) needles and MC, CO 53/59/61 sts, and for hem ribbing, work 2 in. (5 cm) (= 14 rows) in ribbing; *at the same time,* in the last row, evenly distributed, dec 4 sts (= 49/55/57 sts). Change to US 6 (4.0 mm) needles, and cont in St st in stranded pattern, beginning with the 4th/12th/9th st of the chart, and ending with the 10th/10th/9th st of the chart.

For the pocket slit, after having worked 5.7 in. (14.5 cm) (= 44 rows) from end of ribbing, cont as follows: 8 sts in stranded pattern, 33 sts ribbing in MC, 8/14/16 sts in stranded pattern. Work in this pattern for 5 rows (here, for the stranded pattern to the right and to the left of the ribbing section, at times, it will be necessary to work from 2 separate skeins CC). In the next WS row, BO the 33 sts of the ribbing section. In the following RS row, cont as follows: 8 sts in stranded pattern, place the formerly held sts of one pocket lining onto the right needle (right side facing out), 8/14/16 sts in stranded pattern. Now, cont to work over all sts again in stranded colorwork pattern. After having worked 6.7 in. (17 cm) (= 52 rows) from end of hem, continue in St st as follows: 2 rows in CC, 2 rows in MC, 2 rows in CC, and then cont in St st in MC.

For the V-neck, after having worked 15/15/15.4 in. (38/38/39 cm) (= 114/114/118 rows) from end of ribbing, work an accented decrease at the left edge. Rep this accented decrease in every other row another 21/23/23 times. At 21/21.3/21.7 in. (53/54/55 cm) (= 158/162/166 rows) from end of ribbing, BO the remaining 27/31/33 shoulder sts.

RIGHT FRONT

Begin as for the left Front, beginning the stranded colorwork pattern with the 4th/4th/5th st of the chart, and ending with the 10th/2nd/5th st of the chart.

For the pocket slit, after having worked 5.7 in. (14.5 cm) (= 44 rows) from end of ribbing, cont as follows: 8/14/16 sts in stranded pattern, 33 sts ribbing in MC, 8 sts in stranded pattern. Work in this pattern for 5 rows. In the next WS row, BO the 33 sts of the ribbing section. In the following RS row, cont as follows: 8/14/16 sts in stranded pattern, place the formerly held sts of one pocket lining onto the right needle, 8 sts in stranded pattern. Now, cont to work over all sts again in stranded colorwork pattern. After having worked 6.7 in. (17 cm) (= 52 rows) from end of hem, continue in St st as follows: 2 rows in CC, 2 rows in MC, 2 rows in CC, and then cont in St st in MC.

After having worked 15/15/15.4 in. (38/38/39 cm) (= 114/114/118 rows) from end of ribbing, work the V-neck the same way as for the left Front, but as a mirror image, this time working the accented decreases at the right edge of the piece. At 21/21.3/21.7 in. (53/54/55 cm) (= 158/162/166 rows) from end of ribbing, BO the remaining 27/31/33 shoulder sts.

SLEEVES (MAKE 2)

Using US 4 (3.5 mm) needles and MC, CO 51/55/59 sts, and for the cuff, work 2 in. (5 cm) (= 14 rows) in ribbing; in the last WS row, evenly distributed, dec 6/4/4 sts (= 45/51/55 sts). Change to US 6 (4.0 mm) needles, and cont in St st in stranded pattern, beginning with the 6th/3rd/1st st of the chart and ending with the 8th/11th/13th st of the chart. After 42 rows from end of cuff (= 3 heightwise patt reps of the chart), cont in St st as follows: 2 rows in CC, 2 rows in MC, 2 rows in CC, and then cont in St st in MC.

At the same time, for sleeve tapering, after having worked 6/8/8 rows from end of cuff, inc 1 st at each end of the row. Rep these incs in every 6th row 13/10/10 times more and in every 8th row 4/6/6 times more (= 81/85/89 sts). At 16.1/16.5/16.5 in. (41/42/42 cm) (= 124/126/126 rows) from end of cuff, BO all sts.

FINISHING

Block all pieces to measurements on a soft surface, moisten, and let dry. Close shoulder and side seams from the wrong side, leaving the upper 7.1/7.5/7.9 in. (18/19/20 cm) open for the armholes. Seam the sleeves right sides facing each other and wrong sides facing out, and then sew the sleeves into the armholes from the wrong side.

Using US 4 (3.5 mm) needles, pick up and knit a total of 307/311/319 sts along the front edge of both left and right Fronts and the Back neckline as follows: 95/95/97 sts from the bottom edge of the right Front up to the beginning of the V-neck, 117/121/125 sts from the beginning of the V-neck over the Back neckline to the beginning of the V-neck on the left Front, 95/95/97 sts from the V-neck to the bottom edge of the left Front. 3 rows in ribbing patt. In the next RS row, work 5 buttonholes as follows: 4/4/6 sts ribbing, *BO 2 sts, 20 sts ribbing; rep from * 3 times more, BO 2 sts, and then cont in ribbing to end of row. In the next WS row, CO new sts over the sts bound off in the previous row. Then work 2 rows more in ribbing, and BO all sts loosely. Weave in all ends. Sew buttons to the left Front band opposite the buttonholes.

SCHEMATIC

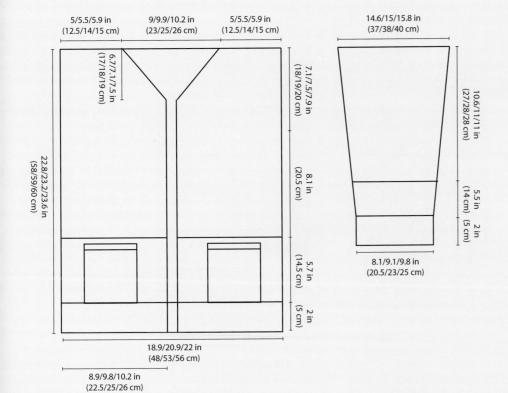

WITH CABLES ALONG THE SIDES

Instructions on page 176

ROUND NECKLINE WITH RIBBED NECKBAND

STRAIGHT SLEEVE TOP

¾ SLEEVE

STRAIGHT BODY

HEM AND CUFFS IN CABLE PATTERN

WITH MOSAIC HEM AND CUFFS AND TURTLENECK

Instructions on page 178

ROUND NECKLINE WITH TURTLENECK

ARMHOLE WITH RAGLAN SHAPING

LONG SLEEVE

HEM AND CUFFS IN MOSAIC PATTERN

STRAIGHT BODY

WITH CABLES ALONG THE SIDES

Pictured on page 174

BUILDING BLOCK PARTS

BODY SHAPE	Straight
BACK	Basic Sweater 6
FRONT	Basic Sweater 6
SLEEVES	Basic Sweater 6
ARMHOLE	Straight
SLEEVE LENGTH	¾ length
NECKLINE	Round neckline with ribbed neckband
HEMS AND CUFFS	Hem and cuffs in cable pattern
SPECIAL FEATURES	In this sweater, the smaller cables from Basic Sweater 6 are shifted to the sides of the Front, the big cable is omitted. Back and sleeves are worked in double seed stitch without cables.

SIZES

Small/Medium/Large (US 6/8, 10/12, 14/16)

Numbers for size Small are listed before the first slash, for size Medium between slashes, and for size Large after the second slash. If only one number is given, it applies to all sizes.

MATERIALS

Schachenmayr Merino Extrafine 120; #3 light weight yarn; 100% wool; 131 yd (120 m), 1.75 oz. (50 g) per skein

- 10/12/14 skeins #113 tan

Circular knitting needles, US 4 (3.5 mm) and US 6 (4.0 mm), each 32 in. (80 cm) long

Cable needle (cn)

GAUGE

In double seed stitch on US 6 (4.0 mm) needles, 22 sts and 34 rows = 4 x 4 in. (10 x 10 cm)

In cable pattern 1 on US 6 (4.0 mm) needles, 18 sts = 3.2 in. (8 cm)

STOCKINETTE STITCH

RS: Knit all sts.
WS: Purl all sts.

STITCH PATTERN CHART C

cable pattern 1 = 18 sts

KNITTING SYMBOLS

■ = knit 1 st

− = purl 1 st

⍺ = slip 1 st purlwise with yarn in back of work

▆▆╱ = hold 1 st on cn in back of work, knit the next 2 sts, and then purl the 1 st from the cn

╲▆▆ = hold 2 sts on cn in front of work, purl the next st, and then knit the 2 sts from the cn

▆▆╱▆ = hold 2 sts on cn in back of work, knit the next 2 sts, and then knit the 2 sts from the cn

RIBBING IN ROUNDS

All rounds (RS): Alternate k1, p1.

DOUBLE SEED STITCH

Row 1: Alternate k1, p1.
Row 2: Knit the knits and purl the purls.
Row 3: Alternate p1, k1.
Row 4: Knit the knits and purl the purls.
Rep Rows 1–4 throughout.

CABLE PATTERN 1

Work from Stitch Pattern Chart C. Only RS rows are shown in the chart; in WS rows, work all sts as they appear (knit the knits and purl the purls), and purl the slipped sts. Work the patt rep (18 sts wide) widthwise across once, and then rep Rows 1–12 heightwise throughout.

CABLE PATTERN 2

Row 1 (RS): *P2, k2, p2, k4, rep from * to last 6 sts of row, ending with p2, k2, p2.
Row 2 (WS): Knit the knits and purl the purls.
Row 3 (RS): *P2, k2, p2, hold 2 sts on cn in back of work, k2, then k2 from cn, rep from * to last 6 sts of row, ending with p2, k2, p2.
Row 4 (WS): Knit the knits and purl the purls.
Rep Rows 1–4 throughout.

INSTRUCTIONS

BACK

Using US 4 (3.5 mm) needles, CO 116/126/136 sts, and work 16 rows in cable pattern 2; *at the same time*, in the last row, evenly distributed, inc 0 sts/inc 2 sts/dec 4 sts (= 116/128/132 sts). Change to US 6 (4.0 mm) needles, and cont in double seed stitch. At 21/21.3/21.7 in. (53/54/55 cm) (= 180/184/188 rows) from hem ribbing, BO all sts.

FRONT

Using US 4 (3.5 mm) needles, CO 116/126/136 sts, and for hem ribbing, work 16 rows in cable pattern 2; *at the same time*, in the last row, evenly distributed, inc 0 sts/inc 2 sts/dec 4 sts (= 116/128/132 sts). Change to US 6 (4.0 mm) needles, and continue in the following pattern: 1 st in St st, 6/10/12 sts in double seed stitch, 18 sts in cable pattern 1, 66/70/70 sts in double seed stitch, 18 sts in cable pattern 1, 6/10/12 sts in double seed stitch, 1 st in St st.

For the neckline, after having worked 19/19.3/19.7 in. (48/49/50 cm) (= 164/166/168 rows) from end of ribbing, BO the middle 28/30/30 sts, and continue both sides separately. For the rounded neckline, BO sts at the neck edge in every other row as follows: BO 4 sts once, 3 sts twice, 2 sts 3/3/2 times, and 1 st 1/2/4 time(s). At 21/21.3/21.7 in. (53/54/55 cm) (= 180/184/188 rows) from end of ribbing, BO remaining 27/31/33 sts for each shoulder.

SLEEVES (MAKE 2)

Using US 4 (3.5 mm) needles, CO 66/66/76 sts, and for the cuff, work 16 rows in cable pattern 2; *at the same time*, in the last row, evenly distributed, dec 6/2/8 sts (= 60/64/68 sts). Change to US 6 (4.0 mm) needles, and cont in double seed stitch. For sleeve tapering, after having worked 14/16/10 rows from end of cuff, inc 1 st at each end of the row. Rep these incs in every 8th row 10/9/1 time(s) more and in every 10th row 0/0/8 times more (= 82/84/88 sts). At 11.8/12.6/12.6 in. (30/32/32 cm) (= 102/108/108 rows) from hem ribbing, BO all sts.

FINISHING

Block all pieces to measurements on a soft surface, moisten, and let dry. Close shoulder and side seams from the wrong side, leaving the upper 7.1/7.5/7.9 in. (18/19/20 cm) open for the armholes. Seam the sleeves right sides facing each other and wrong sides facing out, and then sew the sleeves into the armholes from the wrong side.

Using US 4 (3.5 mm) needles, pick up and knit 126/130/134 sts from the neckline edge, join into the round, and work 1.2 in. (3 cm) (= 8 rnds) in ribbing pattern. BO all sts, and weave in ends.

SCHEMATIC

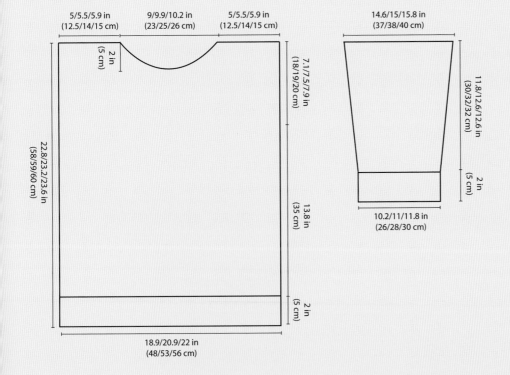

WITH MOSAIC HEM AND CUFFS AND TURTLENECK

Pictured on page 175

BUILDING BLOCK PARTS

BODY SHAPE	Straight
BACK	Basic Sweater 1
FRONT	Basic Sweater 1
SLEEVE	Basic Sweater 1
ARMHOLE	Raglan
SLEEVE LENGTH	Long
NECKLINE	Round neckline with turtleneck
HEMS AND CUFFS	Hem and cuffs in mosaic pattern
SPECIAL FEATURES	This sweater is worked in two colors, which are divided by a mosaic block repeating the hem and cuff pattern.

SIZES

Small/Medium/Large (US 6/8, 10/12, 14/16)

Numbers for size Small are listed before the first slash, for size Medium between slashes, and for size Large after the second slash. If only one number is given, it applies to all sizes.

MATERIALS

Schachenmayr Merino Extrafine 120; #3 light weight yarn; 100% wool; 131 yd (120 m), 1.75 oz. (50 g) per skein

- Main color (MC): 6/7/9 skeins #199 black
- Contrasting color (CC): 5/6/7 skeins #140 cardinal

Circular knitting needles, US 4 (3.5 mm) and US 6 (4.0 mm), each 32 in. (80 cm) long

GAUGE

In stockinette stitch on US 6 (4.0 mm) needles, 22 sts and 30 rows = 4 x 4 in. (10 x 10 cm)

SCHEMATIC

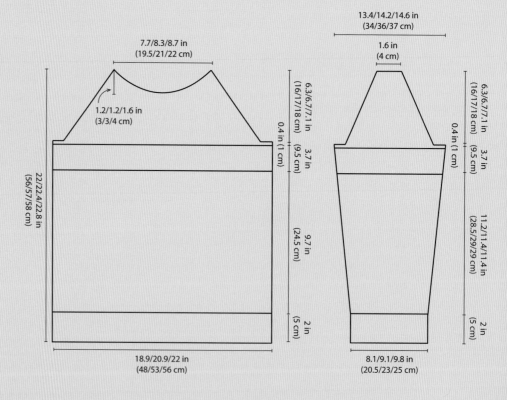

STOCKINETTE STITCH

RS: Knit all sts.
WS: Purl all sts.

MOSAIC PATTERN

RS rows: *K1 in contrasting color (CC), k1 in main color (MC), rep from * throughout, ending with k1 in CC.
WS rows: *P1 in MC, p1 in CC, rep from * throughout, ending with p1 in MC.

GARTER STITCH

All rows (RS and WS): Knit all sts.

RIBBING IN ROUNDS

All rounds (RS): Alternate k1, p1.

ACCENTED DECREASES

Accented decreases are always worked in RS rows as follows: K1, skp, cont in St st to last 3 sts of the row, then k2tog, k1. In WS rows, always purl the first 2 sts and the last 2 sts of the row. In RS rows without decreases, always knit the first 2 sts and the last 2 sts of the row.

INSTRUCTIONS

BACK

Using US 4 (3.5 mm) needles and CC (cardinal), CO 105/117/123 sts, and work as follows: 4 rows garter st in CC, 10 rows mosaic pattern, 4 rows garter st in CC. Change to US 6 (4.0 mm) needles, and cont in St st in MC (black).

After 9.7 in. (24.5 cm) (= 74 rows) from end of ribbing, cont as follows: 4 rows garter st in CC, 20 rows mosaic pattern, 4 rows garter st in MC. Cont in CC in St st.

For raglan shaping, after having worked 13.8 in. (35 cm) (= 104 rows) from end of ribbing, BO sts at both ends of the row as follows: BO 6/7/8 sts once; then, in every other row, 3 sts once, and then 2 sts once. Then, at both ends of the row, work accented decrease of 1 st each in every other row 16/21/22 times, and then in every 4th row 3/1/1 time(s) more. At 20/20.5/21 in. (51/52/53 cm) (= 154/156/158 rows) from end of ribbing, BO the remaining 45/49/51 sts.

FRONT

Work as the Back, but with neckline shaping. For this, after having worked only 19/19.3/19.7 in. (48/49/50 cm) (= 144/148/150 rows) from end of hem ribbing, BO the middle 19/23/25 sts, and continue both sides separately. For the rounded neckline, BO sts at the neck edge in every other row as follows: BO 4 sts once, 3 sts 1/2/1 time(s), 2 sts 2/1/2 time(s), and 1 st 1/0/1 time(s). At 20/20.5/21 in. (51/52/53 cm) (= 154/156/158 rows) from end of ribbing, break the working yarn, leaving a not-too-short end, and pull the tail through the last stitch.

SLEEVES (MAKE 2)

Using US 4 (3.5 mm) needles and CC, CO 45/51/55 sts, and work as follows: 4 rows garter st in CC, 10 rows mosaic pattern, 4 rows garter st in CC. Change to US 6 (4.0 mm) needles, and cont in St st in MC. For sleeve tapering, after having worked 6/8/8 rows from end of cuff, inc 1 st at each end of the row. Rep these incs in every 6th row 7/2/0 times more and in every 8th row 7/11/12 times more (= 75/79/81 sts).

At the same time, after having worked 11.2/11.4/11.4 in. (28.5/29/29 cm) (= 86/88/88 rows) from end of cuff, cont as follows: 4 rows garter st in CC, 20 rows mosaic pattern, 4 rows garter st in MC. Cont in CC in St st.

For raglan shaping, after 15/15.4/15.4 in. (38/39/39 cm) (= 116/118/118 rows) from end of ribbing, BO sts at both ends of the row as follows: BO 6/7/8 sts each once, and then in every other row as follows: 3 sts once and 2 sts once. Then, at both ends of the row, in every other row, work accented decrease of 1 st each 22/23/23 times, and then in every 4th row 0/0/1 time(s) more. At raglan height 6.3/6.7/7.1 in. (16/17/18 cm) (= 50/52/54 rows), BO the remaining 9 sts.

FINISHING

Block all pieces to measurements on a soft surface, moisten, and let dry. Right sides facing each other and wrong sides facing out, sew the sleeves to the Front and Back along the raglan lines. Close side and sleeve seams from the wrong side.

Using CC, pick up and knit 126/130/134 sts from the neckline edge, join into the round, and, for the turtleneck, work in ribbing patt for 9.5 in. (24 cm) (= 72 rnds). BO all sts in pattern, and weave in ends.

ROUND NECKLINE WITH RIBBED NECKBAND

A-LINE SHAPED WITH ELBOW-LENGTH SLEEVES, LACE PATTERN, AND NUPP HEM AND CUFFS

Instructions on page 182

ARMHOLE WITH SLEEVE CAP

ELBOW-LENGTH SLEEVES

A-LINE SHAPED BODY

HEM AND CUFFS IN NUPP PATTERN

RAGLAN WITH ELBOW-LENGTH SLEEVES AND LACE HEM AND CUFFS

Instructions on page 184

V-NECK WITH RIBBED NECKBAND

ARMHOLE WITH RAGLAN SHAPING

ELBOW-LENGTH SLEEVES

STRAIGHT BODY

HEM AND CUFFS IN LACE PATTERN

A-LINE SHAPED WITH ELBOW-LENGTH SLEEVES, LACE PATTERN, AND NUPP HEM AND CUFFS

Pictured on page 180

BUILDING BLOCK PARTS

BODY SHAPE	A-line
BACK	Basic Sweater 4
FRONT	Basic Sweater 4
SLEEVES	Basic Sweater 1
ARMHOLE	Sleeve cap
SLEEVE LENGTH	Elbow-length sleeves
NECKLINE	Round neckline with ribbed neckband
HEMS AND CUFFS	Hem and cuffs in nupp pattern

SIZES

Small/Medium/Large (US 6/8, 10/12, 14/16)

Numbers for size Small are listed before the first slash, for size Medium between slashes, and for size Large after the second slash. If only one number is given, it applies to all sizes.

MATERIALS

Schachenmayr Merino Extrafine 120; #3 light weight yarn; 100% wool; 131 yd (120 m), 1.75 oz. (50 g) per skein

• 10/11/13 skeins #171 olive

Circular knitting needles, US 4 (3.5 mm) and US 6 (4.0 mm), each 40 in. (100 cm) long

GAUGE

In stockinette stitch on US 6 (4.0 mm) needles, 22 sts and 30 rows = 4 x 4 in. (10 x 10 cm)

In lace pattern on US 6 (4.0 mm) needles, 20 sts and 28 rows = 4 x 4 in. (10 x 10 cm)

STOCKINETTE STITCH

RS: Knit all sts.

WS: Purl all sts.

RIBBING IN ROUNDS

All rounds (RS): Alternate k1, p1.

GARTER STITCH

All rows (RS and WS): Knit all sts.

NUPP PATTERN

Work from Stitch Pattern Chart D. Only RS rows are shown in the chart; in WS rows, purl all sts and yarn overs. Repeat the patt rep widthwise across, ending with the 2 sts after the patt rep.

LACE PATTERN

Work from Stitch Pattern Chart A. Only RS rows are shown in the chart; in WS rows, work all sts as they appear, and purl the yarn overs. Begin with the sts before the patt rep, repeat the patt rep widthwise across, and end with the sts after the patt rep. Repeat Rows 1–12 of the chart heightwise throughout.

ACCENTED DECREASES

Accented decreases are always worked in RS rows as follows: K1, skp, work in pattern to last 3 sts of the row, then k2tog, k1. In WS rows, always purl the first 2 sts and the last 2 sts of the row. In RS rows without decreases, always knit the first 2 sts and the last 2 sts of the row.

STITCH PATTERN CHART A
Stitch count is a multiple of 10 + 15

patt rep = 10 sts

STITCH PATTERN CHART D
Stitch count is a multiple of 11 + 2

patt rep = 11 sts

KNITTING SYMBOLS

- ■ = knit 1 st
- – = purl 1 st
- ○ = make 1 yarn over
- ◢ = knit 2 sts together
- ◣ = slip 1, knit 1, pass the slipped st over
- ▲ = slip 1, knit 2 sts together, pass the slipped st over
- ☐ = no st, for better overview only
- N = 1 nupp (= work k1, p1, k1, p1, k1 all into the next st, turn work, purl the 5 nupp sts, turn work again one after another, pass the 2nd, 3rd, 4th and 5th st over the first one)

INSTRUCTIONS

BACK

Using US 4 (3.5 mm) needles, CO 156/167/178 sts, and work as follows: 4 rows garter st, 16 rows in nupp pattern, 4 rows garter st; *at the same time*, in the last row, evenly distributed, dec 11/12/13 sts (= 145/155/165 sts). Change to US 6 (4.0 mm) needles, and cont in lace pattern. For side shaping, after having worked 4 rows from end of hem ribbing, work 1 accented decrease at each end of the row. Rep accented decreases at both ends of the row in every 4th row 8 times more, and then alternatingly in every 2nd and every 4th row a total of 16 times more (= 95/105/115 sts). After this, cont even in lace pattern without further decreases.

For armhole shaping, after having worked 13.8 in. (35 cm) (= 98 rows) from end of ribbing, BO 3/4/5 sts at each end of the row once, and then BO another 2 sts twice and 1 st 1/2/1

time(s). At 21/21.3/21.7 in. (53/54/55 cm) (= 148/152/154 rows) from end of ribbing, BO the remaining 79/85/95 sts.

FRONT

Work as the Back, but with neckline shaping. For this, after having worked only 19/19.3/19.7 in. (48/49/50 cm) (= 134/138/140 rows) from end of ribbing, BO the middle 21/21/29 sts, and continue both sides separately. For the rounded neckline, BO sts at the neck edge in every other row as follows: BO 3 sts 2/3/2 times, 2 sts 3/2/3 times, and 1 st once. At 21/21.3/21.7 in. (53/54/55 cm) (= 148/152/154 rows) from end of ribbing, BO the remaining 16/18/20 sts for each shoulder.

SLEEVES (MAKE 2)

Using US 4 (3.5 mm) needles, CO 68/79/79 sts, and work as follows: 4 rows garter st, 16 rows in nupp pattern, 4 rows garter st; *at the same time*, in the last row, evenly distributed, inc 1 st/dec 6 sts/dec 4 sts (= 69/73/75 sts). Change to US 6 (4.0 mm) needles, and continue

in St st. For sleeve tapering, after having worked 2/6/2 rows from end of hem ribbing, inc 1 st at each end of the row. Rep these incs in every 8th row 2 times more (= 75/79/81 sts).

For the sleeve cap, after having worked 4/4.3/4.3 in. (10/11/11 cm) (= 30/32/32 rows) from end of cuff, BO 3/4/5 sts at each end of the row once, and then, in every other row, BO 2 sts twice, 1 st 10/12/14 times, 2 sts 5/4/3 times, and 3 sts once. At sleeve cap height of 4.7/5.1/5.5 in. (12/13/14 cm) (= 38/40/42 rows), BO the remaining 15/17/17 sts.

FINISHING

Block all pieces to measurements on a soft surface, moisten, and let dry. Close sleeve, shoulder, and side seams from the wrong side, and then sew the sleeves into the armholes from the wrong side.

Using US 4 (3.5 mm) needles, pick up and knit 126/130/134 sts from the neckline edge, join into the round, and work 1.2 in. (3 cm) (= 8 rnds) in ribbing pattern. BO all sts in pattern, and weave in ends.

SCHEMATIC

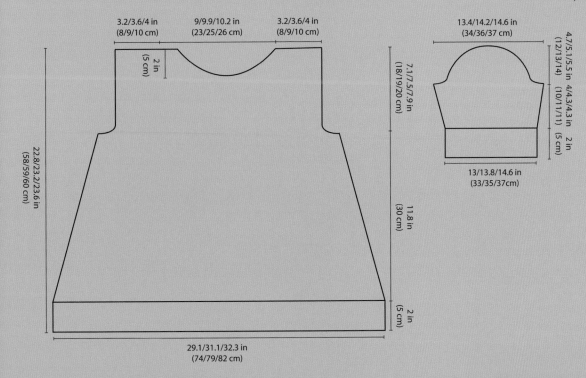

RAGLAN WITH ELBOW-LENGTH SLEEVES AND LACE HEM AND CUFFS

Pictured on page 181

BUILDING BLOCK PARTS

BODY SHAPE	Straight
BACK	Basic Sweater 1
FRONT	Basic Sweater 1
SLEEVES	Basic Sweater 1
ARMHOLE	Raglan
SLEEVE LENGTH	Elbow-length sleeves
NECKLINE	V-neck with ribbed neckband
HEMS AND CUFFS	Hem and cuffs in lace pattern
SPECIAL FEATURES	This sweater is made longer by working the lace pattern on hem and cuffs 3 times in a row.

SIZES

Small/Medium/Large (US 6/8, 10/12, 14/16)

Numbers for size Small are listed before the first slash, for size Medium between slashes, and for size Large after the second slash. If only one number is given, it applies to all sizes.

MATERIALS

Schachenmayr Merino Extrafine 120; #3 light weight yarn; 100% wool; 131 yd (120 m), 1.75 oz. (50 g) per skein

• 9/10/12 skeins #172 fir

Circular knitting needle, US 6 (4.0 mm), 32 in. (80 cm) long

GAUGE

In stockinette stitch on US 6 (4.0 mm) needles, 22 sts and 30 rows = 4 x 4 in. (10 x 10 cm)

In lace pattern on US 6 (4.0 mm) needles, 21 sts and 32 rows = 4 x 4 in. (10 x 10 cm)

STOCKINETTE STITCH

RS: Knit all sts.
WS: Purl all sts.

LACE PATTERN

Work from Stitch Pattern Chart E. Only RS rows are shown in the chart; in WS rows, purl all sts and yarn overs. Begin with the 7 sts before the patt rep, repeat the patt rep widthwise, and end with the 6 sts after the patt rep. Work Rows 1–14 a total of 3 times heightwise, and then work only Rows 15 and 16 once more.

RIBBING IN ROUNDS

All rounds (RS): Alternate k1, p1.

ACCENTED DECREASES

Accented decreases are always worked in RS rows as follows: K1, skp, cont in St st to last 3 sts of the row, then k2tog, k1. In WS rows, always purl the first 2 sts and the last 2 sts of the row. In RS rows without decreases, always knit the first 2 sts and the last 2 sts of the row.

INSTRUCTIONS

BACK

CO 103/113/123 sts, and for hem ribbing, work 44 rows in lace pattern; *at the same time*, in the last row, evenly distributed, inc 2/4/0 sts (= 105/117/123 sts), and then cont in St st.

For raglan shaping, after having worked 13.8 in. (35 cm) (= 104 rows) from end of ribbing, BO at both ends

STITCH PATTERN CHART E
Stitch count is a multiple of 10 + 13

patt rep = 10 sts

KNITTING SYMBOLS

■ = knit 1 st
− = purl 1 st
○ = make 1 yarn over
◢ = knit 2 sts together

◣ = slip 1, knit 1, pass the slipped st over
▲ = slip 1, knit 2 sts together, pass the slipped st over

SCHEMATIC

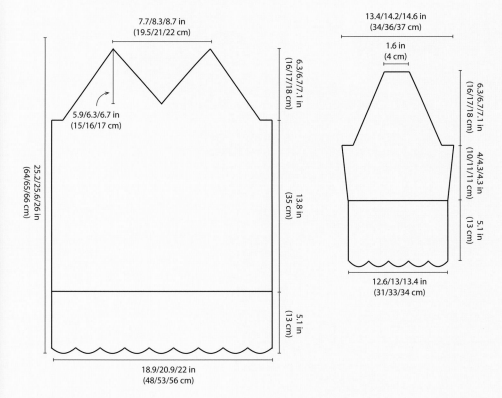

7.7/8.3/8.7 in
(19.5/21/22 cm)

5.9/6.3/6.7 in
(15/16/17 cm)

6.3/6.7/7.1 in
(16/17/18 cm)

25.2/25.6/26 in
(64/65/66 cm)

13.8 in
(35 cm)

5.1 in
(13 cm)

18.9/20.9/22 in
(48/53/56 cm)

13.4/14.2/14.6 in
(34/36/37 cm)

1.6 in
(4 cm)

6.3/6.7/7.1 in
(16/17/18 cm)

4/4.3/4.3 in
(10/11/11 cm)

5.1 in
(13 cm)

12.6/13/13.4 in
(31/33/34 cm)

of the row as follows: BO 6/7/8 sts once; then, in every other row, 3 sts once, and then 2 sts once. Then, at both ends of the row, work accented decrease of 1 st each in every other row 16/21/22 times, and then in every 4th row 3/1/1 time(s) more. At 20/20.5/21 in. (51/52/53 cm) (= 154/156/158 rows) from end of ribbing, BO the remaining 45/49/51 sts.

FRONT

Work as the Back, but with V-neck. For this, after having worked only 14.4/14.2/14.2 in. (36.5/36/36 cm) (= 110/108/108 rows) from end of ribbing, BO 1 st in the middle, and continue both sides separately. For the sloped neckline, at the neck edge, in every RS row, work accented decrease of 1 st each 21/23/24 times. After having

worked 20/20.5/21 in. (51/52/53 cm) (= 154/156/158 rows) from end of ribbing, break the working yarn, leaving a not-too-short end, and pull the tail through the last stitch.

SLEEVES (MAKE 2)

CO 73/83/93 sts, and for hem ribbing, work 44 rows in lace pattern; *at the same time*, in the last row, evenly distributed, dec 4/10/18 sts (= 69/73/75 sts). After this, cont in St st. For sleeve tapering, after having worked 2/6/2 rows from end of cuff, inc 1 st at each end of the row. Rep these incs in every 8th row 2 times more (= 75/79/81 sts).

For raglan shaping, after having worked 4/4.3/4.3 in. (10/11/11 cm) (=

30/32/32 rows) from end of cuff, BO 6/7/8 sts at each end of the row once, and then in every other row as follows: 3 sts once and 2 sts once. Then, at both ends of the row, in every other row, work accented decrease of 1 st each 22/23/23 times, and then in every 4th row 0/0/1 time(s) more. At raglan height 6.3/6.7/7.1 in. (16/17/18 cm) (= 50/52/54 rows), BO the remaining 9 sts.

FINISHING

Block all pieces to measurements on a soft surface, moisten, and let dry. Right sides facing each other and wrong sides facing out, sew the sleeves to the Front and Back along the raglan lines. Close side and sleeve seams from the wrong side.

Using US 4 (3.5 mm) needles, and beginning at the right edge of the Back neckline, pick up and knit a total of 156/162/168 sts for the V-neck neckline as follows: 51/53/55 sts along the Back neckline, 52/54/56 sts along the left sleeve and the left Front to 1 st before the deepest point of the V-neck, 1 st from the tip of the V-neck, 52/54/56 sts along the sts of the right Front and the right sleeve. Join into the round, and work ribbing as follows:

Rnd 1: Work in ribbing pattern.
Rnd 2: Work in ribbing to 1 st before the tip of the V-neck, work cdd over 3 sts (= slip 2 sts together knitwise, knit the next st, and pass the slipped sts over the knitted one), ribbing to end of rnd.
Row 3: Knit the knits and purl the purls. Rep Rnds 2 and 3 twice more, and then BO all sts.
Weave in ends.

STRAIGHT
BODY

HEM AND
CUFFS IN
STRANDED
PATTERN

IN A PATTERN MIX AND WITH MOCK TURTLENECK

Instructions on page 188

STRAIGHT ARMHOLE

ROUND NECKLINE WITH MOCK TURTLENECK

LONG SLEEVE

IN A PATTERN MIX AND WITH MOCK TURTLENECK

Pictured on pages 186 and 187

BUILDING BLOCK PARTS

BODY SHAPE	Straight
BACK	Basic Sweater 5
FRONT	Basic Sweater 6
SLEEVES	Basic Sweater 2
ARMHOLE	Straight
SLEEVE LENGTH	Long
NECKLINE	Round neckline with mock turtleneck
HEMS AND CUFFS	Hem and cuffs in stranded pattern
SPECIAL FEATURES	This sweater is a composite of 3 different Basic Sweaters.

SIZES

Small/Medium/Large (US 6/8, 10/12, 14/16)

Numbers for size Small are listed before the first slash, for size Medium between slashes, and for size Large after the second slash. If only one number is given, it applies to all sizes.

MATERIALS

Schachenmayr Merino Extrafine 120; #3 light weight yarn; 100% wool; 131 yd (120 m), 1.75 oz. (50 g) per skein

- Main color (MC): 5/6/7 skeins #191 flannel heathered
- Contrasting color 1 (CC1): 1/1/2 skeins #150 marine blue
- Contrasting color 2 (CC2): 4/4/5 skeins #142 red
- Contrasting color 3 (CC3): 1/1/1 skein #101 white
- Contrasting color 4 (CC4): 1/1/1 skein #171 olive

Circular knitting needles, US 4 (3.5 mm) and US 6 (4.0 mm), each 32 in. (80 cm) long

Cable needle (cn)

GAUGE

In stockinette stitch on US 6 (4.0 mm) needles, 22 sts and 30 rows = 4 x 4 in. (10 x 10 cm)

In double seed stitch on US 6 (4.0 mm) needles, 22 sts and 34 rows = 4 x 4 in. (10 x 10 cm)

In cable pattern 1 on US 6 (4.0 mm) needles, 58 sts = 8.3 in. (21 cm)

In lace pattern on US 6 (4.0 mm) needles, 20 sts and 28 rows = 4 x 4 in. (10 x 10 cm)

In stranded colorwork pattern on US 4 (3.5 mm) needles, 22 sts and 30 rows = 4 x 4 in. (10 x 10 cm)

STOCKINETTE STITCH IN ROWS

RS: Knit all sts.
WS: Purl all sts.

STOCKINETTE STITCH IN ROUNDS

All rounds (RS): Knit all stitches.

GARTER STITCH IN ROWS

All rows (RS and WS): Knit all sts.

GARTER STITCH IN ROUNDS

Knit all sts in odd-numbered rnds, purl all sts in even-numbered rnds.

SCHEMATIC

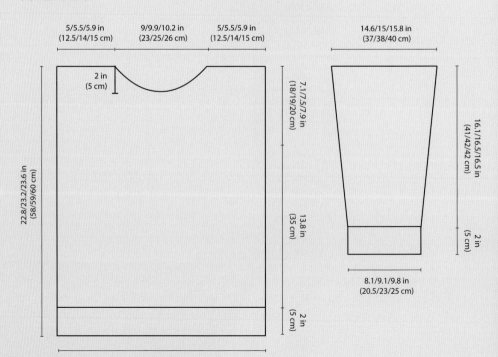

5/5.5/5.9 in (12.5/14/15 cm)

9/9.9/10.2 in (23/25/26 cm)

5/5.5/5.9 in (12.5/14/15 cm)

14.6/15/15.8 in (37/38/40 cm)

2 in (5 cm)

7.1/7.5/7.9 in (18/19/20 cm)

16.1/16.5/16.5 in (41/42/42 cm)

22.8/23.2/23.6 in (58/59/60 cm)

13.8 in (35 cm)

2 in (5 cm)

2 in (5 cm)

8.1/9.1/9.8 in (20.5/23/25 cm)

18.9/20.9/22 in (48/53/56 cm)

LACE PATTERN

Work from Stitch Pattern Chart A. Only RS rows are shown in the chart; in WS rows, work all sts as they appear, and purl the yarn overs. Begin with the sts before the patt rep, repeat the patt rep widthwise across, and end with the sts after the patt rep. Repeat Rows 1–12 of the chart heightwise throughout.

STRANDED PATTERN IN ROWS

Work in stockinette in stranded color-work pattern from Colorwork Chart C. The chart contains both RS and WS rows. Sts are shown as they appear from the RS of the fabric. Repeat the patt rep (6 sts wide) widthwise across, ending with the 3 sts after the patt rep. Work Rows 1–6 of the chart twice heightwise.

STRANDED PATTERN IN ROUNDS

Work in stockinette in stranded color-work pattern from Colorwork Chart C. The charts shows all rounds as stitches appear on the right side of the fabric. Repeat the patt rep (6 sts wide) width-wise around; ignore the 3 sts after the marked repeat—these will not be worked. Work Rows 1–6 of the chart twice heightwise.

DOUBLE SEED STITCH

Row 1: Alternate k1, p1.
Row 2: Knit the knits and purl the purls.
Row 3: Alternate p1, k1.
Row 4: Knit the knits and purl the purls.
Rep Rows 1–4 throughout.

CABLE PATTERN 1

Work from Stitch Pattern Chart B. Only RS rows are shown in the chart; in WS rows, work all sts as they appear (knit the knits and purl the purls), and purl the slipped sts. Work the patt rep (58 sts wide) widthwise across once, and then rep Rows 1–12 heightwise throughout.

STRIPE SEQUENCE A

Alternate 2 rows in MC, 2 rows in CC2.

STRIPE SEQUENCE C

This stripe sequence is worked only once.
18 rows in stripe sequence A, 6 rows in MC, 12 rows in CC4, 22 rows in stripe sequence A, 14 rows in CC1, 10 rows in CC2, 10 rows in CC3, 6 rows in CC1.

STITCH PATTERN CHART A
Stitch count is a multiple of 10 + 15

patt rep = 10 sts

COLORWORK CHART C

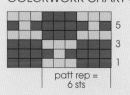

patt rep =
6 sts

KNITTING SYMBOLS

☐ = St st in MC (flannel heathered)
■ = St st in CC (red)

STITCH PATTERN CHART B

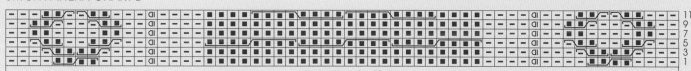

cable pattern 1 = 58 sts

KNITTING SYMBOLS

■ = knit 1 st
− = purl 1 st
○ = make 1 yarn over
◢ = knit 2 sts together
◣ = slip 1, knit 1, pass the slipped st over
▲ = slip 1, knit 2 sts together, pass the slipped st over

☐ = no st, for better overview only
⊡ = slip 1 st purlwise with yarn in back of work
= hold 1 st on cn in back of work, knit the next 2 sts, and then knit the st from the cn
= hold 2 sts on cn in front of work, purl the next st, and then knit the 2 sts from the cn

= hold 2 sts on cn in back of work, knit the next 2 sts, and then knit the 2 sts from the cn
= hold 4 sts on cn in back of work, knit the next 4 sts, and then knit the 4 sts from the cn
= hold 4 sts on cn in front of work, knit the next 4 sts, and then knit the 4 sts from the cn

INSTRUCTIONS

BACK

Using US 4 (3.5 mm) needles and CC2 (red), CO 105/117/123 sts, and for hem ribbing, work as follows: 4 rows garter st in CC2, 12 rows in stranded colorwork pattern, 4 rows garter st in CC2; *at the same time*, in the last row, evenly distributed, dec 10/12/8 sts (= 95/105/115 sts). Change to US 6 (4.0 mm) needles, and cont in CC2 in lace pattern. At 21/21.3/21.7 in. (53/54/55 cm) (= 148/152/154 rows) from hem ribbing, BO all sts.

FRONT

First, begin the hem as for the Back, but, in the last row, evenly distributed inc 11/11/9 sts (= 116/128/132 sts). Change to US 6 (4.0 mm) needles, and cont in MC (flannel heathered) in the following pattern: 1 st in St st, 28/34/36 sts in double seed stitch, 58 sts in cable pattern, 28/34/36 sts in double seed stitch, 1 st in St st.

For neckline shaping, after having worked 19/19.3/19.7 in. (48/49/50 cm) (= 164/166/168 rows) from end of ribbing, BO the middle 28/30/30 sts, and continue both sides separately. For the rounded neckline, BO sts at the neck edge in every other row as follows: BO 4 sts once, 3 sts twice, 2 sts 3/3/2 times, and 1 st 1/2/4 time(s). At 21/21.3/21.7 in. (53/54/55 cm) (= 180/184/188 rows) from end of ribbing, BO the remaining 27/31/33 sts for each shoulder.

SLEEVES (MAKE 2)

Using US 4 (3.5 mm) needles and CC2, CO 45/51/57 sts, and for the cuff, work as follows: 4 rows garter st in CC2, 12 rows in stranded colorwork pattern, 4 rows garter st in CC2; *at the same time*, in the last row, evenly distributed, dec 0/0/2 sts (= 45/51/55 sts). Change to US 6 (4.0 mm) needles, and cont in St st in stripe sequence C. After having completed stripe sequence C, finish the piece in St st in stripe sequence A.

At the same time, for sleeve tapering, after having worked 6/8/8 rows from end of cuff, inc 1 st at each end of the row. Rep these incs in every 6th row 13/10/10 times more and in every 8th row 4/6/6 times more (= 81/85/89 sts). At 16.1/16.5/16.5 in. (41/42/42 cm) (= 124/126/126 rows) from hem ribbing, BO all sts.

FINISHING

Block all pieces to measurements on a soft surface, moisten, and let dry. Close shoulder and side seams from the wrong side, leaving the upper 7.1/7.5/7.9 in. (18/19/20 cm) open for the armholes. Seam the sleeves right sides facing each other and wrong sides facing out, and then sew the sleeves into the armholes from the wrong side.

Using US 4 (3.5 mm) needles and MC, pick up and knit 120/126/132 sts from the neckline edge, join into the round, and work as follows: 4 rnds garter st in MC, 12 rnds in stranded pattern, 4 rnds garter st in MC. BO all sts, and weave in ends.

MY SWEATER DESIGN

Now it's your turn! Become creative, and combine elements into your personal sweater. With the help of this checklist, this will be very easy, and you will be able to start your project in no time.

You don't want to write into the book? No problem! Make a photocopy of this page and use it as your worksheet.

SWEATER FOR	**GAUGE**
SIZE	**STITCH PATTERN**
YARN	**ON NEEDLES**
NEEDLE SIZE	**STS AND ROWS = 4 X 4 IN. (10 CM X 10 CM)**

1. My stitch pattern(s) from Basic Sweaters 1–6
☐ Stockinette stitch (page 12)
☐ Stripes (page 14)
☐ Patterned border (page 15)
☐ Stranded colorwork (page 20)
☐ Lace pattern (page 21)
☐ Cable pattern (page 26)

2. My body shape
☐ Straight body (page 12ff)
☐ Oversized/boxy body (page 68ff)
☐ A-line body (page 76ff)
☐ Fitted body (page 84ff)

3. My cuffs
☐ Ribbing (page 34)
☐ Seed stitch (page 35)
☐ Cable pattern (page 36)
☐ Stranded colorwork (page 37)
☐ Mosaic pattern (page 38)
☐ Nupp pattern (page 39)
☐ Lace pattern (page 40)
☐ Rolled edge (page 41)

4. My neckline finishing
☐ Crewneck (page 42)
☐ Ribbed neckband (page 44)
☐ Rolled neckband (page 44)
☐ Turtleneck (page 45)
☐ Mock turtleneck (page 45)
☐ V-neck with ribbed neckband (pages 43 and 46)

5. My armhole
☐ Straight sleeve (page 12ff)
☐ Sleeve cap (page 47ff)
☐ Raglan sleeve (page 53ff)

6. My sleeve length
☐ Long sleeve (page 59ff)
☐ ¾ sleeve (page 59ff)
☐ Short sleeve (page 59ff)

7. My stitch pattern alternatives
KNIT-PURL PATTERNS
☐ Knit-Purl pattern 1 (page 104)
☐ Knit-Purl pattern 2 (page 105)
☐ Knit-Purl pattern 3 (page 105)
☐ Knit-Purl pattern 4 (page 105)
STRANDED COLORWORK PATTERNS
☐ Stranded pattern 1 (page 106)
☐ Stranded pattern 2 (page 106)
☐ Stranded pattern 3 (page 107)
☐ Stranded pattern 4 (page 107)
LACE PATTERNS
☐ Lace pattern 1 (page 108)
☐ Lace pattern 2 (page 108)
☐ Lace pattern 3 (page 109)
☐ Lace pattern 4 (page 109)
CABLE PATTERNS
☐ Cable pattern 1 (page 110)
☐ Cable pattern 2 (page 110)
☐ Cable pattern 3 (page 110)
☐ Cable pattern 4 (page 110)

STARTED (DATE)	**FINISHED (DATE)**

KNITTING BASICS -

HOW TO WORK

MATERIALS AND GAUGE SWATCH

Knitted fabric is a material with very unique properties. It is very elastic, so that garments with no or even negative ease can be worn comfortably. Properly fitted garments will adjust to any movement.

The finished fabric contains isolating air pockets, which keep the wearer warm and create a pleasant microclimate on the skin. Wool fiber additionally enhances this effect through the air trapped in the curled fibers and their high moisture-retention rate.

GRIP AND DRAPE

Grip means how soft and stretchable, or how stiff and rigid, a knitted piece feels. Grip also determines how well a garment clings to the body and yields to movement.

The drape states how tightly or loosely the stitches interlock—whether they are meshed so loosely into each other that the knitted piece will not hold shape, or whether the stitches are squeezed so tightly together in both directions that the finished knitted piece keeps its shape. Drape is determined by the yarn, a looser or tighter gauge, and the stitch pattern used.

Soft, flowing knit designs or details that don't need to hold shape, but shift loosely around the body, are worked with thicker needles than stated on the ball band. This creates a more meshy knitted fabric than normal. When using wool or mohair yarns and wet-blocking the knitted piece until dry, the fibers of the yarn will lock, and the knitted piece will become open and airy. This method is mainly used with knitted lace shawls and stoles. Smooth and slippery yarns, however, should not be knitted on thicker needles, because the knitted fabric would not keep shape and would easily stretch out.

Loosely spun wool yarns are suitable for soft, figure-hugging garments with details such as flowing collars. The shape of these garments is mainly determined by their measurements and the seams.

For firm, shape-holding knitted pieces, such as jackets, bags, stuffed toys, or pillowcases, thinner needles than normal are used. The stitches in the knitted fabric are smaller, firmer, and denser, and the knitted fabric feels stiffer to the touch. These should be worked in firm stitch patterns with solid increases and decreases. Tightly plied yarns will enhance this effect, and they are also more robust than loosely plied ones.

A garment with high-elasticity features should fit close to the body and at the same time stretch easily and conform to all movements without constricting or pinching. This should be said especially about sleeve cuffs, neckline finishing, or hem ribbing on sweaters. Yarns plied medium tight to tight, with a larger percentage of wool fiber, which by themselves are already elastic, should be worked with a medium needle size. A knit-purl ribbing will add more elasticity. Cuffs worked in nonelastic yarns, such as cotton, obtain the needed elasticity solely from the ribbing pattern. To avoid unwanted stretching in ribbed cuffs, yarns from these fibers should be knit up using a smaller needle size.

Tip: **If a yarn with a different fiber content than stated in the pattern will be used, the required total amount should be calculated by yardage, not weight. For this task, multiply the number of skeins needed listed in the pattern by the number of yards or meters per skein. This yields the total length of yarn needed for the project. You can then calculate how many skeins of your chosen yarn you will need.**

COLOR AND STITCH PATTERN CHOICES

Most stitch patterns will look their best when worked in smooth yarns in light colors. Using darker colors, or multicolored or textured yarns, makes the stitch pattern lose much of its dimensional appeal.

Tightly plied yarns produce a clear and crisply defined stitch appearance. Loosely plied yarns result in softer stitch transitions.

The heavier a knitted piece is patterned, the more yarn will usually be required. This should be considered especially with cable, nupp, and brioche patterns, so either a more lightweight yarn should be used or shaping calculations should account for the higher weight of the finished piece from the beginning.

GAUGE SWATCH

Based upon the planned finished dimensions desired for your knitted piece, the exact widthwise and heightwise stitch count needs to be calculated before starting work.

Since a knitted stitch is usually less high that it is wide, you will first need the exact measurement of a sample in the planned stitch pattern, which is called a gauge swatch. With the help of the gauge swatch, the required stitch count can be calculated.

The gauge swatch depends mainly on the yarn weight: the thicker a yarn, the fewer the stitches that will fit into a certain width.

Additionally, the stitch pattern used will have an impact on the gauge. Cables will heavily constrict the knitted fabric, while lace patterns with a multitude of holes need significantly fewer stitches to cover the same width. With stranded colorwork, the knitted fabric will constrict, but often fewer stitches are required heightwise than with one-colored stockinette.

Needle size, individual gauge, and the fiber content of the yarn all will affect the gauge, too. Before starting a knitting project, time should be taken to make a gauge swatch. Only with a matching gauge can you be sure to achieve the fit of the original pattern or to match the measurements of your own calculations. Afterthought cutting of knitted garments should be avoided at all costs. The seams that would be required to secure the cut stitches would be hardly elastic anymore and, therefore, always present a disruptive element in the future garment.

A good starting point for determining the gauge is the information on the ball band. It will list how many stitches a swatch worked in stockinette stitch on a certain size needle will have over 4 x 4 in. (10 x 10 cm).

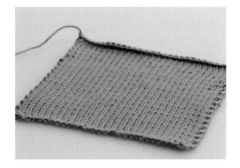

Cast on one-and-a-half times as many stitches as stated for 4 in. (10 cm). Work to a height of 6 in. (15 cm) in the stitch pattern for the gauge swatch.

Bind off all stitches loosely, and then steam block the swatch, or wash by hand, pin down with tailor pins onto a suitable surface, and let dry.

Use tailor pins to mark a section of 4 in. (10 cm) widthwise and heightwise, and count the stitches. Write down the stitch count widthwise, the number of rows heightwise, and the needle size used. This is your personal gauge with this particular yarn in this specific stitch pattern on needles of this exact size.

Now compare the stitch count of your own sample to the numbers listed in the pattern, or check whether the stitch density of the sample is how you would like to have it throughout the whole knitted piece. If you count more stitches than stated in the pattern, or if the swatch seems too densely knit, choose a larger needle size for your next swatch. If you count fewer stitches than stated in the pattern, or if the swatch seems

too loosely knit, choose a smaller needle size for your next swatch.

When using a yarn with a different fiber content than the one listed in the pattern, it can happen that either the stitch count widthwise or the row count heightwise match, but not both at the same time. In this case, choose the needle size that gives you a matching stitch count widthwise, and adjust the height according to the schematic by working fewer or additional rows.

Often, the second gauge swatch is skipped—for fear of having not enough yarn! Make a habit of always buying a skein more than anticipated, and you will be able to swatch for the fitting needle size until your gauge matches, without having to be afraid of running out of yarn. In most cases, leftover full skeins can be returned to the store during a certain time frame.

With the results of your gauge swatch and the measurements from the schematic, you can use the ratios to calculate your stitch counts. Even easier than that, use a knitting calculator: just turn the rotating disc to the appropriate gauge for your yarn, and read off stitch counts for different lengths.

If pieces will be seamed afterward, selvedge stitches at the side edges of the knitted pieces always have to be accounted for additionally. After seaming, they will be on the inside of the finished garment, where they won't add extra width.

Tip: Even when you have arrived at a matching gauge with the help of your gauge swatch, it is still a good idea to recheck how many stitches widthwise and rows heightwise you end up with in 4 in. (10 cm) after having worked in pattern to a height of 11.8 in. (30 cm).

BODY MEASUREMENTS AND KNITTING PATTERNS

Taking exact measurements correctly is crucial for a well-fitting garment. For this reason, body measurements are taken in accordance with defined rules in relevant places on the body that are anatomically important for the garment.

BODY MEASUREMENTS

When taking individual body measurements, the tape measure should be held snugly against the body, but not cut into it. Measurements are taken in an upright standing position, in a naturally relaxed posture, and noted in a measuring table in inches or centimeters. It is recommended to wear a close-fitting t-shirt. This way, beginning and ending points can be pinned on if needed. To determine the correct position of the waist, it can be marked using a narrow ribbon or piece of yarn. As a general rule, the closer a garment is cut to the body, the more detailed measurements should be taken and matched to the pattern's schematic.

MEASURING FOR OVERGARMENTS

CHEST CIRCUMFERENCE: Measure the maximum circumference, horizontally over the fullest part of the bust, underneath the armpits and slightly extending over the bottom point of the shoulder blades.

WAIST CIRCUMFERENCE: Measure at the narrowest part, closing the measuring tape in the front. This measurement is needed for form-fitting tops.

HIP CIRCUMFERENCE: Measure horizontally around the fullest part of the hip. Let the measuring tape slowly slide over the posterior horizontally, and adjust the length to the fullest spot.

SHOULDER WIDTH: The shoulder width is measured from the lateral base of the neck to the beginning of the highest point of the upper arm.

UPPER ARM WIDTH: With arms loosely hanging down, measure the circumference of the arm below the armpit. The circumference of the dominant arm will often be about 0.8 to 1.2 in. (2 to 3 cm) larger. This difference should normally be absorbed by the elasticity of the knitted fabric. Only for very snug-fitting sleeves might it become necessary to note different arm circumferences and adjust the sleeves accordingly during knitting.

ARM LENGTH: Measure the outer arm length from the tip of the upper arm over the bent elbow to the outer wrist joint. Rest the closed fist on the waist so that the elbow is bent approximately 90 degrees.

ARMHOLE DEPTH: Have the person to be measured pin a sheet of paper under their armpit with the top edge going horizontally over the spinal column. Measure from the seventh vertebra along the spinal column downward to the top edge of the paper.

BACK LENGTH: Place the measuring tape along the spinal column from the seventh vertebra to the waist marker.

BACK WIDTH: Measure at the level of the bust circumference line, with arms hanging down, from one side where the shoulder blade transitions into the armpit to the other side. This is the spot where the sleeve seams should end up later.

Please note: A measurement not originating from the tailoring business, but which is very helpful for designing and grading knitted garments, is the height of the sleeve cap. To determine, place a tape measure directly under the armpit around the upper arm. Starting at this tape, place a second measuring tape over the shoulder joint to where the arm starts, and read the measurement.

Size, US	6	8	10	12	14	16
Bust circumference	33.5 in. (85.5 cm)	34.6 in. (88 cm)	36.2 in. (92 cm)	37.8 in. (96 cm)	39.4 in. (100 cm)	41.7 in. (106 cm)
Hip circumference	37 in. (94 cm)	38.2 in. (97 cm)	39.8 in. (101 cm)	41.3 in. (105 cm)	42.9 in. (109 cm)	45.1 in. (114.5 cm)
Height	66.1 in. (168 cm)	66.1 in. (168 cm)	66.1 in. (168 cm)	66.1 in. (168 cm)	66.1 in. (168 cm)	66.1 in. (168 cm)
Waist circumference	27.2 in. (69 cm)	28.3 in. (72 cm)	30.3 in. (76 cm)	31.5 in. (80 cm)	33.1 in. (84 cm)	35.4 in. (90 cm)
Shoulder	4.8 in. (12.1 cm)	4.8 in. (12.2 cm)	4.8 in. (12.3 cm)	4.9 in. (12.4 cm)	4.9 in. (12.5 cm)	5 in. (12.7 cm)
Arm length	23.6 in. (59.9 cm)	23.6 in. (60 cm)	23.7 in. (60.2 cm)	23.8 in. (60.4 cm)	23.9 in. (60.6 cm)	24 in. (60.8 cm)

BASIC LONG-TAIL CAST-ON

The basic long-tail cast-on produces a cast-on edge of medium elasticity. Because the long-tail cast-on is worked using two strands of yarn, before casting on the first stitch, the beginning tail has to be at least 3 times as long as the cast-on edge of the finished piece will be. If an even longer beginning tail is left hanging, it can be used later for seaming pieces.

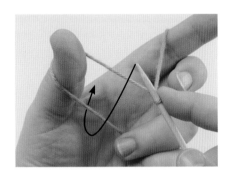

1 Make a slipknot and hold it in place on the working needle using the index finger of your right hand. Spread thumb and index finger of your left hand. Lead the yarn tail over the thumb and the working yarn over the index finger, grasping them with the free fingers of your left hand to pull them taut.

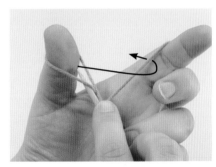

2 Lift the thumb and pull the working needle downward in front of the thumb until the thumb strands cross each other in the front (thumb cross). Pass the tip of the needle below the outermost thumb strand, and lead it from right to left behind the index finger strand in the direction of the arrow as shown.

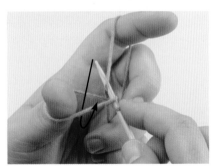

3 Grasp the index finger strand with the needle, and pull it through the thumb loop in the direction of the arrow. Let the loop slip from the thumb and pull the yarn tail with the thumb until a stitch has formed on the working needle. Lift the thumb, and lower the needle. Repeat the steps until the desired number of stitches has been cast on.

BASIC KNIT STITCH

A regular knit stitch is worked off the needle in the direction shown by the arrow in the photo.

To work a knit stitch, the stitch created in the previous row is located on the stitch-bearing needle, which holds the stitches to be worked now and is held in the left hand. All stitches are mounted on the needle with the right leg in front of the needle, and the left leg behind the needle. The working needle is held in the right hand.

There are two main ways that knitters create the knit stitch: picking (also known as Continental) and throwing (also known as English). I will demonstrate both, and you can use whichever you find most comfortable.

PICKING (CONTINENTAL)

1 The working yarn goes over the index finger of the left hand behind the needle. Insert the working needle from the front, from left to right, between the two legs of the next stitch, so that the working needle is underneath the stitch-bearing needle. Lead the tip of the working needle in the direction of the pictured arrow around the working yarn.

2 Lead the working yarn around the working needle, and pull it through the stitch. Let the stitch from the previous row slip off the stitch-bearing left-hand needle. The new knit stitch is now on the right-hand working needle.

Repeat these two steps to knit all stitches from the left needle. After completion of the row, all stitches are located on the right-hand working needle. In the knitted fabric, a knit stitch looks like the letter *V*.

THROWING (ENGLISH)

1 The working yarn goes over the right index finger (the working yarn is located behind the right-hand needle), and the working needle is inserted from the front, from left to right, under the front leg of the stitch. The working needle is located underneath the stitch-bearing needle. Using your right index finger, lead the working yarn behind both needles and bring it to the front from left to right between the needles.

2 Pull the working yarn through the stitch and slip the stitch from the previous row off the stitch-bearing needle. The new stitch is now on the right-hand working needle.

Repeat these two steps until all stitches from the stitch-bearing left-hand needle have been worked.

Remember: Knit stitches wear "V-necks." Purl stitches wear "turtlenecks."

Please note: When comparing how the stitches are created and how they look from the right side and wrong side of the fabric, you can see that the back side of a knit stitch looks like a purl stitch and vice versa.

BASIC PURL STITCH

A basic purl stitch is worked off the needle in the direction shown by the arrow in the photo.

To work a purl stitch, the stitch created in the previous row is located on the stitch-bearing needle, which holds the stitches to be worked now and is held in the left hand. All stitches are mounted on the needle with the right leg in front of the needle, and the left leg behind the needle. The working needle is held in the right hand.

PICKING (CONTINENTAL)

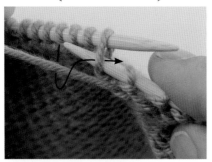

1 The working yarn goes over the index finger of the left hand in front of the needle. If necessary, it can be slightly pushed down with the tip of the left index finger. Insert the working needle from the front, from right to left, between the two legs of the next stitch, so that the working needle is atop the stitch-bearing needle. Lead the tip of the working needle in the direction of the pictured arrow around the working yarn.

2 Lead the working yarn downward between the needles, and pull it through the stitch. Let the stitch from the previous row slip off the stitch-bearing left-hand needle. The new purl stitch is now on the right-hand working needle.

Repeat these two steps until all stitches from the stitch-bearing left-hand needle have been worked. The stitches are now located on the right-hand working needle. The purl stitch features a horizontal strand of yarn, the purl bump.

THROWING (ENGLISH)

1 The working yarn goes over the right index finger (the working yarn is in front of the right-hand working needle), and the right-hand working needle is inserted from the front, from right to left, under the front leg of the stitch to be worked. The right-hand working needle is located atop the stitch-bearing left-hand needle. Using your right index finger, lead the working yarn counterclockwise around the front needle.

2 Pull the working yarn through the stitch. The new purl stitch is now on the right-hand working needle.

Repeat these two steps until all stitches from the stitch-bearing left-hand needle have been worked.

Please note: The new stitches—the knit as well as the purl ones—are again mounted on the needle with the right leg in front. If the stitch sits the other way around, with the left leg in front, the needle has been led around the working yarn in the wrong direction.

DECREASES

Single decreases produce a right- or left-leaning decrease line in the knitted fabric. The stitch count decreases by one.

KNITTING 2 STITCHES TOGETHER (RIGHT LEANING)
Several right-leaning decreases stacked atop each other result in a clean decrease line that slants leftward.

1 Insert the working needle in both stitches together from left to right as you would do for a knit stitch.

2 Grasp the working yarn as if working a knit stitch, and pull it through both stitches at once.

KNITTING 2 STITCHES TOGETHER WITH PASSING OVER (LEFT LEANING)
When stitches knitted together with passing over are worked staggered, the decrease line will look jagged.

1 Slip the first stitch knitwise, and knit the second stitch.

2 Insert the left needle from left to right under the front leg of the slipped stitch, loosen up the stitch a little bit, pass it over the stitch worked last, lift it over the tip of the needle, and let it slip off the left needle.

Please note: When decreases of the same type are worked in the same spot stacked atop each other in subsequent rows, a subtle twined line will appear in the knitted fabric.

INCREASES

Increases as well as decreases are important shaping elements for a knitted item, and they are frequently used for decorative purposes, too. The stitch count increases by one.

SINGLE INCREASE FROM THE BAR BETWEEN STITCHES

When the picked-up bar between stitches is worked the regular way, a small eyelet will form in the knitted fabric, and the increase is not slanted in either direction.

To make a single increase from the bar between stitches, insert the left needle from front to back under the bar between the stitch worked last and the following not-yet-worked stitch. Lift the bar between stitches onto the left needle. It should be oriented on the needle the same way as the other stitches.

For a knitted increase, the lifted bar can now be knitted.

For a purled increase, the lifted bar needs to be purled.

The new column of stitches created atop the small eyelet is not slanted in either direction. When a purl increase is worked in a wrong side row, the right side of the fabric will look in this spot as if a single knit increase had been worked here.

When single increases from the bar between stitches are worked to the right (before) or to the left (after) of a stitch or group of stitches in subsequent rows, little eyelets will emphasize the symmetrical increase. Owing to the additional stitches, the knitted fabric will be slanted.

TWISTED INCREASE FROM THE BAR BETWEEN STITCHES

Twisted increases from the picked-up bar between stitches will appear slanted to the right or to the left in the knitted fabric, depending on whether the bar between stitches was placed on the needle the regular way or twisted.

LEFT-LEANING KNITTED TWISTED INCREASE

1 Insert the left needle from the front to the back to pick up the bar between stitches.

2 To work the bar twisted, insert the right needle from right to left under the back leg of the loop, grasp the working yarn, pull it through, and lift the loop from the left needle.

RIGHT-LEANING KNITTED TWISTED INCREASE

1 Insert the left needle from the back to the front to pick up the bar between stitches.

2 To work the bar twisted, insert the right needle from left to right under the front leg of the loop, grasp the working yarn, pull it through, and lift the loop from the left needle.

SINGLE INCREASE WITH YARN OVER

In a single increase with yarn over, the new column of stitches will emerge from a hole. The increase spot is not slanted. Increases from yarn overs may be used without problems in rows or rounds immediately following each other.

In the increase spot, make a regular yarn over slanted the same way as the other stitches.

Depending on how the increase should appear on the right side of the fabric, either knit or purl the yarn over in the following row or round.

Single increases, placed symmetrically before and after a center stitch or group of stitches in subsequent rows, produce an increase line emphasized by two eyelet columns.

BINDING OFF

When binding off by passing over, you always work over two stitches. The first stitch will then be passed over the second stitch and the tip of the needle so that the top of the stitch will drape like a noose around the legs of the stitch on the needle.

BINDING OFF KNITWISE

Binding off knitwise is the easiest and most common way to bind off stitches. Worked in a right side row, the bind-off edge will blend in with stockinette fabric. To prevent the bind-off edge from pulling in, work the bind-off row loosely if possible. It might be helpful to use a larger needle size for this. With regular working yarn tension, you will get a bind-off edge of medium elasticity.

At the beginning of the bind-off row, knit 2 stitches. Insert the left needle from left to right into the front leg of the right stitch, pass it over the left stitch and over the tip of the needle, and let it slip off the needle. Do not further tighten the working yarn.

* Knit another stitch, again pass the right one of the two stitches over the left stitch and the needle tip, and let it slip off the left-hand needle. Repeat the working steps from * across the row. For the last stitch, cut the yarn, leaving a long tail, and pull the end through the last stitch to secure. Weave the end into the knitting or use it for seaming.

BINDING OFF PURLWISE

Binding off purlwise is worked in a similar way as binding off knitwise, with the difference that stitches are purled instead of knitted before binding them off. An edge bound off this way will blend in smoothly with inverted stockinette fabric; the bind-off edge will look from the wrong side the same as the knitted bind-off from the right side. This way, stockinette stitch fabric can be bound off in purl in a wrong side row.

First, purl 2 stitches. Pass the right one of the 2 stitches on the right needle over the left stitch and over the tip of the needle, and let it slip off the left needle.

* Purl the next stitch and again pass the right one of the two stitches over the other stitch and the needle tip, and let it slip off the left needle. Repeat the working steps from * across the row. For the last stitch, cut the yarn, leaving a long tail, and pull the end through the last stitch to secure. Weave the end into the knitting or use it for seaming.

ACKNOWLEDGMENTS

This book would not have been possible without the help of my wonderful team of sample knitters. While working on this book, we've gone through a lot, debated, and of course knitted together. I would like to thank all of you for your tireless dedication. The valuable contribution of every single one of you is greatly appreciated!

PETRA CARLL
Thank you for working in secret so unflinchingly and surprising me that quickly with the finished project!

JUTTA FISCHER
Thank you for always having time for a cup of coffee and never feeling intimidated— not even by stranded knitting in an oversized format!

CHRISTINE GAHBLER
Thank you for not despairing over those lace pattern increases and for your valuable support in correcting this pattern!

ROMY HOFFMANN
Thank you for always making me laugh in your unrivaled way during these hectic times!

VIOLA KELLER
Thank you for staying on top of things despite the adverse circumstances and for doing everything to keep deadlines!

KATHARINA KLUSMANN
Thank you for always finding time for our collaborative project between playing the violin and commuting by car!

SUSANNE KOTAN
Thank you for your wonderful participation as a newcomer to our team and for creating a fabulous sweater!

ASTRID KREDEL
Thank you for waiting so patiently for the start of our project and knitting so quickly as soon as it was ready.

HEIKE KUBAN
Thank you for supporting me with great zeal at the eleventh hour for this project, too!

MAREIKE LACHMANN
Thank you for tolerating my math error with just a shrug of the shoulders and frogging and starting anew!

MONICA LAUENSTEIN
Thank you for not letting yourself get discouraged by a knitting error and just starting all over!

SUSANNE MÖHLER-BEINROTH
Thank you for tackling a project despite all the stress in connection with launching your store!

IRENE MÜLLER
Thank you for tirelessly offering your help again and again and for even working on two projects!

DANIELA SEINSOTH
Thank you for having been so supportive for so long with your contagious great zeal and for having completed three wonderful projects for this book!

YVONNE WEBER
Thank you again for enabling us to laugh about all our mistakes and for staying with this project from the beginning through the end.

CHRISTIANE WERKER
Thank you for lowering my stress level by filling in when additional help was needed, despite having your own plans.

Last but not least, my thanks go to RAINER GRÜBL—the man who, with stoic calm, put up with rushing and time pressure throughout a whole year and kept me alive with the world's best lasagna!

ABOUT THE AUTHOR

For RITA MAASSEN, designing is a passion. The web and graphic designer has been enthralled with knitting since childhood. Very early on, she became enthusiastic about creating her own designs, and ever since then, she has been creating new knitting designs in her small studio in Germany's Lower Rhine region. Since 2010, she has been offering her handmade fashion and numerous knitting patterns under her own Fashionworks label in her online shop (www.fashionworks.de). Her work has been published in a variety of print magazines and online editions, and her Facebook page and blog enjoy a steadily growing fan base as well.

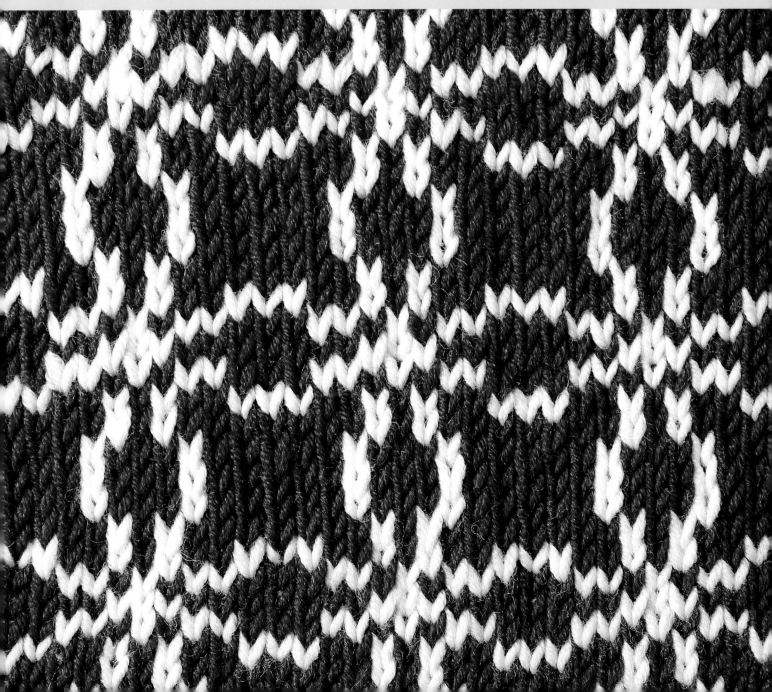